Laughing

through the

Tears

by

Christine Houston

Life To Legacy, LLC

Presented to

To order this book, please go to

Amazon.com or BN.com.

To contact the author, send an e-mail to:

Sugardoo227@yahoo.com

Dedicated to the Memory of

Ike Houston, Sharron White-Fleming, Irma (Sugardo) Brown,

Albert Dickerson Jr., Daisy Petra Nelson, Ruby Lee Fuller,

Judi Ann Mason, Alaina Reed-Hall-Amin

Special Thanks To

Marshaund Chandler, Dorothy Fraction, Valerie Burse, Betty Robertson,

Dr. Christine List, Prof. Sandra Jackson-Opoku, Bill Duke, Anthony

(Bear) Adams, Dr. Shelly Williams, Johnny C. James Sr., Sasha Daltonn,

Dahnetta Ousley, and Dr. Dennis Woods.

My Sincere Gratitude To

Juanita Passmore, Theodore Williams Jr., Phillip Williams, Spencer Leak,

Ernesto Bourges, Bill James, Nancy Newburg, Alice Smith-Jones,

Larry Dulaney, And Shaya Gardner-Hayum.

Table of Contents

Acknowledgments

Giving all praises to God for without Him I couldn't have written one page of this sometimes humorous, sometimes painful story about love, faith, friendship, family, and . . . dementia. How can I begin to thank all those who encouraged me to write this story, especially during the times when I was under a tremendous amount of stress? Perhaps I'll just rewrite and edit something I wrote when my husband Ike made his transition in 2004.

Thanks for the Memories

So many places, so many faces, thanks for the memories.

My life with Ike began more than fifty years ago. The important things that enabled our relationship to thrive were the many occasions of happy times we shared with you; our family, our friends, our co-workers and our neighbors.

We started off with two sons, added another, next came a daughter and then a "god-sent-son"; so much laughter, so much fun, so much happiness. I wish I could call the names of our relatives, one by one; maternal, paternal, great and grand, first and second and twice removed; in-law and out-of-the-law; past and present—who helped shape the course of our lives. Each one of you are special and dear to our hearts; so much happiness, so much fun.

What a joy it was for me, a CTA ticket agent, to see my husband, a CTA motorman pull into my station. And he knew to wait a few seconds in order to make sure he wasn't leaving any of my passengers behind. The friends we made at work have been many and so have the joyful picnics, Christmas parties and Friday night fish fries Ike and I enjoyed with them; so much happiness so much fun.

How can I express the joy we experienced when we joined the Greenville Mississippi Club? The good times, the friends, the traveling, the food, the entertainment, the Fabulous Kings' band, the clubhouse, the club members . . . so much fun, so much happiness, so much love.

When we moved into our new home, we were so excited. We didn't socialize with our neighbors—they were too busy—taking flight to farther away "all-white" suburban areas. Maybe that was a good thing because our new neighbors the Robertson's became more than just neighbors; they became our friends for life; so much fun, so much happiness. Thanks for the memories.

The churches we worshiped at; First Church of Deliverance, Apostolic, True Believers, New Christian Valley; we believed in worshiping at the nearest church. They all helped to shape our lives and supply our spiritual needs. So much love, so much happiness. Thanks for the memories.

ETA Creative Arts Foundation, where Ike and I attended more than thirty plays over twenty-five years; made an important contribution, helping to shape our cultural beliefs and extend our knowledge of the history of Black people throughout the Diaspora. So much fun so much camaraderie.

To the hundreds of people that I've been blessed to meet as I've traveled across these United States; so much fun, so much joy.

Thanks for the memories.

Preface

DURING THE SEVEN YEARS I TOOK CARE OF MY HUSBAND, most of those years were spent in denial. Although, I have to admit I didn't want to accept what was obvious to everyone—including me. For none other than selfish reasons (I now know this to be the case)I didn't want to let go of the man I had met, fell in love with, married, and together raised four children. I refused to believe that the life we had planned to enjoy after his retirement was never going to be. All of my life I'd had a man taking care of me; God, my father Albert, Uncle Sam, and Ike.

Ike and I were supposed to grow old together—I mean really "OLD." Would things have been different if I had heeded the early warning signs, hadn't been in denial, gotten medical help sooner? Maybe, maybe not, but I do believe that in a lot of cases early detection can help to some degree. Through it all, I have learned the true meaning of "commitment". That is the reason I want to share my story. Hopefully, it will lend encouragement to the thousands (maybe millions) of families facing the challenge of caring for a loved one suffering from Alzheimer's or dementia. I am sure that many who read this account of my own challenge will be able to relate to some of the incidents described in the various chapters.

The fact is, although the task isn't an easy one, it is by no means all gloom and doom. Certainly there will be periods of overwhelming sadness brought on by the inability to comprehend or alleviate the situation. But, I strongly recommend that those who will become the care givers should possess a lot of love, patience, fortitude and understanding. A spiritual foundation will certainly be extremely helpful and necessary.

While those of us who are not in the medical profession have a hard time understanding the nature of this disease; we still have to address the situation and adjust our lives accordingly. And, while no cure has yet been discovered, much research is being done towards the treatment and prevention of both Alzheimer's and dementia.

While writing this story, I changed most names and places and even a few dates and times; but almost all of the incidents are true. They actually did happen. People who know me, know I am a writer capable of finding humor in almost any situation. It was devastating for me when I realized that while the body still resembled Ike, the person I knew and loved was no longer visible. Or maybe I should say he was..... just a different individual. But, I've learned how really important it is to find the humor in dealing with this disease.

Ike is no longer with me now. I miss the wonderful man I loved and lived with before and even after the disease, and yes, I miss the funny things he did once I stopped denying that he had it. And ... despite the disease, I never stopped loving him.

I still cry sometimes when I think about some of the things that happened during that time, but I am "laughing through the tears", I really am. It has been said, somewhere and by someone, "Laughter is the best medicine", and sometimes ... it really is.

Prologue

ALL DAY AT WORK, Crystal Haywood had thought about soaking in a tub of hot, bubbly, fragrant water. She would relax and close her eyes and dream of soft music and candle lights surrounding the tub. In her dream, Eric would be his old self again and join her.

Well, she thought as she stood at her opened front door, awaiting her best friend's arrival, Sherry had better make this quick because as soon as she leaves, I'll give Eric some Sleepy Time tea, put him to bed, add more bubbles and hot water, jump in the tub, and soak away my blues.

It was almost nine p.m. when Sherry Green's beige 1983 Lincoln Continental turned into the circular driveway of Crystal's mini-mansion. The car had barely stopped moving before Sherry exited and rushed up to the already opened door.

"Come on in the kitchen, girl," Crystal said, closing the door behind them. "This had better be important. I was just about to put Eric to bed and soak myself in some fragrant, warm bubbles."

"It is important. I've decided to have Thanksgiving dinner at my house this year," Sherry said with excitement as she followed Crystal into the kitchen.

"That's good, but couldn't you have told me that on the phone? Thanksgiving is almost three weeks away."

"I'm just so excited. I've never cooked an entire Thanksgiving dinner," Sherry countered.

"Like I said, that's good but ..."

"Please Crystal, share my enthusiasm," Sherry interrupted. She sounded like a little kid begging for candy.

"I'm trying, but it's not like it's the second coming of Christ. Let me guess, Leonardo's coming to dinner."

"Yes! Now didn't you get excited the first time you invited Eric to taste your cooking?" Crystal heaved a sigh.

"Okay, let's get this over with. I'll help you plan the menu, suggest the guests, help shop for the food, help cook it, bless it, and make sure Eric and I come over and eat it. Is that enough enthusiasm for you?"

"It had a hint of sarcasm, but I'll take it," Sherry said, hugging Crystal. "I'm not inviting any outside people either. Since this is my first big dinner I want everything to go smoothly."

"You don't have to worry," Crystal said, sensing Sherry's concern. "Eric has been acting like his old self lately."

"Look Crystal, you know you and Eric are like family to me and you know I love him, but ..."

"But you're afraid he might say or do something embarrassing and mess up your big day," Crystal said, finishing Sherry's sentence.

"Come on Crystal, don't take it ..."

"It's okay," Crystal said, interrupting Sherry again. "Like I said, Eric is fine."

"Ooh, this is going to be the best Thanksgiving ever," Sherry said gleefully, trying to put the excitement back into the conversation.

Sherry realized she'd hit a nerve with her friend. She hadn't mentioned it, but she felt that lately Crystal seemed overly defensive when it came to discussing Eric.

"If I didn't know better, I would think you are really in love," Crystal said jokingly. She too realized her comments had been a bit edgy.

"Isn't it wonderful? This means Leonardo is ready to move back to Chicago."

"Is he ready to take on a twice-married widow with three children?" Crystal hoped Sherry wouldn't be offended by the question.

Ignoring the question's implementation, Sherry said, "If he's ready, I'm ready."

"Good, and I'm ready to jump in the tub," Crystal said as she pushed Sherry toward the front door. "I can't believe you drove all the way over here, this time of night, just to tell me you're cooking dinner in three weeks," she added.

"If I didn't know better, I'd suspect you're actually trying to put me out," Sherry said jokingly.

"If you knew how bad I want to splash in those bubbles, you wouldn't have to suspect. Now goodbye, good night, and good riddance," Crystal said, laughing as she opened the door. "

Alright, but we need to start planning. I'll call you tomorrow," Sherry said as she jumped in the car and quickly pulled off.

Crystal watched her friend drive away before going back into the house. "Okay honey, let's call it a night," she called to Eric as she headed into the den where she'd left him watching television. Surprised to see he wasn't there, Crystal turned off the television and the lights, and headed up the stairs. She hoped Eric had remembered to put on his pajamas. Sometimes he would forget and get into bed naked. She laughed at the thought. When they were younger, he would playfully suggest they sleep naked and lay their pajamas beside the bed ... in case of fire. Entering the bedroom, Crystal was surprised again. Eric was not in bed. She crossed to the bathroom. There he was splashing in the fragrant bath oils and bubbles she had prepared for herself. Determined not to get upset, she laughed.

"Those bubbles were not meant for you. Come on, let's rinse you off and get you out of here."

"I'm not getting out," Eric said emphatically.

"Come on, honey, you've been in there long enough. You can't stay in the tub all night." Feeling the water, Crystal realized it was barely warm. "You've got to get out before you catch a cold," she said trying not to sound harsh.

"I'm not getting out until Jesus comes and tells me to get out," Eric said, showing no intentions of backing down.

Crystal stood looking at him for a moment, not knowing how she was going to get him out of the tub. Finally, she went back into the bedroom and sat on the bed trying to think of what to do. Every now and then she would get up and peep around the doorway to see what Eric was doing. He continued to splash and play in the bubbles. After deciding to give it one more try, Crystal grabbed a bed sheet, draped it around herself, covered her hair with a white sleeping cap, and entered the bathroom. Changing her voice to sound deep and masculine, she walked slowly toward the tub and said, "I am Jesus. Eric Haywood, step out of that tub."

At first Eric just stared at her. Then he let out a loud laugh and said, "You're not Jesus. Jesus was white with long brown curly hair." He continued to play in the bubbles that were now beginning to dissolve. Crystal sighed. She didn't know what else to do, but she knew she couldn't leave him in the tub all night. She couldn't call her best friend; Sherry couldn't help her ... not with this one. Crystal went back into the bedroom to call the only person she knew who could coax Eric out of the tub. She picked up the phone and dialed.

"Hello ... Shaun?" She asked her middle son, almost in tears. "Can you come over here right now? Your father is in the bath tub and refuses to get out. I'm so tired, I don't know what to do. Please, can you come? ... Alright, but please hurry."

Crystal hung up and went back into the bathroom. She stood watching Eric splashing in the water. All of the bubbles were gone now, but that didn't seem to bother him. She finally said,

"Alright, I'm through playing with you. You have gotten on my last nerve!"

There was no softness in her voice now: no patience, no trying not to get upset, no handling him with kid gloves. She was tired. She didn't even want to run more bath water and put in new bath oil and make bubbles for herself. She just wanted him out of the tub and in the bed so she could go to bed.

"I'll just remove the stopper and let all the water out. That ought to make you get your butt out of this tub."

As Crystal was bending down to remove the stopper, Eric grabbed her arm playfully trying to pull her into the tub with him. Crystal let out a loud scream as she attempted to break her fall. She felt the bones in her right wrist and left elbow crack as they hit the side of the tub. She felt a terrible pain as her forehead hit the faucet.

Crystal blacked out.

One
The Grand Retirement Party
Four years earlier...

CRYSTAL STOOD IN FRONT OF THE FULL LENGTH BEDROOM MIRROR admiring the gold lamé dress she had designed. As she slipped into the accompanying gold mesh jacket, with its hand-sewn gold roses, she couldn't help complimenting herself. She would be celebrating her fiftieth birthday in a few months, and she was still attractive, managing to keep her weight down around 150 pounds. She was proud of her reputation for choosing elegant and one-of-a-kind outfits. Crystal knew everyone would be watching to see what she was wearing. She'd made sure they would not be disappointed. She was also praised by her family and friends for dressing her husband Eric in the latest fashions for men. By his own admission, Eric was color-blind and had absolutely no ability to "mix-or-match."

Crystal and Eric had met shortly after she graduated from college. A mutual friend had thrown a party and invited them. After being properly introduced, Eric wasted no time showing his instant attraction to Crystal. During the years while majoring in theater at the University of Illinois, she'd had several dates but nothing really serious. Besides, most of the guys she'd dated had been her own age or no more than a couple of years older. She was flattered by the interest Eric showed, especially after learning he was thirty-eight, fourteen years her senior. But the age difference became more intriguing when Eric began showering her with gifts combined with other gestures of genuine love and affection. After a whirl-wind courtship, they were married. Although she wanted one, it wasn't a big church wedding with bridesmaids and groomsmen and Crystal wearing a flowing white gown. It was just a marriage at the minister's home with a few close friends and family members present. Still, Crystal looked elegant in a knee-length green three-tiered chiffon dress. She promised herself a real wedding when she and Eric celebrated their fiftieth anniversary.

It was during the early days of their courtship that Crystal realized Eric's inability to coordinate his wardrobe. As soon as they were married, she took over choosing everything he wore—from his hat and tie, down to his socks and shoes. After receiving endless compliments from friends and relatives, Eric had no problem allowing Crystal to groom and dress him. It would be putting it mildly to say Eric began to depend on Crystal to dress him for every occasion, and she welcomed the confidence he had in her choices.

Eric was a very hard worker, sometimes holding two jobs in order to save for the down payment on a house. After three years, they were able to purchase a modest two-bedroom home. Crystal taught theater courses at a junior college when she wasn't pregnant, and they continued to save. By the time they'd had their third—and what they thought would be the last—addition to their family, they sold their small house and purchased a more spacious one: five bedrooms, five bathrooms, a gigantic living room, a formal dining room, and a den. They also had a laundry room and a full basement. The house sat on a quarter of an acre with beautifully manicured shrubbery and trees. Several years later, Eric had a friend to put in an in-ground swimming pool. Eric had teased Crystal, asking her why she had to be the proud owner of a "mini-mansion."

"Do you plan to trick me into fatherhood a fourth time?"

"No," Crystal had laughed. "I've dreamed of owning a house big enough to have a wedding in. Besides, I didn't trick you; you were a willing participant," she'd added.

As Crystal continued to primp in the mirror, Eric emerged from the bathroom. She turned to inspect his progress. Even at sixty-five, she thought, he's still a handsome hunk of a man. Slightly graying at the temples, his hair was beginning to thin, but he still had enough for her to run her fingers through. Satisfied that he too had managed to keep his weight down, she was proud of the way he looked in the white-on-white plaid silk suit she had chosen for him.

"Where's your bow tie?" she asked.

Eric took the gold tie that matched his gold shirt, which matched her gold lamé dress, and handed it to Crystal, who placed it around his neck. "Only the rich and famous get to have a valet dress them. I'm neither," Eric teased.

"In this family, you are the rich and the famous ... and the color-blind," Crystal reminded him, laughing.

Eric laughed too as he took a pair of socks from the drawer. Sitting on the edge of the bed, he started to put them on. Crystal let out a loud shriek startling him.

"Those are not the brand new socks I laid out for you! They don't match a thing you have on!"

"Okay, okay, so where are the ones you laid out?"

"They're on your butt."

"On my butt?" Eric gave Crystal a puzzled look.

"You're sitting on them," Crystal said laughing.

Eric grabbed her and pulled her into his arms. "You know something? I'm lucky to have such a beautiful, sexy, intelligent, thoughtful ..." He paused for a moment.

"Don't stop," Crystal urged. Eric continued, "... kind, color-coordinated, fashion-wise expert who ..." Crystal interrupted.

"Now you're making fun of me."

"No, really, you are all those things. Who else has a wife who is throwing him a retirement party fit for a king?"

"You are my king," Crystal replied as Eric kissed her lips. Suddenly, Leonardo poked his head in the doorway.

"Hey, what's going on in here?" he asked with a sly Jack Nicholson grin.

Leonardo was in his early fifties and looked quite handsome in his black-and-white tuxedo. He always did have a boyish look about him. He and Eric had worked together for eight years. Eric was the motorman, and Leonardo had been his conductor on the el train for the CTA (Chicago Transit Authority). That was up until six years ago, when Leonardo quit and left town to find his niche as a stand-up comedian in Hollywood. Despite the twelve years difference in age, Leonardo and Eric became close friends. During the years they worked together, they spent many hours fishing and hunting. Eric treated Leonardo like a son and included him in all family events and functions. Leonardo had been raised by a foster mother who died when he was eighteen. He had no knowledge of any of his blood relatives. Crystal knew she could not give Eric a retirement party without asking Leonardo to fly in from L.A. and emcee what she hoped would be an event all who attended would never forget. Leonardo and Eric had a habit of joking and signifying with each other.

"Hey, I heard screaming in here. You two are supposed to be getting dressed, not getting your freak on," Leonardo said, pretending to be upset.

"Whatever we're getting on, we're getting it on in the privacy of us's bedroom," Eric snarled, pretending to be upset too.

"Crystal, I thought you told me you'd taught this corn-fed, pig-feet-eating, biscuit-sopping, teeth-sucking Negro how to speak English," Leonardo laughed.

"She didn't have time, so your mama taught me," Eric snapped back. Crystal laughed.

"Okay you two, save the face-off for our elegant and elite guests."

"Honey, I find it hard to believe you're paying his monkey-ass to tell his tired-ass jokes to our elegant, elite guests," Eric joked.

Leonardo fired back, "What you should find hard to believe is the amount of money she's spending on a party for your retarded ass."

Crystal laughed, "Will you two stop? It's after six. Cocktails will be served at seven. Let's go. The limo is waiting outside."

"I thought we were waiting for the boys," Eric said.

"If you're referring to those grown sons of ours, they're supposed to go straight to the ballroom from the airport." Leonardo leaped at the chance to signify with Eric again.

"Crystal, don't tell me you've still got him thinking those kids are his?"

Eric shot right back, "For twenty years, your mama had your daddy thinking you were his."

"You two don't ever quit!"

Crystal tried to sound irritated while trying to suppress her laughter.

She really missed the clowning around the two of them did. She had to admit both of them were quick with the retorts, and quite funny. As they headed down the stairs, Crystal told them she knew nothing she said would stop them, but she urged them to continue their "love fest" as they head out the door. She steered them toward the foyer and reminded Leonardo to keep his jokes clean.

"Not even if he washed his mouth with Tide and bleached his tongue with Clorox," Eric said, getting in the last dig.

As the three exited the house, a few neighbors had gathered to take pictures and express their admiration for the handsome couple. The Limo driver hopped out and opened the door for them. While Crystal and Eric entered the limo, Leonardo couldn't resist hamming it up for the cameras. Suddenly, a big ferocious-looking dog broke away from a boy who obviously lacked the ability to assert muscular authority. The dog headed straight toward Leonardo. Both he and the limo driver leaped into the backseat with Eric and Crystal, slamming the door and locking it. Eric roared with laughter.

"What? You think the dog can open the door? Is that why you locked it?" Eric laughed. "The next time you mouth off at me, I'll just borrow that boy's dog," Eric added, unable to control his laughter. With the help of one of the neighbors, the boy regained control of the dog. After making certain the animal was in tow, the limo driver emerged from the backseat. He hurried around to the driver's side, jumped in, and quickly pulled off.

"I hope your jokes are as funny as seeing you two leap back here with us," Eric said, still unable to stop laughing.

"Hey, I could have handled that mutt; I just didn't want him biting into the legs of this rented tux."

"Your leg wasn't the body part he was getting ready to bite," Eric said, still unable to stop laughing.

The sleek, white 1986 Cadillac limousine cruised through the early evening traffic along Chicago's beautiful lakefront. It was the middle of June, and the flowers in Grant Park were in full bloom. Water from Buckingham fountain spewed high into the air, splashing back down again. Daylight saving time had allowed the city to show off its "downtown" elegance. Despite Leonardo's constant bragging about the star-studded glamour of Los Angeles, Crystal and Eric were quite proud of their city. The limo cruised through the Loop, which displayed some of Chicago's famous elite apparel shops. Along Michigan Avenue, Crystal proudly pointed to Sax Fifth Avenue, Neiman Marcus, and Lord and Taylor, as if she owned them. Her friend Sherry would have said, "She should own them as much money as she spends in them."

The limo finally pulled into the circular driveway of the plush La Cynthia Nightclub, located on what resident Chicagoans called, Michigan Avenue's "Magnificent Mile." Two male guests emerged from the club and began rolling out a red carpet. Two more men came out. One carried a long red velvet robe trimmed in white faux fur, and the other held a "costume" bejeweled crown. The limo driver got out, walked around, and opened the door. Leonardo exited first; Eric and Crystal followed. After realizing the cape and crown were for him, Eric allowed the men to bedeck him while he assumed a majestic pose. The men rushed to hold the double doors open as Eric strutted inside, leaving Leonardo and Crystal to follow behind him like two adoring peasants.

As Eric entered the grand ballroom, the band began to play a medley of pageantry music including the United States' "Hail to the Chief" and

England's "Royal Fanfare." The guests all stood, cheering and applauding while Eric strutted pompously, commanding some of them to bow down before him, while others did it automatically. The royal party was led to a special table with one of the chairs shaped like a throne. Eric milked the moment until he saw his three sons—Mark, 30; Shaun, 28; and Jay, 25—bowing in acknowledgment of their "King Father." Mark and Shaun had features favoring their mother, but Jay was the spitting image of his father. As the photographer lined them up, Crystal and Eric's adopted daughter, Anna, entered with her husband, Abraham, who could have easily been mistaken for—anybody. Anna was cute, petite, and shapely. She had a smile that lit up her whole face. One could tell she was a dancer merely by the way she glided across the floor when she walked.

Tony, Crystal's godson, rushed in behind them. He looked like a young Teddy Pendergrass, not quite as tall and definitely without the ability to launch a singing career. They were just in time to be included in the family portrait. As the photographer instructed them to hold for another shot, Leonardo jumped into the picture holding up two fingers behind Eric's head in the shape of rabbit ears. Of course, after Crystal jokingly chided Leonardo, the photographer reshot the picture.

During the cocktail hour, the guests mingled, exchanging greetings with those they knew and making new acquaintances. Excitement reined as the ballroom became filled with a remarkably festive ambiance. Sherry was serving as chief hostess and assistant coordinator. She moved among the guests, greeting them and showing them to their pre-assigned seats.

Sherry was eighteen years younger than Crystal, but they had become close friends when Sherry married Herbert, one of Eric's close CTA buddies. Crystal befriended Sherry after she became a prime target for juicy CTA gossip. Folks couldn't understand why Herbert had gone to Arkansas on vacation and returned with a bride twenty-five years younger than he. The fact that she had three kids, ages two, four, and five, made them talk even more. They also made fun of the way Sherry talked and the way she dressed. Crystal found it much easier to show Sherry how to dress, but after a while, Sherry's speech did improve ... a little.

Sherry looked radiant in her sequined gold and white form-fitting dress. She was a very attractive woman with an infectious smile. Leonardo had met Sherry and her husband, Herbert, through his close association with Eric, but he hadn't spent much time in their company except maybe at dinner on Thanksgiving. Leonardo would always either bring a date or leave early to go meet someone. But now, he could barely keep his eyes off Sherry. It was as if he was seeing her for the first time. Noticing this, Crystal looked at Leonardo and nodded her head in disapproval. She thought to herself, Your chances are slim with this one, buddy. When Leonardo was able to move closer to Crystal, he asked her what she meant by shaking her head.

"I meant that after nine years of marriage to a man who spoiled her and her children before his sudden and untimely death, Sherry is not a good candidate for a long-distant relationship. Besides, she's only been a widow for two years. She's still in mourning," Crystal informed Leonardo, sounding like a mother hen. She started to mention the fact that Leonardo probably had oodles of lady friends in L. A. since he was single and in show business, but she thought that would be guessing on her part and probably wouldn't help to deter him.

"Two years of mourning is long enough," Leonardo replied in a voice that inferred he liked what he saw, and nothing Crystal said was going to stop him from going after it.

Crystal was about to say something else but realized her point had not been well received. She watched Leonardo inch his way over to Sherry until the two were face to face. Leonardo just stood there staring at Sherry as if he couldn't believe she was real. Sherry stared back with a puzzling look. Feeling very uncomfortable with Leonardo's stare, she glanced away just in time to see Crystal point to the time. This gave Sherry her method of escape. She apologized and quickly moved toward the stage. She reached the podium without looking back, but she knew Leonardo's eyes were roaming over the lower extremities of her body. Somehow she didn't like the warm and fuzzy feeling it gave her—or maybe she didn't want to like it.

At the podium, Sherry welcomed the guests, trying hard not to look at Leonardo, who clung to her every word and gesture. Crystal decided to make a mental note to include Leonardo's obviously sudden obsession whenever she and Sherry discussed the events of the evening—of course without being too intrusive. She was already helping Sherry with her attire and her speech; she didn't want Sherry to think she was trying to run her love life.

Sherry urged the guests to continue to enjoy the cocktails and chatting with their friends while dinner was being served. She promised them that live entertainment would follow dinner and warned them they were about to experience an unforgettable evening of music, dining, dancing, with entertainment straight out of Hollywood.

And what an evening it turned out to be. Leonardo was the perfect host, telling side-splitting jokes and signifying about Eric's family and his three sons. When Leonardo had finished his last joke, he made an announcement.

"Before you party reptiles hit the dance floor, you must hear a word from 'His Royal High-ass', oops ... I mean, 'His Royal Highness' King Eric Haywood."

The guests responded with laughter and cheers. As Eric strutted up to the podium, the band played "Hail to the Chief." Crystal beamed with pride. Eric spoke into the mike.

"Thank you, thank you all for coming. I don't know about you, but because of you I'm having the time of my life. I promise I will never forget this night. I am extremely grateful and fortunate to have friends and family like you." Then he turned to Crystal and said, "But I am truly blessed to have you for my wife." He grabbed Crystal and planted an adoring kiss right on her lips. The guests went wild. Leonardo grabbed the mike from Eric.

"Okay, so much for the porno part of the entertainment. Now let's put this fabulous band to work. Come on everybody, get on the floor and dance."

The guests' response was immediate as they took to the floor with joyful enthusiasm. The band, The Fabulous Kings, Eric and Crystal's favorite group, had been brought in from neighboring Gary, Indiana. They played fast-tempo music that made the guests move to the beat, as well as soft, slow music that made them sway in the arms of their spouse or significant other. When the band played a popular slow number, Leonardo took the opportunity to ask Sherry to dance. Sherry started to make an excuse, but he placed her hand in his and before she could respond she was on the dance floor and in his arms. It has only been two years, she thought to herself. It's too soon to even think about starting a new relationship, especially with a man who lives two thousand miles away. Sherry stiffened when Leonardo tightened his arm around her, pulling her closer. The tingling sensations she felt left her breathless.

"Relax, I won't harm you," he whispered in her ear.

Sherry felt embarrassed, thinking that Leonardo must certainly feel her heart pounding against his chest.

"Relax," he whispered again.

Sherry tried but still couldn't relax. She decided closing her eyes might help. Crystal noticed her friend dancing with her eyes closed and quickly danced Eric over toward the couple. When she was close enough, she nudged Sherry with her elbow. Startled, Sherry opened her eyes to see a smiling Crystal, but she knew that look in Crystal's eyes. She could almost read her mind. She knew that despite the smile, Crystal was saying, Girlfriend, this is something we need to talk about. When the song ended, Sherry hastened over to a nearby table pretending to have been summoned by the occupants. She knew Leonardo was still watching her but prayed he wouldn't follow her.

The band finally took a break and the DJ took over. When he played a popular "get down" number, Anna, who was an excellent dancer, showed off her talent. Abraham tried hard to keep up with her, but it was obvious he was used to allowing her to do her "thing." Shaun had found himself a pretty good dance partner and was doing his own "thing." Mark, who had traveled without his wife, was content to converse with Tony, whom he hadn't seen in quite a while. And of course, Jay was displaying his charms while being surrounded by several admiring young ladies.

When the DJ switched to James Brown's "I Got the Feeling," Anna and Shaun took over the dance floor. The guests stepped back, cheering them on. Mark and Jay joined in, and the crowd went wild. Jay performed some of James Brown's moves, while Mark acted as his female counterpart. Tony refused to be left out and joined them, adding his own special hilarious antics. Eric and Crystal watched proudly as their children showed off their unique ability to provide fun and entertainment. Eric looked at Crystal as he slipped her hand in his.

Softly he said, "I adore you." Crystal smiled and said, "Back at you."

Hours later, the once exuberant guests started to wind down. As they prepared to say farewell, Crystal grabbed the mike and announced the location of the "after-party." Eric and Crystal belonged to a private social club called The Greenville Mississippi Club. The members, most of them from Greenville, had purchased their own clubhouse, which was open on weekends for rest and relaxation with their family and friends. The members also hosted many other occasions such as family reunions, birthday and anniversary parties, wedding receptions, cookouts, and seasonal celebrations. They sometimes rented the club to non-members for their special functions. Crystal and Eric were very proud of their clubhouse. It was hard to believe that so many of the guests actually showed up since the clubhouse was smaller, and not nearly as elegant. The "after-party" included more dancing with music played by the tired but well-paid DJ. The breakfast fare included eggs, bacon, sausage, grits, hash browns and rice, with a choice of biscuits or toast and coffee or juice.

It was four o'clock in the morning when the door to the foyer swung open, and Crystal entered wearing the king's cape and crown. Eric and Leonardo stumbled in behind her. Leonardo was holding Eric up while the limo driver held them both up.

"How about having one for the road?" Eric said to the driver, slurring his words.

The driver laughed saying, "No thanks, it's against company rules.

Besides, the road is already laid out."

"Hey, that's funny; the road's already laid out. We should have paid you to tell jokes instead of this monkey's ass," Eric said, pointing to Leonardo.

"Your mama should've thrown you away and kept the afterbirth," Leonardo said, slurring his words. Eric motioned the driver toward the den.

"Just put me down gently in there on the sofa," he said.

"Put me down over there, too. Only gent-ly—er," Leonardo echoed. The limo driver obeyed, steering them to the sofa and releasing them. Eric flopped down, and Leonardo flopped down on top of him.

"Maybe you should just cover them up and leave them here," the limo driver suggested.

"Maybe I should just cover them up and leave them here," Crystal said, repeating the suggestion. They both laughed.

As Crystal walked the limo driver to the door, she apologized for the long night and thanked him for his patience. He smiled and replied, "No need to apologize, those were the best parties I have ever attended. I had a great time."

As the limo driver was leaving out, Anna and Abraham entered. Jay, Shaun, and Mark followed with their arms around each other singing "For he's a jolly good fellooooow ..." When they reached the den and saw Eric and Leonardo sprawled on the sofa, they changed the lyrics to "For they're two jolly good fellooooows ..." Crystal interrupted, reminding them that the party was over and they should call it a night before the neighbors called the police. Abraham and the singing trio headed upstairs while Anna helped Crystal cover Eric and Leonardo. Crystal decided it really was a good idea to leave them on the sofa rather then watch the slightly inebriated trio try to get the totally inebriated duo up the stairs. As she and Anna headed up to bed, Crystal told Anna how happy she and Eric were to have all of them home. She also said she was glad they had five bedrooms and five bathrooms.

"See you in the morning, Mom," Anna yawned as she headed toward the bedroom to join Abraham. Crystal yawned back, "Anna baby, it's already the morning".

The next morning, Crystal thought she might sleep a little later than usual, but the bright sunlight that poured through the unclosed blinds had other plans. The clock on the night stand displayed ten a.m. It was Sunday, and Crystal always enjoyed walking to her church, which was only a block away. She especially enjoyed the walk when the weather was nice. I'd like to go this morning, but my get-up-and-go got up and went. Besides, God knows my heart, she thought to herself. And Pastor Cooper should know how tired I must be after last night and all the previous weeks of planning. She smiled at the afterthought. Reverend Cooper and his wife had attended the party, but congratulating Eric after dinner, they left.

Crystal decided to lie in bed a little longer. After all, her kids were home and she and Eric wanted to spend some "family only" fun time with them. She closed her eyes, reliving the events of the previous evening. She smiled again as she thought about what Eric's reaction would be when he awoke to find Leonardo lying almost on top of him. Or maybe they rolled over onto the floor. Crystal laughed as she glanced again at the clock. It was almost ten thirty now. She decided not to waste anymore precious family time. A quick shower should refresh her before going downstairs to administer "hangover medication" to the menfolk and prepare for another full day of activities.

Without looking in, Crystal tiptoed pass the den; she didn't want to wake Eric and Leonardo. While making coffee and heating up the homemade rolls she had managed to keep hidden until now, Crystal thought about her children. Mark, the oldest, was a bit more sensitive than the other two. He would burst into tears if he saw a dead animal lying in the street. He had gone to college for two years while working part-time as a cashier. After discussing it with his parents, he had decided to take the band he formed in high school to L.A. and test their talent. He'd majored in music, taken keyboard lessons from a well respected teacher, and felt it was time to make a move. After all, he was still young and at 25 still single, and had not been informed of any potential heirs. That was five years ago. The band didn't make the big time, but Mark remained in L.A., got a job, got married, and became a father. Not exactly the life Crystal would have mapped out for him but as long as he was happy—and Crystal was certainly happy to have a grandson.

Shaun was two years younger than Mark. He didn't develop MCS, "middle child syndrome," until after Jay came along. MCS really stands for "I'm too young to do what the oldest one does, and I'm too old to do what the youngest one gets away with." By the age of twelve, Shaun showed talent for the theater. Crystal became a stage mom when Shaun won a role in a professional traveling production of "Nobody Knows Me." By age thirteen, his voice changed and so did his ambition to become a Broadway star. Shaun also attended college (Crystal had told all her children, either work or go to college), and soon he became what Crystal called a professional student. After admitting that he loved campus life, Crystal suggested that he graduate and become a professor; then he could be on campus every day. She warned him his parent-supported school days were about to come to an end. That's when Shaun decided to follow in Mark and Jay's footsteps.

Jay was two and a half years younger than Shaun. Jay was the opposite of his siblings. He was always early to bed and early to rise, while the other two were night owls and had to be dragged out of bed each morning. He didn't take chastising too kindly either, so he tried to stay out of trouble. Jay loved sports and steered clear of the girls. That is, until he reached high school. After that it was girls, girls, and more girls. They loved him ... like a brother, and he loved them like ... a sister. At least that's what he'd told Crystal. But his "sisters" came in all sizes, ages, and conditions. One of them even had a baby. He swore she had the kid when he met her. Crystal reminded him that if he dated the mother, he should become involved with the kid. That meant he needed a job because the kid needed milk and diapers. After doing three years at a two-year college, Crystal felt Jay needed a change of scenery away from all of his "sisters." So she shipped him off to live with Mark in L.A. She often wondered why he was still single since he was so popular with the girls.

Crystal had always dreamed of having a little girl to dress in frills and ruffles. Every time she became pregnant, she'd hoped for a girl. After Jay was born, Crystal decided she would give up trying for a girl. When a close friend of hers died, she convinced Eric they should adopt her friend's daughter Anna. Anna was ten, the same age as Mark. The boys knew her and had no problem accepting her into the family, especially since Anna didn't mind helping them clean their rooms and iron their clothes. Shaun thought she also possessed great dishwashing skills. Crystal treated Anna just like she had given birth to her. Although Anna was too old for the frilly ruffles, Crystal still loved the chance to shop for a girl. She always enjoyed dressing the children in the latest fashions. She went to great lengths to make sure they wore good quality and proper-fitting shoes.

Crystal had treated Anna the same way. She knew Anna had a talent for dancing, so she decided Anna should take lessons from one of the community's prominent dance instructors. Anna loved to dance. She even made up her own dance moves. Crystal always believed that someday Anna would become a professional dancer and choreographer. She was happy when Anna decided to move to New York. Her chances for a career in dancing would be much better than if she remained in Chicago. Crystal wasn't too happy when Anna wrote and said she and Abraham, a guy she had met while working at the New York Stock Exchange, were getting married. Of course Crystal wanted Anna to come home and have a big wedding, but Anna chose to quietly marry and remain in New York. Again, not a choice Crystal would have made for her only daughter.

Crystal knew her children weren't perfect, but they got along well with each other—most of the time and they were obedient—most of the time. She also knew that she and Eric weren't the perfect parents, but they did the best they could without a manual—most of the time. There was one rule that she strictly enforced. Crystal did not want her children fighting amongst themselves. Her rule was, if they fought, whenever they finished their fighting, she would take on the winner—the loser had already gotten his butt whipped. She also taught them to look out for one another. She taught them to fight for and protect each other.

Once when they were teenagers, Crystal was visiting her next-door neighbor. The neighbor's daughter rushed in announcing that Shaun and Jay were fighting. Although the fight was over by the time Crystal reached home, she demanded to know what the fight was about and who had won. When she learned that Shaun had gotten the better of Jay and that Shaun had actually started the fight, she lit into Shaun. She was both surprised and amused when Jay interceded on Shaun's behalf. She later explained that while they should protect each other, they should think twice before doing so against her. She also emphasized that they should come to each other's aid, but that they should never use or parasite off one another.

Their children had most of the necessities and a few unnecessary luxuries. She didn't mind spending money on them, but she demanded obedience and respect, and she received it. Crystal spent a lot of time with them, taking them skating, visiting friends and relatives, and dining out. There was plenty of togetherness. Crystal did not believe in "sparing the rod," but there was still plenty of love—tough love.

Crystal's thoughts were interrupted as Shaun entered the kitchen carrying a flight bag. He gave his surprised mother a kiss on the cheek.

"I had a wonderful time, Mom. I really hate to cut out so soon. My flight leaves in an hour. Tell Dad I didn't want to wake him to say goodbye."

"That's because you knew he would be upset, you coward." Crystal laughed. She had hoped all of them would be able to stay at least through the weekend. Shaun hugged her, reminding her they would all be together for Christmas in L.A. He grabbed a couple of rolls as he explained that he had to be back at work on Tuesday and hadn't been able to get a flight out on Monday. Crystal followed him to the door.

"Your father is going to be so upset," she reiterated.

"He'll get over it," Shaun said. "The party was fabulous. You really did it up for the old man. I hope I find me a woman just like you."

"Stop lying, boy. You ain't even looking for a woman like me," Crystal fired back.

"Well, almost like you. Dad got lucky. They just don't make them like you anymore." Shaun kissed Crystal's forehead and hurried toward the waiting limo. "I love you," Shaun yelled over his shoulder as he climbed into the limo.

Though barely audible, Crystal replied, "I love you, too." The limo driver waved at her as he closed the door and rushed around to the driver's side. Crystal realized he was the same driver from last night and wondered when he ever slept. She stood watching as the limo exited the driveway, turned onto the street, and slowly faded into the distance. Heaving a sigh, Crystal returned to the kitchen. She hoped the others wouldn't spoil her plans for the day. She began removing various items from the refrigerator. She thought about the big breakfast they had eaten at the after-party and began putting the items back. They can just have rolls, coffee and juice, she thought, maybe we can all go to a restaurant for an early dinner. She decided to wake Eric and Leonardo so they could at least take off the clothes they had obviously slept in.

As she was about to exit the kitchen, Crystal noticed an envelope with her name on it. She hadn't seen it before. She picked it up and opened it. It was a short note from Leonardo. She sat down and began to read it:

> *Dear Crystal,*
>
> *Sorry I had to leave so early. I didn't have the heart to wake you. I admit I was a little upset when I awoke to find Eric's toes in my mouth—just joking. Thanks for allowing me the privilege of being a part of one of the most wonderful evenings I have ever spent—well, maybe not ever. Because you and Eric are such special friends of mine, I tore up the check*

you wrote me. Like I said, it was a privilege. Your limo driver is taking me to the airport. Thanks for everything.

Love, Leonardo

P.S. I'll be back sooner than you think. Like I said, two years is long enough to mourn.
P.P.S. I didn't want you to think I was ungrateful, so I glued the check back together. Rent's due next week."

Crystal laughed out loud as Eric entered. He still had on the pants to his suit but he was also wearing the king's cape and crown. When Eric asked if she was laughing because of the way he looked, she handed him the note from Leonardo. Eric read the note and laughed too but couldn't hide his disappointment that his friend had left without a goodbye.

"He could have at least allowed me to thank him. That was the best party I have ever attended, and he certainly helped to make it. And now that I'm officially retired, I'm going to chase you all over the house and make mad love to you in every room," he said, grabbing her and kissing her passionately as Jay entered.

"You're too old for that," Jay laughed, "both of you."

"If you don't hurry up and get married, you'll be too old for this ... for real," Eric chided.

"Alright, time to change the subject," Jay laughed. When Eric said he was happy to have his entire family home, Crystal regretfully told him Shaun had left. Now Eric really expressed disappointment, but Crystal smoothed things over by explaining Shaun's dilemma. When Eric mentioned how he wished they would all just come back home for good, Crystal reminded him that they were grown and chose not to deal with the harsh winters in Chicago. She silently hoped Eric wouldn't remind her that she was the one who had encouraged them to follow their dreams. Crystal changed the subject, "Jay, you want some coffee?"

"Yep, and some bacon and eggs and rice and hash-browns and grits and rolls and jelly and ..."

"Whoa," Eric interrupted, "It's time the royal family showed some compassion for the Queen Mother. Let's all get dressed and go out to eat."

"Sounds like a plan to me," chimed Mark as he entered still clad in pajamas and robe.

Crystal didn't let on that she had already thought of dining out. Instead she agreed it was an excellent idea. When the bell rang, she warned Eric that he'd better have plenty of cash since it was probably Tony coming over to hang out with the guys ... and eat. "By the time you pick up the tab for Anna and Tony, plus the rest of this family, you might be glad that Leonardo and Shaun had to leave", Crystal said laughing.

Realizing that Crystal had a point, Eric said, "If we hurry, we might be able to catch the six ninety-nine all you can eat buffet."

As Jay answered the door, Crystal pushed Eric toward the stairs, urging him to go take a shower and wake Anna and Abraham. Mark grabbed a roll as she pushed him behind Eric. Tony entered, giving Crystal a big bear hug and praising her for orchestrating the greatest retirement party ever. He sat down at the table and grabbed a couple of rolls while expressing his delight about the prospect of dining out with the family. When Tony complimented Jay on his ability to attract the ladies at the party, Crystal jumped at the opportunity to question Jay.

"Were any of them eligible prospects for marriage?" It had always been Eric who asked Jay when he planned to settle down and get married, but now Crystal was admitting she wouldn't mind helping him plan a wedding. Mark had gotten married in L.A. with no fanfare and no celebration, causing Crystal to count from the day of the marriage to the date of her first grandson's birth. Not wanting to be labeled a nosy mother-in-law, she never mentioned the seven months difference. Much to Crystal's disappointment, Anna had also married with no fanfare.

"Come on Mom, it's bad enough I have to listen to Dad prodding me about getting married. Do I have to hear it from you, too? If it pleases you, I am seeing a young lady in L.A., but I have no plans to marry her. I'm just not ready for the responsibility of providing for a family. When I'm ready and I find the right woman, I'll get on my knees and beg her to marry me." Clowning, Jay dropped to his knees, demonstrating. Tony pretended to be the intended bride with a high-pitched response.

"Oh yes Jay, yes, yes, yes, I'll marry you!"

"One knee should be sufficient," Crystal said, laughing and shaking her head at the two.

Crystal left them discussing old times while she went to help Eric get dressed. She was thinking about her youngest son and his desire to remain single and happy. Crystal hoped Eric wouldn't pressure him about marriage. She didn't want anything to spoil the day. Maybe when we get back, we can spend the rest of the time playing Monopoly before dinner, she thought. Crystal also thought about calling her friend Sherry and inviting her to go with them, but she remembered it was Sunday and Sherry and her kids usually spent the day in church. She hummed as she climbed the stairs, thanking God for her husband and her family.

On Monday morning, Eric managed to get Jay alone before he had to leave for the airport.

"Man, I really enjoyed my trip home. That was some retirement party."

"Did you meet any marriage potentials?" Eric asked.

"Here we go again," Jay said trying not to sound irritated. Jay knew Eric wouldn't let him leave without bringing up the subject of marriage.

"I'm not trying to pressure you, son. I just want to see you ..."

"Married," Jay said finishing Eric's sentence.

"And happy," Eric added.

"I am happy ... happy to be single, and I'm not ready to get married."

"Well you need to get ready," Eric said as if giving him a direct order.

"Dad, when I'm ready to make that move, you and Mom will be the first to know."

"In that order?"

"In that order," Jay replied.

"Promise?" Eric asked.

"I Promise," Jay said, smiling.

"Before you tell your mother?" Eric asked.

"What do you want, a promissory note?" Jay laughed.

"No, just a wedding."

"Well, there won't be one today, or next week, or next month. Now you promise me you won't keep badgering me." When Eric didn't respond, Jay asked again, "Promise?" Finally Eric said okay.

"That's not a promise," Jay laughed.

"It's the best I can do," Eric said.

"I'll take it," Jay said hugging him. "I love you, man."

"I love you too, son."

"Alright, spread some of that love around," Crystal said entering and handing Jay his garment bag. "The limo is outside waiting for you." Jay hugged Crystal. She and Eric followed him. They stood in the doorway watching until the limo was out of sight before going inside.

"Okay baby, put on your running shoes because the chase is on," Eric said. Crystal knew what that gleam in his eyes meant.

"No, wait," she laughed. "Anna and Abraham are due back from the gym any minute."

"Well let's make haste, woman." Crystal ran, taking the stairs two at a time. Like two children playing tag, Eric was right behind her.

Two
In Denial

A LITTLE OVER A WEEK HAD GONE BY SINCE THE RETIREMENT PARTY. Anna and Abraham had been the last to leave. Eric didn't hide the fact that he was glad he finally had Crystal to himself. Although they talked on the phone, Sherry had not visited Crystal. She knew they needed some time alone. Eric kept his promise about chasing Crystal around the house. He had retired in April, but during the months leading up to the retirement party, Crystal had been pretty busy planning for the big night. Now with the celebration over and the children gone, Eric wanted to enjoy spending his days—and nights—alone with Crystal.

Whenever Crystal tried to coax Sherry over so they could discuss the party—and Leonardo—Sherry would hedge, reminding Crystal she and Eric needed some private time by themselves. Crystal suspected Sherry was stalling. She accused her friend of not wanting to let on how she really felt about Leonardo. Sherry insisted she was giving them some much needed private time. She reminded Crystal how Eric had made that very clear. It wasn't that he disliked Sherry; in fact, he and Sherry's husband Herbert had made a pact: if something were to happen to either of them, the one remaining would look after the other's wife. While Eric tried to live

43

up to this "obligation," he did wish Sherry would, as he put it, "find herself a man." Then she wouldn't have so much time to spend visiting Crystal. Sherry knew Eric loved to tease her, and it didn't seem to bother her. In fact, Eric teased and joked with everybody. Although lately everybody didn't always think he was joking.

Crystal and Sherry normally spent time together during the week, especially when Crystal was off and Eric was still at work. On weekends the two women attended to their own family's personal needs, except for the Saturdays they went grocery shopping together. During most evenings and on weekends, Eric wanted Crystal all to himself. Crystal hoped that Eric would be cordial when Sherry did come over so they could do their "girl talking" without any interruptions.

Crystal loved her job teaching theater at the nearby junior college, but she usually took the summers off. She loved having the freedom to enjoy the nice weather and spend time just hanging out with Sherry. She and Eric had a pretty good marriage, but of course they had their ups and downs. Eric was a stay-at-homer, while Crystal liked to go. This never seemed to cause a problem. Soon after the kids had all left home, one of Eric's co-workers invited him to join the Greenville Mississippi Club. Members consisted of folks born in Greenville and within a fifty mile radius. Since he was born in Mound Bayou, he was eligible. His spouse could join too, regardless of where she had been born. After they joined the club, they spent more time together, attending the various festive activities and club functions

There were times when they disagreed, but whenever that happened, Eric would go around pouting and not speaking. Crystal would allow him to continue his "little boy" act for a few days, but then she would finally coax him into talking about the situation until some sort of compromise was reached. She was a firm believer that in a marriage, it was important to keep the lines of communication open. "Talk it out" was her philosophy.

Crystal had finished cutting up the tomatoes for the salad just as the doorbell rang. Wiping her hands on the dish towel, she went to let Sherry in. She hoped Eric was still engrossed in the White Sox's ball game. On the way to the door, Crystal thought, *Maybe Sherry could stay for dinner since her kids are away at camp."*

"Girl, I didn't know how much I missed your company until I was holed up in here with Eric for almost two weeks," Crystal said as she led Sherry into the kitchen.

"Hmmm something sure smells good in here." Sherry lifted the top to the Dutch oven as she sniffed again. "Ooh ox-tails, my favorite."

"Good, I was going to ask you to stay for dinner," Crystal admitted. "Come on, you can help me finish the sides. The cornbread is just about done."

"Hold on, I brought you a copy of the *Defender,*" Sherry said with excitement. "Listen to this. CTA motorman Eric Haywood retired after twenty-five years. Back in December, for the third consecutive year, Eric was awarded Motorman of the Year, and a huge celebration took place. But that was nothing compared to the "show-stopping" retirement party his theatrical wife, Crystal, threw for him at the elegant La Cynthia Grand Ballroom. The invitation proclaimed that the "king" was retiring to sit on his throne and do nothing forever, and the party was truly a celebration fit for a king." Sherry stopped reading. "Shall I read on?"

"No," Crystal replied, "I was there, remember? But you can buy you another paper and leave that one here."

"I'm way ahead of you. I bought two, this one is yours. I figured you and Eric were too busy to run out and buy a paper," Sherry said, winking.

Crystal took the paper and laid it aside. Putting her hands on her hips she said, "Okay, stop stalling." Sherry knew exactly what Crystal meant, but she gave her a blank stare pretending ignorance.

"I'm listening," Crystal said, folding her arms.

"Listening to what?" Sherry teased as a sly grin crossed her lips.

"Don't play with me girl," Crystal warned jokingly. Sherry knew Crystal was dying to hear the facts, so she began relating how Leonardo had pursued her all night like a dog in heat, and at the after-party he had begged her to at least give him her phone number.

"Did you give it to him?" Crystal asked, hoping she didn't but knowing she probably did. Sherry didn't answer, but the look on her face said she had. When Crystal reminded her she was supposed to be in mourning, Sherry described the feelings Leonardo had aroused in her. She told Crystal that she'd found herself anxiously awaiting a call from him.

"And he didn't," Crystal assumed aloud.

"Oh but he did," Sherry said smiling. "In fact he's called every day, sometimes twice in one day."

"Okay, so I'm glad to see you coming back to life, but you need to think twice before entering a long distant love affair." Sherry assured her that she was far from being in love and really hadn't planned on responding to Leonardo's advances via long or short distant.

"Sure," Crystal responded with a knowing look. But deep down inside she agreed with Leonardo: two years was long enough to grieve. She also felt Eric was right. Sherry needed a man, and her children could use a father. But she wondered if Leonardo was the right one. Of course she would never express that thought to Sherry. Crystal felt that no one should choose another person's mate—not even a best friend.

Sherry changed the subject by bringing up Crystal and Eric's planned trip to Las Vegas and the seven-day cruise they would be taking a few weeks later. "I really envy you, taking two romantic trips with your husband. I kind of wish I were in your shoes."

"You'll get your chance," Crystal said soothingly, "as soon as your kids are grown."

"That long huh? Thanks a lot, friend," Sherry said pretending to be disappointed. The two women were satisfied they'd had a chance to chitchat without interruptions. Crystal suggested they set the table before she called Eric to come down and eat, but Eric beat her to the punch with a surprise entrance that startled both women.

"Honey, your king is ready to dine," he belted out as he entered. At first he pretended not to see Sherry, but then, "Oh, hi Sherry. So you're what's holding up my dinner."

"She's not holding anything up," Crystal replied in Sherry's defense. "Come on Sherry, let's set the table."

"Shouldn't she be setting the table at her own house?" Eric asked.

Crystal started to admonish him for being rude, but Sherry stopped her. For some reason, Sherry sensed Eric was not in a good mood. Maybe it was the underlying tone in his voice.

"It's okay. I don't pay Eric any attention," Sherry admitted. "Besides, he's right. I should be setting my own table."

"Right, if you had someone to set it for," Eric said. It was becoming obvious, Eric wasn't joking.

Crystal jumped in, explaining that since Sherry's kids were away at camp she had invited her to stay for dinner. Sherry insisted that Eric meant no harm. She assured Crystal that she knew he was just joking around like he always does. Somehow Crystal sensed this was not Eric's usual way of joking with Sherry. Maybe it was the way he'd said it. She reminded Eric of his commitment to Herbert. In defense, Eric said he was just trying to get Sherry to see that she needed a man. Crystal was further disturbed when Eric added that this time Sherry should marry a man who was not twenty-eight years older than her. He came right out and said that her youthful affection was probably the cause of Herbert's heart attack.

The usually unaffected Sherry fired back, "Are you insinuating that I killed Herbert?"

"If the shoe fits, wear it," Eric said, a hint of malice in his tone.

"Eric, what's gotten into you? That was out and out rude!" Sherry grabbed her purse and started to leave. Suddenly she stopped and turned to face Eric.

"Have you forgotten the age difference between you and Crystal? And how dare you insinuate that Herbert's death was due to any vigorous sexual act I might have performed on him. Despite our age difference, Herbert could handle any situation ... with loving tenderness and so could I," she finished angrily as she stormed out. Crystal ran behind her trying to smooth things over and trying to convince her to stay to no avail. When Crystal returned to the kitchen, Eric grabbed her playfully.

"Now I've got you alone again."

"Stop it, Eric! I can't believe you joked about the intimacy between Sherry and Herbert. You've never done that before. She left here in tears."

"Aw, it ain't like she's never coming back. I've always teased her. I don't understand why all of a sudden she's so sensitive. I really did it on purpose so we could be alone. I missed you."

"Stop it, Eric! How could you miss me? And that was certainly no way to joke with her," Crystal added angrily. She wondered if this was the way he was going to act from now on whenever Sherry came over.

"We've been together almost every hour of every day since your retirement party."

"And that's the way it should be, just you and me," he said as he kissed her cheek and moved around to her lips. Pushing him away, Crystal asked him what he intended to do in the fall when she returned to work. Eric said exactly what she knew he was going to say.

"You can quit that job now. I'm receiving a nice pension, and soon I'll be collecting a pretty big social security check. We also have a nice little nest egg saved up."

"We can't pay these bills with your pension and a Social Security check. We still need my pay check. Besides, I love my job and I'm not ready to retire." Crystal thought about her students. *They seem to enjoy my classes. The whole school looks forward to the plays I produce twice a year. I want to work at least five more years ... maybe even ten.* Eric interrupted Crystal's thoughts.

"Tomorrow, I'm taking you shopping, how about that?"

"Ooh," Crystal said, allowing her anger to subside. "You know how I feel about shopping. I love it! I love it!"

"And I love you," Eric said.

"I love you too, honey, but ..."

"No ifs, ands, or buts. Now feed me, woman, before I eat you," Eric joked.

The next day Eric kept his promise. After breakfast, he and Crystal set out for the mall. Since they lived close to the River Oaks Mall, Crystal assumed that's where they were going. Instead, Eric headed straight for the expressway. When Crystal questioned him, he told her to just sit back and enjoy the ride. Eric turned the radio on to a popular local station. The D.J. was playing Michael Jackson's "Billie Jean." Crystal leaned back and closed her eyes. She began to think about the vacation she and Eric have planned. Every now and then she would open her eyes and look at Eric. He seemed so happy. She thought about all the years they had been together. She thought about how blessed she was to have a husband who worked hard, always brought his money home, and never gambled instead of paying the bills. If he chased women, she never knew it. He drank socially, and rarely ever got really drunk, except on special occasions, like on the night of his retirement party. Eric wasn't abusive. He would never even think about hitting her. In fact, he seldom if ever, hit their children who felt that some of his sermons lasted far longer than any punitive measures he could dish out. So he left most of the chastising up to Crystal. She didn't mind because she made it very clear, she was not in a popularity contest when it came to her children. She taught them to be obedient and respectful and warned them she was not going to get them out if they did anything to land themselves in jail.

Eric wasn't perfect, and at times, he did some things that really irritated her. For instance, when she was having a really good time at a party, he would want to go home before she was ready to leave. He would threaten to leave her. Since they only owned one car, unless she could hitch a ride, she would have to leave with him. But to complain about that would be nit-picking. Besides, she knew that she herself was far from perfect. Eric put up with her shopping sprees and acted like it really wasn't a big deal. He knew that's what most women liked to do, and Crystal was no different. Everyone said Eric adored Crystal, and she adored him back.

Crystal might have fallen asleep had not the D.J. played Eric's favorite song and he sang right along with the recording. He might be a good husband and father, but a gifted singer he was not. When Crystal finally opened her eyes and looked out of the window, she saw a sign with an arrow pointing toward the Gurney Mills Shopping Mall. She sat straight up. She had heard it had lots of wonderful stores. Crystal had always wanted to shop there. Although she shopped in the various malls on the south and west sides of Chicago, she had never ventured so far north. Eric loved to surprise her. Crystal squealed with delight when he turned into the mall's parking lot.

Their first stop was a high-fashion men's store. Whenever they shopped together, Crystal always shopped for Eric first so if he got tired or became impatient, they could go home and he would be happy. She knew she could always go back another day, alone or with Sherry and finish her own shopping. Eric tried on several outfits, modeling each of them for Crystal's approval or disapproval. Surprisingly, after going into two more stores for men only, and making several purchases for Eric, he didn't mind it when Crystal began shopping for herself. Eric was very patient as Crystal shopped first for sexy lingerie, next for several sundresses, and last, the latest in footwear. Eric knew she would have to buy at least two pairs of shoes despite the fact that her closet shelf held over seventy-five pairs stacked neatly in their original boxes.

They stopped by a travel agency to pick up some brochures for the cruise they were planning. Finally, when Eric began to look like he'd about had it, Crystal suggested they rest over lunch at a quaint little outdoor cafe.

Eric ordered two glasses of Merlot red wine. Afterwards, they sat for a while laughing and talking. Eric told Crystal she should really think about retiring after the next semester. He said they could travel all year to any place she wanted to go. He took her hand in his and promised he would never forget the love she'd shown him and he would spend the rest of his life keeping her happy. Crystal smiled as she said, "You'd better not forget that."

Eric and Crystal spent the next two weeks preparing for their vacation. In three days they would be on their way to Vegas. Sherry stopped by for last-minute instructions from Crystal. She had managed to get over the inconsiderate way Eric had joked with her. He had apologized a couple of days later and promised he would try not to hurt her feelings again. Crystal handed Sherry a list of important things to do. She and Eric would be leaving on Friday, returning the following Wednesday. They would be staying at Caesar's Palace. Crystal instructed Sherry to call them for emergencies ... only.

Sherry reminded Crystal that she and Eric had a doctor's appointment the day before their departure. They had been going to the same doctor for five years. It was Dr. Winter's practice to examine a husband and wife in the same room at the same time if they agreed. Crystal was happy because this way they would both be aware of each other's health issues. Sherry admired the closeness they had in their marriage. She asked Crystal about their sex life now that Eric had retired. Crystal's eyes twinkled as she described how amorous Eric had become. Sex between them had always been great but now it was as if they were on a never-ending honeymoon.

"I'll have to remember to tell Dr. Winter about that," Crystal said.

"I take it that means it's good," Sherry said.

"Better than good," Crystal replied with a sly grin. "Believe me when I tell you, the man is on fire!"

"Be careful," Sherry playfully warned, "remember what Eric said about how the age differences could lead to fatal consequences."

"You know he didn't really mean that. Besides, he'll probably kill me before I kill him." Crystal laughed at the thought. She was glad Sherry had accepted Eric's comments as a joke and hoped she realized he hadn't meant to hurt her feelings. Suddenly Eric entered, startling the two women. He was dressed in a black-and-red wool plaid winter jacket, light blue plaid summer pants, a yellow-and-black striped shirt, a red tie, and white shoes.

"Is this okay?" he asked as he spun around modeling his attire.

"Okay for what?" Crystal asked, trying not to show how irritated she was.

"Our doctor's appointment," Eric replied with innocence. Sherry covered her mouth with her hand as she tried unsuccessfully to stifle a laugh. Crystal was used to Eric putting the wrong outfits together, but this one bordered on the ridiculous.

"Eric, this is July. It is too hot for almost everything you have on. Besides, nothing matches. Plus, our appointment isn't until tomorrow, okay?"

"Okay, but you don't have to raise your voice. I just forgot, that's all," he said, raising his voice. As Eric retreated, he mumbled a short greeting to Sherry, acknowledging her presence.

"Now that's what I call 'sho' nuff' color-blindness," Sherry said as she removed her hand from her mouth so she could laugh out loud.

"I'm glad you think it's funny," Crystal said, making no attempt to hide her irritation. "Now you see why I lay out his clothes?"

"But you really shouldn't get upset since you said he does it all the time", Sherry said while still laughing. Crystal didn't tell Sherry, but Eric had never looked that wild before. Lately his clowning around had begun to get on her nerves. This incident was cause for her to worry. Sherry noticed Crystal's worried expression.

"I think he did that just to get your attention. You know he hates it when you spend a lot of time with other people, especially me. It's really your fault. You spoiled him, buying his clothes, combing his hair, treating him like a king—it's your fault," Sherry reiterated as she laughed.

"You're right, but I'm starting to worry about him."

"But why," Sherry queried as Eric returned. Seeing Eric, Crystal pointed.

"That's why." Eric was still dressed as before.

"Baby, what time is our appointment?" he asked.

"Four-thirty," Crystal said emphatically. "Four-thirty tomorrow," she continued. "Now will you please go take off those hot clothes?"

"Okay, okay, I'm going," Eric said as he left mumbling something inaudible. Now he was the one who seemed irritated.

"Maybe I'm the one who should be going," Sherry said as she started to leave. "No, please stay. I enjoy your company. You know, years ago when Eric and I first got married, he used to intimidate my friends. I've always been a "people" person. Eric never minded being alone, and he didn't care what he said to people or how he said it. What came up usually came out. But over the years he's become more amiable and a bit more considerate, and I don't intend to let him revert back to his old bad habits."

"Really, most of the time it doesn't bother me. I know him and I don't pay him any mind."

"Well I know him a little better than you, and it bothers me. I don't want to have to keep apologizing for him. I refuse to allow him to act like he used to act."

"I told you, he's just doing that to make me leave so he can have you all to himself," Sherry said as she sat back down. They went over the list of instructions again, making sure they'd covered everything.

"Don't forget about the mail," Crystal said.

"I won't. I'll check your box every day."

"Yeah, providing your long-distant lover doesn't keep you on the phone all day," Crystal teased.

"Well in that case maybe I won't check every day," Sherry said, laughing. Their conversation was interrupted again when Eric entered; this time without the jacket and tie, but the rest of his attire was the same.

"Honey, I don't mean to interrupt you and your company, but when did you say we go to the doctor?"

"I swear Eric, if you ask me that one ..."

Sherry interrupted laughing, "It's okay, Crystal, I can take a hint. The kids will be home soon, so I have to go anyway. You take care of your husband. I can let myself out." Sherry was still laughing as she headed out. Eric playfully grabbed Crystal, pulling her into his arms.

"Come on upstairs, honey, and show me what to wear."

"Eric, if you don't take those hot clothes off, I'm going to show you a straight jacket."

"That'll be okay, as long as you get in it with me," Eric joked as he pulled Crystal toward the stairs.

On Thursday, the day before their Vegas trip, Eric and Crystal sat in the examining room awaiting Dr. Winter. Crystal had already decided not to take up a lot of time with new concerns. A quick exam is all they needed. Dr. Winter entered with a smile. He was in his early sixties, medium build with mingled gray hair. He had a rugged attractiveness—for a doctor. Eric and Crystal felt very comfortable with his old-fashion bedside mannerisms. He always called them by their first names and proclaimed them his "favorite" patients. Eric liked to joke with the doctor, and the doctor enjoyed Eric's humor. Sometimes Crystal would join in with a little humor of her own. Dr. Winter would laugh at them both.

When Dr. Winter asked how they were doing, Eric said, "I'm fine, but you need to check out that grumpy old woman."

"He may be fine, but since he retired, I'm not doing so well." Crystal said, adding her contribution. Dr. Winter knew they were both joking and laughed.

"Okay, who wants to be first?" Dr. Winter always asked that question, but he always examined Crystal first. He performed a routine exam on both of them, making small talk as he checked their blood pressure; listened to their hearts; checked their ears, eyes, and throats; and tapped on their knees with a little hammer-like instrument. When Crystal told him they were leaving the next day for Vegas, Dr. Winter teased them.

"You'd better get plenty of rest before you go. Las Vegas is The City That Never Sleeps. You won't get much either." The mentioning of the word sleep made Eric remember to tell the doctor that he had been having trouble sleeping and that sometimes he awoke during the night with a terrible headache.

"Honey, you never told me that," Crystal said, surprised that Eric would keep something like that from her.

"Why should I have? You're not my doctor," Eric teased.

"Thank goodness I'm everything else," she teased back. Crystal was making a joke, but she still wondered why Eric hadn't mentioned his headaches. They really did have a good relationship, especially when it came to telling each other about their aches and pains. Dr. Winter asked Eric how often he was experiencing the headaches.

"Not every day. But since I've never been bothered with headaches before, I just thought I would mention it. Maybe you can prescribe something."

"Stop by the lab on your way out. I'll order some tests, have them take some blood, and see what's going on."

"You know how I hate needles, doc."

"Yes, but they are a necessary evil. We'll do an EKG and an EEG, and when you get back from your trip, we'll make an appointment for you to have an echocardiogram. In the meantime, it's okay for you to take a couple of Tylenols whenever you get a headache. Now go and enjoy your vacation. I'll see you both in two months."

"But what about all those tests you just ordered? When will we find out the results," Crystal questioned, showing her usual concern when it came to Eric's health. "And when will he take the echocardiogram?"

"My nurse will call you. There's nothing to worry about."

Crystal heaved a sigh of relief as she thanked the doctor.

"Come on, honey, we might as well get this over with," she said as they headed down to the lab. While Crystal never really dwelled on the age difference between them, Eric's health was always a matter of concern. When he had a cold, she was all over him like Florence Nightingale. She and Sherry laughed about the way men became big babies when they suffered the slightest bit of discomfort. She still wondered why Eric had not mentioned the headaches or his inability to sleep. Then she thought about the fact that she neglected to tell Dr. Winter about Eric's loud snoring. He'd always snored a little, but lately it had gotten really loud. *That's probably why he can't sleep,* she laughed at the thought. His snoring probably wakes him up.

They had always slept together in the same bed, even when twin beds had become a popular trend. She and Eric had said they wouldn't think of sleeping in separate beds. Crystal laughed again as she thought, *Eric's loud snoring might cause us to sleep in separate rooms.* Sitting in the waiting room while Eric was in the lab, Crystal closed her eyes as she turned her thoughts toward their vacation. *Eric and I definitely need one. In fact, we deserve one.*

Eric's childhood wasn't filled with great memories. He never knew his father, and his mother never talked about him. When Eric was thirteen, his mother sent him to Chicago to live with her brother. Her brother owned a funeral home and was married but didn't have any children of his own. She felt Eric would have an opportunity for a better life, better than the one she was able to provide for him. At that time, Mississippi didn't look kindly on little colored boys. Eric had told Crystal that living with his uncle made him experience even less of a childhood. After school, weekends, and all summer, he had to work at the funeral home. Eric never had a birthday party until Crystal gave him a surprise party on his fiftieth; boy was he surprised. He had never worn a Halloween costume until Crystal dressed him as a Japanese pimp. They won first place at the Halloween party, and of course she was dressed as a Geisha woman. Soon she would be taking him on his first cruise. She had promised him he would love it so much that he would want to take one every year. Eric had reminded her that it is the man who is supposed to take the woman on romantic escapades, but Crystal loved introducing Eric to new and exciting things. She had told him they would have wonderful memories to cherish in their "old age." Eric would always joke saying, "I'm already old, but I'll just wait until you catch up with me."

Eric emerged from the lab, interrupting Crystal's thoughts as he loudly complained about the technician's inability to find a vein and the need to stick him twice.

The following afternoon the airport limousine pulled into the circular driveway of the Caesar's Palace Casino and Hotel. Eric and Crystal exited the limo, and for a moment they just stood, taking in their surroundings. The driver placed their luggage on the cart the hotel bellboy had awaiting them. Crystal had been to Vegas with several of her girlfriends, but this was Eric's first trip and he was in awe. Crystal smiled while Eric's eyes danced as he looked around like a little boy on his first visit to Disneyland.

"If you think this is something," Crystal said, "wait until tonight when everything is all lit up. It's not only the city that never sleeps, it's the city of lights." In their hotel room, after tipping the bellboy and closing the door, Eric grabbed Crystal spinning her around.

"I finally have you all to myself," he said. "No phone calls, no door bells, just you and me."

"Hold on, I won't mind hearing a few bells when I hit one of those big jackpots. The bells are part of the excitement," Crystal informed him. Suddenly Eric noticed there were two full-size beds.

"Hey, we don't need two beds."

"Oh, yes we do," laughed Crystal. "You like to go to bed early and when I hear those one-arm bandits calling me back down to the casino, I want to answer the call without disturbing you."

Eric shook his head. "Uh uh, we're sleeping in the same bed and we won't be doing much sleeping." He plopped down on one of the beds. "This is the life." Crystal sat down beside him.

"I'm glad you're happy," she said. "It's five o'clock, let's eat. Then I'll show you how to play the slots."

"Okay, and I'll show you how to shoot craps," Eric said, pulling her on top of him.

"Oh, oh, let's go eat before you get ideas."

Crystal convinced Eric to have the prime rib dinner while she opted for the jumbo fried shrimp. Eric was surprised at how reasonable everything was. After dinner, they walked around the casino, trying their luck at the various games. Finally they sat down at the one-dollar slot machines. Crystal explained to Eric how to play and he quickly caught on. Several minutes passed when suddenly Eric's machine lit up and bells began to ring. He had hit a jackpot. Dollar coins began falling into the tray that was attached to his machine. Eric was excited, but Crystal was the one who made all the noise.

"Beginner's luck!" she cried as she grabbed one of the nearby plastic buckets and began helping Eric fill it up with the silver coins. People around them smiled as they watched the jolly pair. When the ringing finally ended, they had filled three buckets with coins. Eric suggested they cash in his winnings and go up to their room and relax.

"Not already," Crystal cried. "We came to have fun. It's still early. My machine was ready to hit, too."

"I just want to rest for a short while. We can come back down later. I promise," Eric said trying to comfort her.

Recognizing the gleam in Eric's eyes, Crystal said, "I know what you're up to, and we've got plenty of time for that too, Romeo."

"No really, after eating that prime rib dinner, I just want to relax—for a minute," he said with a sly grin.

"Alright, but no hanky-panky," she said, laughing.

Crystal cashed out her coins and accompanied Eric to the cashier. Eric grinned widely as the cashier counted out ten one hundred dollar bills, three twenties, and two fives.

"Now that's the way to start a vacation." He beamed.

"You can give me my cut when we get up to our room," Crystal said, pouting to evoke sympathy because she hadn't won. Eric grabbed her by the arm leading her to the elevator.

"What's mine is yours baby."

"Amen," Crystal said, "what's yours is mine." Then added jokingly, "And when I win, what's mine—is mine."

It was after nine o'clock when Crystal awoke. She and Eric had slept over two hours. Eric wasn't kidding when he said the prime rib had filled him up and made him need to take a nap because he was still asleep. It was probably his snoring that had awakened her, but it wasn't disturbing him at all. He had said he would be ready to hit the slots again after he'd had a power nap. He must have meant "powerful" nap. Crystal had been able to resist Eric's passionate kisses, convincing him they would have plenty of time for lovemaking. She had even agreed to lay down with him but hadn't figured she would go to sleep too. What would Sherry think if she knew they were both asleep in Vegas ... at nine o'clock? Crystal smiled as she looked over at Eric, who was still sleeping like a baby. Well I didn't travel two thousand miles to lay up and sleep, she thought. I'll just go down and play for an hour, and then I'll come back up and wake him. Crystal primped in the mirror. Satisfied with her appearance, she glanced over at Eric again and then tipped-toed out, easing the door closed.

Crystal entered the casino, hoping she could find the same machine she had been playing earlier. She also hoped others had played it but hadn't won so it would be ripe for her. After trying several machines, she found one she felt would be the lucky one. She was right. A few moments later, she hit a small jackpot but moved on trying several other machines. She finally found one she thought might be lucky and decided to stay at that one for a while. Two hours later, Crystal checked her watch and thought, I'd better go wake Eric. She hadn't lost, but she hadn't won a lot so she cashed out and headed for the elevator leading to their ninth-floor room.

As she exited the elevator, Crystal's eyes were drawn to a pair of brown suede loafers sitting right beside the elevator. At first she thought that was an odd place for someone to leave their shoes. Whoever did it must have had one too many cocktails. They looked brand-new, just like the ones she had picked out at the mall for Eric. She couldn't explain it, but suddenly a tinge of fear made her examine the shoes. They were Eric's size, but why would she think they were his? Questions and thoughts began to emerge. Did someone drop them or lose them? No, they looked as if they had been neatly placed there. Could they be Eric's? Of course not, there must be hundreds of men who had brown suede shoes like these. Why would Eric's shoes be sitting out here beside the elevator anyway? Should she take them to her room? No, whoever lost them will probably come looking for them.

Crystal hurried down the hall toward their room, unable to ignore the uneasy feeling that had begun to creep into the pit of her stomach. She nervously pushed the key in and turned the knob. As she threw the door open she was consumed with fear. Both beds were empty. She rushed into the bathroom. It was empty too. Eric was not there. She looked beside the bed and in the closet. Eric's brown suede shoes were not there. The clothes he had worn that day were on the extra bed. Crystal checked his pockets. The money he had won was still in his wallet. She checked his clothes hanging in the closet. They were all still there, just the way she'd hung them. Had someone come in and kidnapped him? Don't be silly, who would do that? He couldn't have gone out without any clothes on. Why would he?

Crystal rushed back out to the elevator. Terrible thoughts raced through her mind. Did Eric slip out of his shoes just before he fell down the elevator shaft? Why didn't he put back on the clothes he had worn earlier? What is he wearing now? Where could he have gone? She had only been gone two hours and he was sound asleep when she'd left. Could he have gone back down to the casino looking for her? If so, what is he wearing? Oh God, she prayed, please don't let anything happen to him. Tears swelled in her eyes. I shouldn't have left him. But ... why not? There was no reason why Eric couldn't be left alone. Crystal realized she was thinking out loud as she nervously awaited the elevator. She would check at the front desk. Please God, let him be alright, she prayed. She grabbed the brown suede shoes as she entered the elevator.

As Crystal exited the elevator and turned the corner, she saw a group of people at the front desk. There, in the middle of the group was Eric. He was barefoot with a towel wrapped around him. Eric smiled when he saw Crystal. A look of sheer relief encompassed his face. The rest of the group looked over in her direction.

"Honey, am I glad to find you. I thought you were lost. I didn't know where you were."

"What happened?" Crystal asked trying to mask her terror mixed with confusion. The desk clerk spoke up.

"Are you his wife?"

"Yes I am," Crystal said with apprehension, not knowing whether to display concern or embarrassment.

"He got off of the elevator obviously very confused. He was barefoot, wearing only his underwear. Since he knew his name, we checked the registry to see what room he was in; but when he was escorted to the room, he didn't recognize the men's clothes in the closet."

"That's because most of his clothes are brand-new," Crystal said defensively as she tried to calm her shaking voice.

"We were just getting ready to notify the police," the manager admitted.

"The police? Has he committed some kind of crime?" Fear was beginning to creep into her voice. "If you had checked his wallet you would have realized it was his room." Crystal also wondered why they hadn't seen his shoes sitting there beside the elevator.

"Your husband is relieved to see you, and so am I. We covered him with this towel ma'am. Is he on some kind of medication?" the manager asked.

"Yes," Crystal lied.

She wanted to hurry and get Eric up to their room so she could question him in private. She prayed there would be a logical explanation for his embarrassing if not outrageous behavior.

"I'll give it to him as soon as we get back to our room. I'm sorry about the disturbance."

"No problem, ma'am. Are you sure he's okay? I can call an ambulance if you like."

"No ... no thanks," Crystal quickly replied. "He'll be okay once he's had his medication. Come on, honey," she said, forcing a smile.

Unable now to conceal her embarrassment, Crystal led Eric to the elevator. They got on the elevator with several other people who kept staring at Eric.

"Did you enjoy your swim, honey?" Crystal asked Eric, hoping he would play along with her and save her from any further embarrassment.

"You know I can't swim," Eric said without cracking a smile. He had no idea Crystal was trying to save face. She was glad when the elevator stopped on their floor. An elderly couple got off with them, so Crystal remained silent. But as they headed toward their room, and she realized the couple had gone in the opposite direction, Crystal let go.

"What made you decide to leave the room without getting dressed, Eric?"

"I'm sorry baby, but when I woke up and didn't see you I thought something had happened. I went looking for you."

"In your underwear? Why didn't you put your clothes back on?" Crystal no longer tried to maintain self-control. "And why did you leave these shoes sitting by the elevator? You scared the crap out of me."

"Those are not my shoes."

"Eric, we bought them when we went shopping. You wore them here."

"I knew you were going to be mad," he said, almost childlike.

"I'm not mad; I'm just wondering what's going on with you."

"There's nothing going on with me. I told you I was looking for you." Crystal also wondered what she should do since there wasn't any medicine to give him. Eric grabbed her playfully, pulling her into his arms.

"I missed you baby."

"Stop it, Eric. You're not funny. You really scared me."

"Okay, I'm sorry. I won't do it again."

"How do you know you won't do it again when you don't even know why you did it."

"I said I'm sorry. Come on, honey, we're on vacation. Don't spoil it."

"Me spoil it? You ..." Crystal was about to really let Eric have it but stopped because he was standing there with his eyes closed and his lips puckered, waiting for Crystal to kiss him. Crystal sighed but still refused to kiss him. Finally, he pulled her into his arms and forced her to kiss him. He kept kissing her until they were on the bed. She couldn't believe he wanted to make love after what had just happened. After they'd made love, Eric fell asleep right away, but Crystal remained awake. What was really going on in Eric's head? she thought as she watched him sleeping. Could the headaches Eric had mentioned to Dr. Winter be causing his strange behavior? In all the years they'd been married, he had never ever acted like this. Crystal felt exhausted and drained, both physically and mentally. Finally she slowly drifted off.

The next morning when Crystal awoke, Eric was already up. She could hear him humming as he showered and shaved. She remained in bed thinking about what had happened and wondering if it had all been a dream. When Eric emerged from the bathroom, she started to question him.

"Honey ... last night you ..."

"I'm sorry, baby; I guess I was really tired. I sure didn't mean to fall asleep as soon as we got in the bed. I promise I'll make it up to you tonight. Okay?" Eric interrupted Crystal before she could finish her sentence. "Now get up, sleepyhead, and let's go eat breakfast. After that, we can explore this town. I've got plenty of money, so you can shop until you drop," he added as he pulled her out of the bed. Crystal was both surprised and puzzled. Eric was acting like nothing had happened.

"Honey ... how do you feel," she asked.

"How do I feel? I feel great—and hungry. Now come on, get in that bathroom and make it snappy. Time's a wasting. We're in Vegas!" Crystal looked at Eric for a moment. He looked and acted as though he really did feel great. She decided to continue their vacation in the same happy and excited mood Eric was in. She really didn't want to have anything negative interrupt the wonderful time they had planned. Since he didn't seem to remember or want to discuss it, she pushed the scary episode of the night before to the back of her mind, as if it had been a bad dream. Eric was acting as if it had never occurred, so Crystal decided to act like it hadn't happened too—at least until they got back to Chicago. Silently she prayed that there wouldn't be any similar incidents.

She and Eric really enjoyed the next few days. They rented a car, and Eric drove them around exploring downtown Las Vegas. They shopped and ate and attended several of the highly entertaining extravaganzas that Las Vegas was noted for. Every night they gambled a little and then went to their room and made love like newlyweds. Eric was having the time of his life. Although Crystal had enjoyed other visits to Vegas, seeing how much fun Eric was having certainly made this trip much more memorable. She was glad he had decided to retire. She thought about all the vacations and exotic, faraway places they would travel to in the future.

Life was good, and Crystal was grateful. The only time she thought about the events of their first night was the one and only time she came face-to-face with the same manager who was on duty that night. Since he didn't mention it, neither did she. She had already begun to convince herself it never happened. And of course Eric never mentioned it either. He continued to enjoy being in Vegas, hitting small jackpots and spending most of his winnings on anything and everything that Crystal expressed a desire to have. When it was time to leave, he made her promise they would come back at least once a year.

As the limousine pulled into the driveway, Sherry opened the front door. She knew just what time to expect them back and stood in the doorway grinning.

"Welcome home," she said. "I see you have an extra piece of luggage. Is this the one with all the winnings," she asked, grabbing the extra suitcase. Crystal and Eric followed her into the foyer.

"The money would have made our bags too heavy so the casino manager wrote us a check," Eric teased, trying to sound serious.

"No kidding?" Sherry squealed.

"Yes kidding," Crystal said, shaking her head. "I can't believe you actually thought Eric was telling the truth. We won a little and we shopped a lot. And before you ask, yes I brought you something. Now tell me, how did things go back here?"

"Let me get my pad; I wrote everything down," Sherry said as she led the way into the kitchen.

"Eric, take our bags upstairs. I'm too tired to tell Sherry about the fun we had so I'll be up in a minute," Crystal promised.

"Okay but remember, a minute is only sixty seconds," Eric joked as he lugged their bags toward the stairs.

"Hey, what about the present you brought me? Don't let him take it upstairs," Sherry squealed.

"It's not anything to get excited about. You'll get it when I unpack."

Crystal sat down at the table as Sherry handed her a stack of mail. Trying not to show her disappointment, Sherry began to read the list of calls she had written down.

"Did Dr. Winter's office call," Crystal asked.

"I didn't take a call from him, but he may be on your answering machine. Now come on, it's not that late. Tell me a little bit about the fun you two had on your trip," Sherry said as she sat down.

"Why don't we do lunch on Saturday? I promise I'll give you every exciting detail," Crystal said.

"And I have to wait until then to get my gift too?"

"If you don't mind," Crystal said with a hint of fatigue.

"Okay, okay, I guess I can wait until then," Sherry said, still sounding a bit disappointed. "But you need to call Mark. He wants to make sure you and Eric are still coming for Christmas."

For the past three years, Crystal and Eric had spent Christmas and New Year's in L.A. Crystal wouldn't think of missing a chance to spend Christmas with her only grandchild. Mark was managing a small hotel and had combined a room and a suite and turned it into an apartment for him and his family. Crystal and Eric would be staying in another suite right across the hall. She assured Sherry that she was definitely going to L.A. for Christmas and asked her what she and her kids planned to do for the holidays.

"I might be having an out-of-town guest," Sherry said smiling.

"Oh?" Crystal waited, expecting a more detailed explanation. She figured Leonardo was the guest, but she wanted Sherry to confirm. The telephone interrupted the two women. It was Dr. Winter's nurse, asking Crystal if she and Eric could come in at ten o'clock on Friday. Crystal agreed, repeating the date and time for confirmation. As she hung up, she forced a smile, hoping Sherry hadn't noticed her worried expression. It was too late, but before Sherry could question Crystal, Eric made another one of his surprise entrances and announced their little "tete-a-tete" had gone way past the promised sixty seconds.

"Eric, I'm coming," Crystal said, showing a little bit of impatience.

"Eric, I'm going, Sherry laughed. "Here, you can read the rest of this yourself," she added, handing the list to Crystal. "I'll let myself out. Goodbye, Scrooge," she teased as she made a face at Eric.

"Bah humbug," Eric teased back, giving her a "raspberry."

"You still didn't tell me who your holiday guest is," Crystal reminded Sherry as she started to walk her to the door.

"I know, but I did tell you I'd let myself out, so goodbye." Sherry exited quickly, closing the door behind her.

"What guest?" Eric asked. When Crystal told Eric she suspected that Leonardo and Sherry were about to engage in a long-distant relationship, Eric quickly responded.

"That's a good thing. I think it's time for her to get on with her life."

"Is that what you would want me to do?" Crystal teased, knowing exactly what he was going to say.

"No baby—uh, uh—it's you and me forever. Now let's put a little icing on that cake, if you know what I mean."

"Yes I do, and let's not forget to tell Dr. Winter how amorous you're getting in your old age," Crystal laughed. Eric bowed and took her hand, leading her up the stairs as if he was her prince and she was his princess.

The next day Crystal unpacked the clothes they'd taken to Vegas and began deciding what they would be taking on their next trip. They had chosen a seven-day Caribbean cruise and the excitement was building in both of them. This was Crystal's first cruise too and she looked forward to experiencing it with Eric. Eric spent his time teasing Crystal about the idle time he had on his hands. He said they should be spending it trying to make a baby. Crystal laughed.

"The next time I deliver a baby, a star will shine in the east and three wise men will show up with enough gold to ensure that no one in our entire family will ever have to work again. But if the wise men don't show up, I can always sue the hospital that tied my tubes."

"Maybe I know how to untie them," Eric said laughing. Crystal loved company, but she really cherished the fun times she and Eric shared, laughing and joking, just the two of them. Since Eric hadn't talked about what happened in Vegas, Crystal decided she wouldn't mention it to Dr. Winter. In fact, she wouldn't even think about it ever again. Since she was convinced that Dr. Winter just wanted to go over the results of Eric's tests, she didn't have any reason to worry. Most of Eric's friends were on some kind of blood pressure medication, she thought, maybe Dr. Winter was going to prescribe something for him. Eric was almost sixty-six and hadn't had any serious medical problems. The tests probably showed Eric had developed hypertension. Dr. Winter would be concerned that Eric might have a stroke, so he would probably prescribe something to control it.

The day before their appointment, Crystal decided to pick out the clothes that Eric would wear in case he tried to put something together himself. She still couldn't forget the way he looked the last time he did the choosing.

Friday morning Crystal and Eric arrived at Dr. Winter's office a little before the scheduled time. Since it wasn't their regular appointment,

Crystal thought it best they be a little early. She figured Dr. Winter might be fitting them into his already busy schedule. The nurse led Eric and Crystal into the examining room where Dr. Winter was already waiting for them. As usual, Eric greeted the doctor with a joke, which usually caused him to laugh, especially when Crystal followed with her own witty response. This routine always created a casual and relaxed atmosphere. But Crystal sensed the doctor was in a serious mood.

Dr. Winter started off by saying, "Eric, you have developed hypertension." Crystal thought, I knew it. I knew it was something simple. She was visibly relieved. "I can prescribe something for that," Dr. Winters continued, "but I'm concerned about something your EKG showed. There's a very slight blockage in one of your arteries. I'm sure the blood thinner Coumadin should solve that problem. Just to be on the safe side though, I want to make an appointment for you to have an MRI and another EKG and an EEG."

Crystal's relief only lasted for a moment. She asked Dr. Winter what the MRI was for. He explained that an MRI would be more conclusive and confessed that he was concerned about what was going on with Eric's heart. He added that he was also concerned about Eric's headaches and wanted to take a look at his brain. Crystal assured Dr. Winter that Eric was not experiencing anymore headaches. Eric agreed.

"Just the one over there, doc," he said, pointing to Crystal. Dr. Winter forced a smile. He glanced at Crystal, sensing her uneasiness. He knew how she hovered over Eric like a mother hen over her baby chicks, so he attempted to quell her fears.

"I recommend the MRI because of Eric's age and because I don't want to guess about anything. The good news is that Eric is in pretty good physical condition. In fact, both of you are."

"She should be. She doesn't do anything. I have to do all the work," Eric joked. Dr. Winter smiled, waiting for a comment from Crystal, but she made none. He knew her thoughts were on the number of tests he wanted Eric to have. Trying to ease her fears, Dr. Winter asked if they were still planning to take a cruise. Eric quickly answered.

"Yep, we leave in two weeks. It's either a cruise or a divorce."

Crystal, feeling a little more at ease added, "It'll probably be both." This time Dr. Winter's laugh was genuine.

"Go on, you two. Enjoy your cruise. Call my nurse when you get back, and we'll schedule an appointment for the MRI and the EEG. And don't forget to have that prescription filled. Eric needs to start taking the Coumadin right away."

Crystal heaved a sigh of relief as they headed home to begin preparing for their cruise. She was glad Dr. Winter hadn't given them a negative report—one that would prevent them from going on their cruise. Next stop—Marshall Fields.

Sherry shared her friend's excitement as they headed to the mall. Crystal had taught her the art of shopping, and she loved it as much as Crystal even if she didn't have the money to shop like her.

"You and Eric are going to be the best-dressed couple on the boat."

"Ship, darling, it's a ship," Crystal said smiling. For a few minutes no one spoke. Finally Crystal said, "I'll give you a penny." That's what they always said to each other whenever one of them wanted to know what the other was thinking.

"I was just thinking that if Herbert were alive, we'd probably be going on that cruise with you and Eric."

Crystal recognized the melancholy tone in Sherry's voice. One minute Sherry was jovial and excited and the next she sounded—sad. Crystal couldn't say she knew how Sherry felt because she didn't, and she hoped she would never know that feeling. But she did know that Sherry was on the verge of tearing up, so she decided to change the subject before they both bawled like babies. That's the way it was with them. They were so close, most times when one cried the other would join in as if they were singing a duet. This always made them both end up laughing.

Crystal thought back to the day Herbert died. It had been early in the afternoon when Sherry had called her. The minute she heard Sherry's voice, Crystal had detected the urgency and the panic.

"Crystal, I think Herbert is having a heart attack, but he won't let me call the paramedics," she'd said. "I had to sneak to call you. Can you come over right away?" Crystal explained that Eric had taken the car and had gone to the barber shop.

"You sneaked and called me, now sneak and dial 911," Crystal ordered.

"He begged me not to do that." Sherry began to cry.

"Where is he now?" Crystal asked.

"He's out in the backyard, lying in the grass, trying to catch his breath."

"What happened?" Sherry spoke while crying profusely.

"Crystal ... we had just finished having sex. I was in the bathroom when I heard him gasping for breath. I made him go outside so he could get some air. Oh please hurry, Crystal! I'm so scared."

"Okay, I'll call the barbershop. As soon as Eric gets back, I'll be right there. Meanwhile, forget what Herbert said. Dial 911 now! Better yet, I'll dial them."

"Okay, and tell them to please hurry!"

Crystal dialed 911 first and then she called the barbershop, but Eric was already on his way home. By the time Eric arrived, Sherry had called back to say the ambulance had come, and they were on their way to the hospital in Hammond, Indiana.

Eric drove while Crystal silently prayed. At the hospital, Eric let her out at the emergency room entrance while he parked the car. Crystal rushed inside not knowing which way to go. A nun approached and asked her if her name was Crystal. Too scared to speak, she just nodded. The nun led her toward a door. The nun pushed open the door. Sherry was inside with another nun and a doctor. Sherry turned around and when she saw Crystal, she began to scream. "He's dead, he's dead! I killed him!" At that moment the two women grabbed each other and they both fell to the floor, hollering and screaming and rolling around like two saints at a Holy Roller's revival. Obviously, Sherry had gone to pieces earlier when Herbert had been pronounced dead because one of the nuns reached down and touched Crystal's arm and said, "Miss, we had hoped you would be able to calm her down." Embarrassed, Crystal picked herself up and helped Sherry to her feet. She managed to calm her down but only until they had left the hospital. Sherry cried every day up until the funeral and every day after the funeral for weeks. Months later, when Crystal reminded Sherry of that day, they both managed to laugh, not only at their actions but at the reactions and expressions on the faces of the nuns. Although they both had to admit it wasn't funny at the time.

Crystal's thoughts were interrupted as they reached the mall. She was sure once they started shopping Sherry's spirits would be lifted. If that didn't do it, she would engage her in a conversation about Leonardo. She knew that would bring back the excitement in her—at least she hoped it would.

Three
Normality Encourages Denial

TWO DAYS BEFORE ERIC AND CRYSTAL WERE TO LEAVE ON THEIR CRUISE, Sherry called and asked if they could stop by and pick up a gift she had bought them. On the way to Sherry's house, Eric complained about having to go with Crystal. He couldn't understand why both of them needed to pick up the gift.

"In fact, she'll be coming to our house tomorrow to get last-minute instructions and pick up the keys," he reminded Crystal, defending his complaint.

"Honey, Sherry cared enough to buy us a gift. The least we can do is go and get it," Crystal said. "Besides, maybe it's so big it'll take both of us to carry it home," she laughed. Eric knew he couldn't win, so he changed the subject.

"You know something? I am really excited about this cruise. I've gotta hand it to you baby, you've planned a great vacation. Now that's one of the advantages gained when an old man marries a young woman."

"You're right," agreed Crystal, "and while you're singing my praises, get your checkbook out; I need some money."

"Did I mention some of the disadvantages?" Eric chuckled as they pulled up in front of Sherry's house. "Maybe I'll just stay in the car. That way she won't hold us up with a long, drawn-out conversation."

"Maybe you'll just get out the car and come with me so she won't think you're unappreciative." Eric got out the car mumbling something incoherently. Crystal rang the bell. It was a while before Sherry came to the door, which prompted Eric to wonder aloud.

"Why is it taking her so long to answer? Are you sure she's expecting us?"

"Stop being so impatient, she might be in the bathroom," Crystal chided. Finally the door opened. As Eric and Crystal entered, a small group of well-wishers greeted them.

"Surprise! Bon Voyage," they all yelled.

"We really surprised you, didn't we," Sherry added. Crystal displayed genuine surprise.

"Not me, I knew it all the time," Eric lied. The group expressed their disappointment and asked him when and how he'd found out. Crystal assured them Eric was lying and hadn't had the slightest inkling. Eric and Crystal were showered with gifts fit for traveling and cruising. Both expressed their genuine gratitude and appreciation. On the ride home, Eric had to admit they were lucky to have a good friend like Sherry. Crystal was happy to hear that coming from Eric. Despite the teasing Eric did with Sherry, Crystal always knew he liked her as a person and would never do anything to jeopardize their close friendship.

It was a hot and muggy Sunday afternoon in August when the limo arrived to take Crystal and Eric to the airport. Assuring them she would handle everything while they were gone, Sherry waved goodbye as the limo took off. They would soon be boarding a plane to Puerto Rico. From there, they would board the ship and sail off on their Caribbean cruise, or as Eric would later describe it, "Heaven right here on earth." Crystal agreed. She thought it was the most wonderful time of their whole life together. Well—maybe one of the most wonderful times.

The ship, named the "Royal Monarch of the Sea," was larger and more majestic than they had even imagined. From the moment they stepped aboard, they were like two kids in wonderland. They were shown to their cabin, which was small but comfortable. The designers knew the occupants would spend very little time in their cabins. Theirs was on level three of the eight levels below the deck. The higher up toward the deck, the more expensive the cabins were.

There was so much to do aboard the ship. The activities were endless. There was bingo, horseracing, shuffle board, bowling, and table tennis. They could attend movies, extravagant shows, and even gamble in the casino. You name it, you could do it. There were shops of all kinds: a beauty salon, a barbershop, a jewelry store, a camera shop, a shop where one could get a manicure or a pedicure or both. There was even a shoeshine stand. Whatever you wanted to buy, you could buy it aboard the ship. There was also a laundry and dry cleaners. And the food! Crystal and Eric marveled at the amount of food one could consume on a cruise. First there was breakfast, and then you snacked, and then lunch. After that, there were more snacks; and in the evening, a seven-course dinner. Before calling it a night, one could feast on a fabulous midnight buffet consisting of various salads, seafoods and desserts. Eric said he had never seen so much food, and all of it was delicious. Crystal just knew they both were going to be at least ten pounds heavier when they weighed in back at home.

"No wonder there's an exercise gym aboard this ship. We are going to use it every day," Crystal informed Eric.

"We need to use it after every meal," Eric added, laughing.

Each day, the ship sailed to a different island. Sometimes they shopped for jewelry, which was a lot cheaper than on the ship or even back in the states; but most times they went swimming off the beach or just walked around exploring the island. The people on the islands were friendly enough, but they were either begging or trying to sell you something you didn't need or want. Crystal wondered if they had access to deodorants. On one of the islands, Eric bought Crystal a beautiful opal and diamond birthstone ring. He told her that every time she looked at the ring he hoped it would remind her of how much he loved and appreciated her. At that moment, Crystal felt no two people on earth could be happier than they were.

On the second night, at dinner they met Adelia and Ricardo Mendoza, a Hispanic couple from one of the suburbs of Chicago. What a coincidence, Crystal thought. Ricardo was a little younger than Eric, but Adelia was about Crystal's age. They spent the rest of the evening with the couple, taking in one of several musical extravaganzas. Adelia and Ricardo proved to be devoted to one another but were different from any couple Eric and Crystal knew. In fact, they were quite comical and very entertaining. They were the total opposite of each other. Adelia was tall; Ricardo was short. He wanted kids; she never did, and so they never had any. He was raised on a farm; she was raised in the city. Ricardo liked to tell corny jokes. Adelia hardly ever laughed at them, but she didn't discourage him from telling them. While they didn't mind hanging out with the couple occasionally, Crystal and Eric had the most fun just enjoying each other.

One of the most memorable events of the cruise was the Captain's Ball.

Everybody was decked out in their finest after- five attire. Crystal was glad she had brought along the dress she'd had made for Eric's retirement party. Eric wore his retirement party outfit too, looking as handsome as ever. Crystal had told Eric, "As much as these outfits cost, we might as well get to wear them again. Besides, no one on the cruise has seen them."

The ballroom was eloquently decorated with beautiful hanging chandeliers. The dance floor was huge, so many of the couples could feel comfortable as they swayed to the romantic music the band played almost non-stop. It reminded Crystal of the ballroom Eric's retirement party was held in.

Eric eased over to the captain and informed him that Ricardo and Adelia were celebrating their tenth wedding anniversary and asked if the band could play "The Anniversary Song." The first words of the song are *Oh how we danced on the night we were wed, we vowed our true love though a word wasn't said.* Eric knew it was also one of Crystal's favorite songs.

When the band began to play the song, the captain announced that it was Ricardo and Adelia's anniversary, and the surprised couple quickly went to the center of the floor and began to dance. Other couples joined them. Eric took Crystal's hand gently in his. He bowed and asked,

"May I have this dance?" Crystal gave an equally dramatic consent as she thought back to the day she and Eric had wed. She felt the same love and adoration for him now as she did then. As Eric pulled her to him, she melted into his arms, pressing her cheek against his. At that moment, she wished time would completely and totally stand still. Eric held her so close to him she could feel his heart beating. When the song ended, Crystal was still swaying.

"Shall we go to our room?" Eric teased.

"Quick, fast, and in a hurry," Crystal teased back as she thought, You may be teasing, but I am dead serious my love.

Crystal was glad she had remembered to bring her camera. Ricardo offered to take pictures of her and Eric. Almost everybody on the cruise was extremely friendly. No one seemed to mind when Crystal asked them to take her camera and snap a picture of Eric and her with Ricardo and Adelia.

Later that night, as they snuggled in each other's arms, Eric whispered, "Let's do this again, same time next year and every year afterwards." Crystal closed her eyes and smiled. Her body answered yes, yes. She made a mental note to speak to Dr. Winter about Eric's heightened sex drive—not that she had any complaints whatsoever.

A few years later, when Crystal would think back to that memorable vacation, if there were any signs that Eric had entered the first stage of dementia, she had to admit she never recognized them. On the last day of the cruise, Eric and Crystal did not want to exit the ship.

"I think our next cruise should last at least two weeks," Eric said.

"You need to think about the cost of such a vacation, Mr. Rockefeller," Crystal said jokingly. "I suggest you go back to work in order to make it happen."

"I'll not only go back to work, I'll get a newspaper route and throw papers on porches on my way to work," Eric joked.

Before Eric and Crystal left the ship, they exchanged addresses and phone numbers with Ricardo and Adelia, promising to keep in touch. Adelia reminded Crystal to call her when she was ready to try some authentic Mexican recipes. Although Crystal was not ready to end their vacation, she was eager to get home and tell Sherry about the wonderful time she and Eric had. In fact, she knew she would be talking about this vacation for months, with pictures to back up her description of each glorious and exciting moment. Boy, will we have some great memories to share during our twilight years, she thought as she turned back to get one more look at the magnificent ship.

When Crystal and Eric arrived home, Sherry greeted them at the door. "Leave your bags down here and come have a cup of coffee with me," she said.

Eric declined, saying, "I'll take a rain check. I'm going to bed. You two can talk 'til Lou gets through." As Eric headed upstairs, Sherry asked, "Who is Lou?"

Laughing, Crystal explained, "It's something the old folks used to say. Somebody named Lou was long-winded I guess."

"Well, talk like Lou and tell me all about the cruise."

"It's too much to tell you tonight, but I will say this, I never dreamed that I could have the fun I had on that cruise. Now, I don't mean to seem rude, unappreciative, or unkind by rushing you out, but we've got the rest of the week to talk."

"Okay, I get the message," Sherry said, pretending to be disappointed. "I wrote down all your phone calls, and here's your stack of mail." Sherry headed for the door as Crystal followed. "You needn't see me to the door; I can let myself out."

"Aw, don't be angry," Crystal said apologizing.

"I'm not angry, I'm jealous. You'd think you and 'Lover Boy' did enough snuggling on the cruise," Sherry said, pretending to be angry.

"Well we didn't, so don't go away mad. Just go away," Crystal teased.

"I'm your best friend, the shoulder you may one day need to cry on.

You know something? You're beginning to sound just like your husband," Sherry snarled. "Don't get upset when I refuse to tell you about my upcoming secret rendezvous."

"Oh you'll tell me alright, you can't wait to tell me. We'll both talk 'til Lou gets through," Crystal promised, laughing.

As Sherry exited she turned back, "Oh, I forgot to write it down, Dr. Winter's nurse called yesterday, but she didn't sound like it was urgent. She said she would give you a call next week or you could call her whenever you got back."

"Thanks, I'll call her tomorrow," Crystal promised.

As she climbed the stairs to join Eric, Crystal thought Dr. Winter probably wants to see how the Coumadin is working and let us know that Eric's tests came out okay. He also probably wants to make an appointment for Eric's MRI. That night, as Crystal slid into bed beside Eric, she whispered a prayer. "Thank you, Lord, for a safe and memorable cruise; and thank you for blessing me with such a wonderful husband and soul mate." As she started to drift off, Eric turned over and grabbed her.

"Gotcha," he said pulling her into his arms. "I thought you'd never come to bed. I'm neither tired nor sleepy."

"Well, I am, and you should be too—old man," Crystal teased as she succumbed to Eric's ardent kisses.

Crystal was still floating on air days after they returned. The first couple of days she managed to unpack and clean the clothes they had worn on the cruise. Sherry stayed away, allowing Crystal to get back into the swing of being "Susie Homemaker" and prepare for the fall semester at the college. Finally, after three days, Crystal couldn't resist any longer. She called Sherry and insisted she come have coffee and some of her homemade rolls. When a couple of Eric's buddies dropped by to tease him about having nothing to do, Eric didn't hesitate to give them the 411 about his Caribbean cruise. He also boasted that he still had plenty to do, which included drinking beer, watching baseball on T.V. and chasing his wife around the house. Crystal was glad Eric was preoccupied. She and Sherry could do their "girl talking" without any interruptions.

Sherry dropped her kids off at day camp and by ten thirty she and Crystal were sitting in the kitchen sipping coffee and sharing information. Sherry listened while Crystal related every exciting and intimate detail of the cruise. Sherry was serious when she told Crystal how lucky she was to have a husband like Eric.

"He's what every girl dreams of."

"Hold on there. He's not perfect."

"I know," Sherry said, "but he's a good man and after all these years you two have been together, he's still in love with you."

"And the feeling is mutual," Crystal assured her. Crystal knew her friend was happy for her, but she could tell by Sherry's tone that she was also envious. "You'll get your turn, you'll see," Crystal said. "So now, tell me about your so called secret rendezvous," she added. Crystal knew her friend was eager to confide in her, but she also knew she wanted to be coaxed.

"Okay." Sherry's eyes lit up as she spoke. "Leonardo called while you were on your cruise." Sherry paused.

"And?" Crystal asked with raised eyebrows.

"Let's just say that the gods have smiled upon us."

"I take that to mean despite my friendly advice, you intend to engage in a long-distant relationship."

"Maybe," Sherry replied with a mischievous grin.

"I hope you know what you're doing," Crystal warned.

"I do," Sherry said with confidence, but she knew her friend was not pleased with her decision.

The next few days were uneventful. Crystal was right, the nurse had called them to make an appointment for Eric's MRI. Dr. Winter had arranged for him to take another EEG as well. Eric tried to persuade Crystal to let him go alone since the MRI would be time consuming, but Crystal insisted she could bring along some reading materials and wait. It had been a number of years since Eric had gone to the doctor alone, and Crystal didn't see any reason things should change now. She was happy that Eric had not been doing or saying anything unusual lately. Hard as Crystal tried, she couldn't get the incident in Vegas totally out of her mind. She kept telling herself that if it wasn't a dream it was probably a sign that Eric was getting older and when people grow old. ... She chided herself for even thinking those thoughts. Eric wasn't THAT old. In fact, he still had a lot of good years ahead. Still, she chided herself for thinking about Vegas since she had vowed she would never bring it up nor discuss it with anyone, including Dr. Winter. Crystal decided that since Eric was only going for tests, he probably wouldn't even see Dr. Winter. The appointment was set for the following week.

Eric was right, it was a long day; and Crystal was also right, they didn't have to see Dr. Winter. Crystal had brought along a magazine to read while she waited. Just as she started to read, a woman seated next to her began to complain about her husband, who was also in having some tests done. It seems that she had caught her husband with another woman and she wanted to tell everybody within listening. She was giving a blow-by-blow description of the melee. Crystal made no comments as she thought about her own marriage. Eric had never been unfaithful. Besides, because of the fifteen years difference in their ages, if he ever yearned for a young woman it would be her. Crystal smiled at this thought. The woman went on and on with her tirade. Crystal found it difficult to concentrate on her magazine. When Eric finally emerged from taking his tests, Crystal was on her feet leading him out before he could finish putting on his jacket.

"Hey, slow down, what's the hurry?"

"I'm sorry, honey. I was tired of listening to that woman describing her husband's extramarital affair. Are you okay? I can drive if you want me to."
"I feel fine. I've been driving since I was sixteen, and I haven't become old and senile yet. I can still drive, and it's my car," he added playfully.

Crystal agreed but wondered why men thought they were better drivers than women. With Eric, Crystal figured driving was a symbol of his manliness. While Crystal didn't mind driving, she also didn't mind being chauffeured. The truth was, she really didn't like driving Eric around because he would tell her how to drive instead of just relaxing and enjoying the ride. On the few occasions when she did drive him, he would attempt to "side-seat drive," but she would remind him that she managed to get to and from her destinations safely when she was by herself. That would always quiet him down—at least for the moment. Anyway, before Eric retired, she always had the car since as an employee he rode public transportation free and as a retiree, he could still ride free for the rest of his life. Crystal wished the CTA would allow the same privilege for the spouses; it would save on gas.

Crystal spent the next few days visiting with Sherry and enjoying Eric's permanent daily companionship. Sometimes he ran errands for her and helped her around the house. But most days they just sat watching television or talking about the good times they'd had and remembering when their kids were young. One day, while reminiscing, Eric closed his eyes as if by doing so, he could relive those good times once more. Crystal didn't notice that Eric had fallen asleep. She told him how she had longed for these days and now they finally had them. She said she almost wished she didn't have to go back to work, although being a professor had its advantages, especially having the choice of not having to work during the summer months. When Eric didn't comment, she started to say that maybe she didn't really want to be home with him all the time. She didn't say it, but she smiled at the thought.

"I really love teaching drama at the college," Crystal said. "I overheard some of my students remarking about what a great instructor I am and how much being in my class has improved their self-esteem and their desire to achieve."

She paused as she beamed with pride at the thought that she had made such an impact on their young lives. Eric's snoring made Crystal realize he was no longer reminiscing. He hadn't heard a word she'd said about her students. Rather than wake him, Crystal closed her eyes and continued to reminisce silently. The ringing of the telephone brought them both back to the present. Crystal managed to get to it first. It was Dr. Winter's office. When she'd hung up, she calmly informed Eric his tests results were back and Dr. Winter wanted to see him on Monday. Since it was Wednesday, Crystal thought, "It couldn't be urgent, otherwise Dr. Winters would have told them to come in on Friday or Saturday. Still, for some reason she felt an uneasiness she couldn't quite explain.

The doorbell rang. When Crystal said it was probably Sherry, Eric headed for the stairs saying, "I'll be upstairs until you two hens finish cackling."

Crystal let Sherry in, and they headed straight for the kitchen where they usually sat and discussed current events. They drank coffee whether it was morning, noon, or night; summer, winter or spring.

"So have you gotten the results of Eric's tests yet?" Sherry asked, hoping she sounded caring instead of nosy.

"We have an appointment on Monday," Crystal replied. "But I'm sure everything's okay. Eric couldn't be healthier. In fact, he's too healthy if you know what I mean."

"Oh stop rubbing it in," Sherry teased. "This time next month I may be grinning from ear to ear."

"Don't tell me Leonardo is coming for more than just a weekend," Crystal said.

"Okay," Sherry grinned. "So I won't tell you—that."

"Come on, girl," Crystal joked, "I know you're not that hard up."

"Oh yes I am," Sherry laughed. "Like you said, two years is long enough."

"I didn't say that, Leonardo did."

"Well, I agree," Sherry said.

"You sound like you can hardly wait, you shameless hussy," Crystal teased.

"I can't. You know something? I knew Leonardo was a close friend of Eric's, and I'd seen him often here at your house. I knew when he moved away, but truly, I hadn't given him a thought. All of a sudden, it's like I'm meeting him for the first time. It's like ... I never knew he even existed, and now ... I can't get him out of my mind. It's crazy." Crystal could tell

Sherry was really serious.

"Even though I warned you, I'm happy to see you so excited. It has been said that man should not live alone—but neither should woman. I hope everything turns out well for both of you. I really mean that."

Sherry smiled as she said, "I know you do."

For a moment neither of them said anything. Then Crystal gave Sherry a hug and told her not to be nervous. She made Sherry promise to let Leonardo know that he has to wine her and dine her before he gets a taste of the "dessert."

"I have no intentions of giving in—at least not on the first date."

They both laughed because they both knew that was a maybe. Crystal was from the "old school," and she knew Sherry was not quite as "old fashion" as she pretended to be.

"And don't forget to tell him to be—gentle."

"Right," Sherry agreed as she laughed.

On Monday morning, Crystal and Eric sat in the examining room as Dr. Winter pointed to the results of Eric's EEG and MRI he had placed on a screen. Crystal sensed the doctor's demeanor was a bit foreboding.

"Eric has had several mini-strokes," he said. "See this small gray shaded area? This area of his brain is slowly losing the ability to function. The MRI confirms what the EEG shows."

"So what does that mean—the shaded area is losing its ability to function?" Crystal asked, fear rising inside her. Dr. Winter admitted he didn't want to make a diagnosis at this time but went on to explain what happens when mini-strokes occur. He ended by saying they may have caused Eric to enter the first stage of his dementia. Crystal didn't know exactly what dementia was, but she had heard it being used in conjunction with the word Alzheimer's.

"But ... Dr. Winter, we just went on a seven-day cruise. Eric was fine then and he's fine now. Evidently the mini-strokes haven't had any effect on him. Tell him, honey," she coaxed Eric. "We've been laughing and joking together, just like we always do. Tell him, honey. Tell Dr. Winter how you feel."

"I feel fine, doc. I could do eighteen holes of golf right now. How 'bout it," Eric joked.

"How about you talk to a neurologist and then we'll see about the golf game, okay?" Dr. Winter didn't crack a smile. His demeanor was very somber, which caused a little knot to form in Crystal's stomach. Crystal was surprised when Eric responded with a quick, "Okay, when do I see him?"

Reluctantly, Crystal told the doctor to make the appointment and she would go with Eric. Dr. Winter tried to lighten the moment by saying he was glad they'd had a nice time on the cruise, but Crystal's spirits were not lifted. She made another attempt to reassure Dr. Winter that Eric was fine. The doctor didn't dispute her but said his nurse would call them after the appointment with the neurologist had been set. Later that afternoon, Sherry stopped by to ask Crystal about Eric's test results.

"So what did the doctor say?" she asked, hoping she didn't sound too nosy."

"Nothing much," Crystal replied, knowing she didn't sound convincing.

"Nothing much? Come on, Crystal. I'm not trying to get in your business ..." Crystal interrupted, abruptly changing the subject.

"Have you taken the kids shopping for their new school supplies?" she asked. "September is right around the corner, you know."

"Oh no you don't, I'm not letting you change the subject on me," Sherry said, her tone demanding an answer.

"I told you it's nothing. Dr. Winter wants Eric to see a neurologist, that's all."

"That's all? Isn't that a doctor who deals with the brain? Don't act like you're not worried, Crystal."

"I'm not, really I'm not," Crystal insisted.

When Sherry suggested that she might be in denial, Crystal became agitated.

"There is nothing to deny. I am positive everything is fine."

Sherry thought it was obvious; Crystal had convinced herself there was nothing wrong with Eric since he'd never had any serious health problems. Besides, Sherry knew Crystal considered Eric to be her "knight in shining armor." She couldn't afford to believe he would ever be sick. At least not the kind of sick Sherry suspected.

"Dr. Winter is over dramatizing the situation," Crystal stated with conviction. Sherry stared at her a moment. Did she hear a bit of concern in Crystal's voice?

"You're talking about the man you and Eric have entrusted with the treatment and care of your health. As friends, we've always shared both our ups and our downs."

"I'm not experiencing any ups or downs," Crystal replied. "If I was, I would certainly share that with you. Listen, do you remember the time Dr. Winter's nurse called and said Eric's x-ray showed there was a spot on his lungs? But then, when we got to the doctor's office, we found out that a mistake had been made. It was someone else's x-ray and not Eric's."

"I remember," Sherry said. "That was two years ago. But something good came out of it. Eric got scared and threw a brand new pack of cigarettes away and hasn't smoked since." Crystal agreed that was good but suggested this could be just another mistake. They went back and forth with rebuttals like students on a debate team.

"Crystal, you and Eric wouldn't keep going to a doctor who continued to make errors, now would you?"

"Sherry, Eric and I have been planning and saving toward his retirement since the day we got married. We've talked about all the places we're going and the things we'll see and do. I've even dreamed about it." Thinking about her own husband and what had happened to him, Sherry took a deep breath before she spoke.

"I think you ought to table those dreams and cancel your next trip. You need to see about your husband's health."

"I don't remember offering you a penny for your thoughts," Crystal fired back at Sherry. "Nor do I remember asking your advice concerning my husband's health." Sherry knew she had pushed the wrong button, but she felt the need to continue. She loved Crystal and Eric and she believed her friends were in crisis. She also believed that Crystal had made up her mind; she wasn't going to accept a negative diagnosis from Dr. Winter or any neurologist. This bothered Sherry because she had begun to notice something was not quite right with Eric. He had always joked around with her, but lately he would say mean things, and the scary part was he sounded like he meant them. Sometimes he even seemed a little disoriented.

"You need to get rid of your chronic envying," Crystal said, her tone unusually harsh and loud.

"My chronic envying?" Sherry couldn't believe the words that she was hearing had come out of her best friend's mouth.

"My husband's health is fine and I intend to go on with our plans to travel."

"And I second that e-motion" joked Eric as he made another one of his surprise entrances. "I just got off the phone with my CTA buddy Cleave. He invited us to go on a bus trip to the dog races in Iowa."

Crystal looked directly at Sherry as she said, "Call him back and tell him we would love to go."

"I knew you'd want to go so I already told him to save us a seat," Eric informed her. "Hey Sherry, maybe you'd like to go too." This was not the first time Sherry and Crystal had disagreed on something, but they had never had an argument like this one. Sherry was hurt and puzzled by Crystal's attitude and sudden harshness.

"Thanks Eric, but I don't think so. I'd better go. I have some business to take care of. I'll let myself out," Sherry said as she headed toward the front door.

"Yes, go handle your business and let yourself out," Crystal said, sounding even harsher. If Eric sensed anything was wrong between the two women, he didn't let on. He grabbed Crystal playfully pulling her toward the stairs.

"Let's go upstairs and wrap a package," he joked. In an obvious attempt to try and calm down, Crystal half-heartedly joked back, "Okay, I've got plenty of wrapping paper. I hope you've got enough ribbon."

The next day, Crystal was sorry she had gotten so upset with Sherry. When she thought about it, she knew Sherry was concerned about both she and Eric. She realized that in the nine years they had been friends, they had never ever disagreed so intensely. She blamed it on—she didn't know what to blame it on. All she knew was that she needed to apologize, and that's exactly what she intended to do the next time she talked to her.

Sherry waited a couple of days before she called Crystal. She knew her friend must be dealing with a serious situation. She wished Crystal would confide in her, but she had to allow her to move at her own pace. Sherry also knew that in time Crystal would tell her exactly what was going on.

"Hi, would you like to see a movie tonight?" Sherry asked hoping Crystal would realize she was trying to bury the hatchet. "The kids are participating in a camp-out, and the White Sox are playing the Yankees. Eric won't even miss you." Crystal laughed as she thought, "She's right about Eric, and maybe the movies will be a good place for me to apologize."

"Sounds like a plan," Crystal said, "I'll be ready in half an hour. You drive." It had been a while since she and Sherry had gone to a movie. Shopping and seeing the latest movies were two important components of their close friendship. In route to the movies, Crystal took the opportunity to apologize for the way she had spoken to Sherry. She made a weak attempt to explain her reason for becoming so agitated. "Maybe I'm going through the change." Crystal thought that would be a sufficient excuse to give her friend. Sherry knew that was not the truth but decided to go along with it—for the moment.

"You could be, but I want you to know that I'll always be here for you no matter what you're going through," Sherry promised.

"Thank you for being such a good friend. I guess I owe you more of an explanation." Crystal said.

"Okay," Sherry said, waiting patiently.

"Sherry, I know you're not going to agree but ... Eric and I have been doing some thinking, and we've decided to go by the old adage, 'if it's not broken, then don't fix it.'"

"And what is that supposed to mean," Sherry asked fearing that she already knew the answer.

"There's no need for Eric to see a neurologist. He just needs to take his blood pressure medication and the blood thinner Dr. Winter prescribed. He also needs to stay busy, take up a hobby and do a little more reading. He just needs to keep busy, keep his mind occupied."

Feeling Crystal was not telling her the whole situation, she asked, "And this will cure ...?" Crystal sensed Sherry was digging a little deeper into a subject she wasn't quite ready to discuss.

"It won't cure anything because there's nothing to cure. Listen Sherry, I don't know how many older people you have been around but ..."

"Excuse me, both my mother and my grandmother were older than me, and my husband was twenty-eight years older than me ... remember? So I think I've been around a few "old" people." Sherry prayed she was not inviting another outburst from Crystal, and she certainly didn't want to upset her by dwelling on the subject but couldn't help asking the next question. "Are you sure you're doing the right thing? I mean about Eric not seeing a neurologist."

"I am positively sure," Crystal replied.

And with that, Sherry knew the subject was closed—at least for now.

Four
Normal Versus Abnormal

IT WAS EARLY FALL, and Crystal had settled into her work at the college. She and Eric had adjusted to a routine that seemed compatible for both. But sometimes she worried that Eric might develop "cabin fever" by staying at home all week with not much to do. She couldn't get him to do any of the activities she suggested. He didn't want to read or try to solve puzzles. A few times she was able to get him to go to the movies. His friends would call, but he would tell her to tell them he was gone or asleep. Baseball season had ended and football was only on the weekend. Basketball wouldn't begin until November. Eric watched a lot of television and to Crystal's surprise, he had become interested in a few soap operas. Finally, she decided that since Eric was a morning person, she would get up two hours early each day, and the two of them could take a forty-five minute walk around a nearby park. This idea pleased Eric. In fact, he looked forward to it and would insist on walking even when Crystal would sometimes suggest they skip a morning. Eric would remind her that they needed to get in as many days before the weather changed and the snow and ice hampered them. She really did enjoy the walks. It made her feel good the rest of the day. Besides, it was something they did together outside of the house.

Crystal was glad that she only taught four days a week. That gave her a three-day weekend. Eric was always in good spirits, and their sex life was better than ever. He hadn't complained about any more headaches, and Dr. Winter didn't attempt to convince him to change his mind about seeing a neurologist. During the week Crystal would be home by four o'clock, and by five-thirty or six they would be eating dinner. Eric didn't cook much— maybe sometimes he'd watch something Crystal had put in the slow cooker before she'd left. They hardly ever had any real big spats, but when they did, Eric would pout and give Crystal the silent treatment; and Crystal wouldn't cook just to get back at him. He was the epitome of the adage, "The way to a man's heart is through his stomach." When she stopped cooking, he resumed talking, at least long enough to ask, "What's for dinner?"

Crystal talked to the kids every other week. Whenever they asked about their father, she always told them he was doing fine. Sometimes she would hand him the phone so he could talk to them. Her godson Tony checked on them every week, either by phone or a pop-in visit. She even gave him a key but informed him to ring the bell first and wait a few minutes to ensure he was not infringing on their privacy. Tony laughed and gave her a look that asked, "Just what kind of privacy could you be talking about?" Crystal smiled as she thought, He'd be surprised if he really knew what she and Eric did in private—and at their ages.

Crystal still talked to Sherry by phone, but they only got together every other Saturday when they went shopping for groceries. Sherry confided that something had come up, and Leonardo had postponed his planned trip in October. He still called, and Sherry said he had even started writing her letters. She was a bit secretive about the contents, but when Crystal teased her saying, "Oh please spare me the gory details," Sherry did tell her that Leonardo was planning to visit the weekend before Thanksgiving. Crystal asked if he would be staying over Thanksgiving since she always cooked and Sherry and her kids always came over to eat. If Leonardo would be coming to dinner too, Eric would like that. Crystal thought it was unusual for Eric not to tell her his pal was coming to town. After all, they always stayed in touch.

When Crystal voiced her thoughts, Sherry said, "Eric just forgot to mention it, that's all."

"Eric has a memory like an elephant; he doesn't forget a thing," Crystal said in his defense. "Sometimes he brings up things that even I've forgotten. He still holds a grudge against a grammar school classmate who switched his bologna sandwich with a peanut butter and jelly sandwich."

Sherry laughed. She thought that was funny. She also thought Crystal sounded defensive but decided not to comment. Crystal was aware of how excited Sherry would get whenever she talked about Leonardo, so she moved the conversation back in that direction.

"So, let's discuss your knight in shining armor," Crystal suggested. Sherry's eyes lit up; her face was aglow. Crystal thought, *This girl is really in love! Dear God, please don't let him break her heart.* She smiled hoping Sherry hadn't read her thoughts as they sometimes did with each other.

"Girl have you looked in the mirror lately? That man has you glowing brighter than the northern star," Crystal laughed.

"Well you're glowing pretty bright yourself," Sherry laughed, too.

"Eric created my glow with years of nurturing and pampering, plus steadfast love and sincere affection," Crystal responded.

"I know what you're thinking, and you want me to compare Leonardo with Herbert. But every relationship is different. People love in different ways for different reasons. I admire what you and Eric have. You two have that real love that only comes once in a lifetime. So don't burst my bubble. Besides, you coaxed me into this," Sherry added.

"Yep, in a way I did but ..." Sherry interrupted Crystal saying,

"Uh uh sister-girl, I don't want to hear any ifs, ands, or buts. Let's just see how it plays out."

"Wow, that was quite a backlash," Crystal said laughing.

"Color me inexperienced, but remember, friends are there to catch you when you fall, so here's my shoulder you can lean on me."

"Hey, that sounds like the words to a song. I've heard them somewhere before," Sherry said.

"They are from a song, but they are appropriate and I mean them."

"Glad to know that. I'm putting you on stand-by," Sherry informed her.

"Okay, I'm on," Crystal confirmed.

Later that night, when Crystal questioned Eric about Leonardo's planned visit, he shrugged it off. "I thought I told you," he said, grabbing her around the waist playfully. "Come upstairs with me, and I'll tell all." He always did that. Whenever he thought the conversation was about to turn into an argument, Eric would joke about it. Maybe that's why they had so few real arguments. Sometimes that was a good thing, but sometimes Crystal was not in a joking mood and this was one of those times. If they were going to have a house guest, she wanted to know.

That year, the weatherman on channel two predicted a warmer than usual Halloween. Since the Greenville Club was sponsoring a Halloween party, Eric suggested that he and Crystal wear a costume that would be sure to win first place. When Crystal asked him what he had in mind, Eric said, "Me Tarzan, you Jane." Crystal burst into laughter as she allowed her mind's eye to picture them in such a getup.

"You'd better come up with another suggestion because that one isn't going to happen, not even if the temperature reaches a hundred. Besides, we already won before—you can't win every year."

"With you, all things are possible."

"Stop it, Eric! It's with GOD all things are possible." Eric tried to defend his statement admitting that he was just joking, but he knew he couldn't win this one because when it came to the Bible, Crystal didn't make jokes.

On Halloween, Eric was as excited as a kid on Christmas morning. They went as "Little Red Riding Hood and the Wolf." Crystal made herself up to look just like the fairytale character; from the golden Shirley Temple curly wig and the red hooded cape, down to the anklets and the red patent leather baby-doll shoes she had found at a resale shop. She made Eric a brown furry jumpsuit, complete with wolf paws and feet that had fake claws. She pinned a long furry tail to the back of the suit, and made his face up to look just like a real wolf, including the fake nozzle and fangs that she'd picked up from the trick shop. Crystal smiled broadly as their costumes drew raves and applauds from the crowd at the clubhouse. Eric was even more jubilant when they won the first-place prize again.

That night when they were undressing for bed, Crystal remarked, "Well we did it again." Eric pulled her into his arms, howling like a wolf. "No honey, you did it again."

Eric had always showered Crystal with praises for the things she did for him, and she never hesitated to give him credit for being a good husband and role model for their children. But lately she felt he was actually depending on her more than ever to do some of the things he used to do for himself. Crystal thought it felt more like he was clinging to her. She decided she should accept the fact that both of them were experiencing deeper feelings of love stemming from their ability to enjoy one another in a way they couldn't when they were raising their kids and maintaining a tight budget. She knew Eric loved her and he knew she loved him and they both felt it was important to say those words to each other—often.

The Saturday before Thanksgiving, Sherry and Crystal were at the grocery store as soon as the doors opened. They'd planned to get the jump on many of the weekend shoppers. When Sherry questioned her about the amount of food she was preparing this year, Crystal explained that she had decided to invite her friends Adelia and Ricardo Mendoza, the couple she had met on the cruise.

"I thought Thanksgiving was more of a family holiday," Sherry said. Crystal thought she detected a hint of jealousy and teased Sherry.

"They don't have any close family in Chicago. Besides, I want you to meet my friends."

"Stop calling them your friends for goodness sakes. You just met them," Sherry said. Crystal laughed as she continued to tease Sherry.

"Don't worry, she'll never be the friend you are."

"I'm not worried about that," Sherry lied, "in fact the more the merrier. It'll be me and the kids and ... I'll be bringing a guest, too." Since she hadn't told Crystal when Leonardo was coming, she decided this was as good a time as any.

"Leonardo is coming in tonight."

"What? Eric didn't tell me Leonardo would be staying with us. Darn it, I've got to get back home and make sure the bedroom next to ours is ..." Sherry cut her off.

"You've got plenty of time; he's checking into the Ramada for a couple of days."

"The Ramada?" Crystal cried. "Leonardo has never come home and stayed in a hotel. Eric will be furious." Crystal paused but only for a second. "Aha, so you two plan to ... okay, okay ... I get it now. You two want a little privacy ... to really get acquainted."

"Right," Sherry admitted, "he plans to check out on Thanksgiving Eve and spend the rest of the time at your place. He's going back to L.A. the Saturday after Thanksgiving."

"Well thanks for telling me. I guess you'll come over and help me start cooking on Wednesday since we're having so many extra guests."

"You bet I will," Sherry smiled. "But you've got more extras than me," she added, laughing.

When Crystal returned home, she asked Eric if he knew Leonardo was coming in for the holiday. He said of course he knew and he thought he had told her. Crystal argued the point.

"If you had told me, I would have gotten his room ready."

Eric brushed her off. "You don't need to do anything special. Leonardo is like family."

Crystal tried not to think about the fact that Eric kept saying he'd told her something when he hadn't.

"Did you know he was checking into a motel?" she asked. "Yep," Eric replied, "And I told you that too."

Crystal decided it wouldn't be any use to continue to argue. It really wasn't that big of a deal. The important thing was that Leonardo was finally coming and Sherry was deliriously happy. Crystal wondered, if anything happened to Eric would I be able to ... She stopped herself; that's something she didn't even want to think about.

At five o'clock, after giving Cinnamon, her teenage sitter, instructions for the evening, Sherry took another look in the mirror. She wanted to look sexy but not too sexy. She had decided on a basic black dress. It would make her look smaller and accentuate her size-ten figure. She had bought the dress for Eric's retirement party, but Crystal had wanted her to wear white since she was the main hostess. It would also fit in with the overall color scheme. Crystal had been very helpful making certain Sherry chose the right clothes for the right occasions. Since the death of her husband, Sherry had not thought too much about clothes, especially dressing to look sexy. In fact, whenever she wore an outfit that caused some of her male church members to give her a compliment, she would thank them but then she would remember not to wear it again. She just wasn't ready for the attention. She had no desire to have a man, neither in her life nor in the lives of her three children. So why am I so excited about Leonardo's visit? Good question, but she didn't have the answer. She forced her mind to wonder about the kind of car Leonardo would be renting. His plane was landing at four thirty-five, and he said he would be picking her up around six o'clock. Carolyne, Sherry's eleven-year-old daughter, came into her room to watch as she got dressed.

"That's a pretty dress, Mommy. You look beautiful ... like Cinderella."

"Why thank you, and I guess I should also thank my fairy godmother, Auntie Crystal."

"I want to be your fairy godmother. Can I? Please, Mommy?"

"Okay, but just for tonight. I don't think Auntie Crystal will mind."

Sherry loved the fact that her children treated Crystal and Eric like family. She was surprised when Carolyne asked her if Leonardo was going to be their new daddy.

"You don't need a new daddy right now," Sherry said, smiling.

"Yes we do," Carolyne replied. Carolyne was smiling, but Sherry knew she was serious.

When the doorbell rang, Cinnamon answered and yelled to Sherry that a limo was outside waiting for her. Sherry laughed thinking Cinnamon was joking, but when she arrived at the front door, Leonardo stepped aside and motioned toward an awaiting sleek, black stretch limo. The driver was standing beside the opened rear door, awaiting them. Leonardo escorted a visibly excited and impressed Sherry to the limo. Cinnamon, Carolyne, Sherry's fourteen-year-old son Johnny, and her thirteen-year-old son Clyde, crowded in the doorway gaping. Sherry looked back at them and waved before she climbed into the limo. Carolyne waved as she shouted, "Goodbye, Cinderella! Goodbye, Prince Charming." Leonardo smiled.

Once inside the limo, Sherry allowed Leonardo to do most of the talking. She was in awe of the way the evening was starting to shape up. She also thought he looked more handsome than ever. When they arrived at the motel, Leonardo had more surprises for the already stunned "Cinderella." He led her into a large, beautifully decorated suite. The plush living room had a gorgeous chrome and glass table decorated with a beautiful center piece of purple and white orchids. There were two place settings complete with long-stem wine glasses and a pair of candles mounted in crystal holders. Mood lights seemed to be coming from both the ceiling and walls. Soft music could be heard from a hidden stereo and sounded more like it was being piped in.

Leonardo invited Sherry to kick off her shoes and relax while he freshened up. When he heard a knock on the door, Leonardo yelled from the bedroom telling Sherry to answer it. She was further surprised when a waiter entered, pushing a cart with several covered stainless steel serving dishes and a bottle of imported Italian wine. The serving dishes contained what turned out to be the most exquisite meal she had ever seen or eaten. Sherry thanked the waiter, but when she tried to give him a tip, he declined saying it had already been taken care of. Sherry had really thought they were going out to dinner. Although she loved the romantic ambience Leonardo had created, she was a little nervous about being alone with him. Leonardo exited the bedroom looking even more handsome in a paisley print trimmed in black satin, smoking jacket.

"I hope you like Amuse-Bouche and Grilled Balsamic Glazed Steak with Melted Parmesan Butter and Baby Arugula, served with Truffle Pureed Potatoes and Braised Bibb Lettuce," he said as he took the cover off each dish.

"I don't know what it is, but if you like it, I'm willing to try it," Sherry said hoping she would like it. She was a finicky eater at times, and nothing would spoil this romantic evening like having to pretend she liked something and then spitting it into the napkin when Leonardo wasn't looking.

"The chocolate mousse dessert is for you, but for me—you're sweet enough." Leonardo gazed deeply into Sherry's eyes.

Sherry blushed, despite her medium tan complexion. Leonardo smiled as he removed their flatware from lace trimmed linen napkins. During their long-distant communications, Leonardo had learned that Sherry was from the South and had been exposed to mostly "soul" foods. He'd decided to choose a more romantic cuisine for this very special evening. Leonardo poured the wine and held up his glass. "May this night represent the first night of many nights like this during the rest of our lives."

Again Sherry appeared flushed as she smiled and touched her glass to his. Leonardo dished up the food while Sherry made small talk. She was trying hard not to show how impressed she was. She also tried hard not to stare into his eyes. The food was delicious, and she complimented him on the choices he had made. During dessert, Sherry decided to turn the conversation toward Eric.

"Did you tell Eric you were coming?" she asked. "Of course I did. He's almost like a father to me. I would never come here and not let him know. I usually stay with him. He wouldn't have it any other way."

"What did he say?" Sherry hoped Leonardo wouldn't think she was interrogating him.

"He told me to come on, he'd be glad to see me. He reminded me that he hadn't seen me since the night of the retirement party. He was disappointed when he awoke the next morning and found out I had left without saying goodbye. We joked back and forth like we always do."

Even though Sherry thought her next question might give Leonardo a reason to be concerned about her inquisitiveness, she asked if he had noticed anything out of the ordinary in Eric's conversation. Leonardo said he hadn't and asked why. Not wanting to explain that she feared something serious was going on with Eric's health and that Crystal was in a deep state of denial, Sherry waved it off and decided to change the subject. Besides, she hadn't really wanted to spend such a special evening discussing Crystal and Eric.

"You went to a lot of trouble—I mean ... to make this night special," Sherry said.

"I'm glad you like it because to me you are as special as the night," Leonardo said in what Sherry later described as one of the sexiest voices she'd ever heard.

They sat talking and sipping wine for almost an hour. Leonardo was trying not to take things too fast, while Sherry was wondering if he noticed her body language was responding to the mere presence of his. Leonardo confessed that he had thought of nothing else since he'd danced with her at the retirement party. Sherry could not explain the burning sensation that suddenly came over her. She was ashamed to admit even to herself how much she was attracted to this man. Even before he led her into the bedroom and introduced her to more passion than she had ever experienced in her whole life, she knew that he was the one. She knew it that night at Eric's retirement party when he asked her to dance and pulled her trembling body into his arms. She knew it when she felt the warm, tingling sensations whenever she talked to him on the phone. She knew it when his trip to visit her in October was postponed and disappointment consumed her. She knew it when he told her that nothing would stop him from coming for Thanksgiving and wild anticipation overwhelmed her. She knew it when Leonardo said she was as special as the night—she already knew he was the one.

It was after midnight when Leonardo and Sherry climbed out of the limo. He walked her to the door. As he was about to kiss her goodnight, Carolyne snatched open the door, startling them. Johnny was standing right beside her.

"Why are you two still up? And where is Cinnamon?"

"The television is watching her. I was just trying to stop your fairy godmother here from turning the limo into a pumpkin," Johnny said, trying to keep a straight face.

"That's not true," Carolyne argued. "He really wanted to make sure the goodnight kiss wasn't a long, mushy, and passionate one."

Sherry blushed but Leonardo laughed, expressing his delight. He asked the children to promise him they wouldn't allow anybody else a chance to give "Cinderella" a long, mushy and passionate goodnight kiss. Johnny promised, adding that he would do it for a small fee. Carolyne blurted out, "If you're paying, I promise too." Sherry laughed as she hustled them off to bed. Then she turned back to Leonardo, who was still standing there as if he hated to leave her.

"Thanks for a wonderful evening. You know something? I think my kids like you."

"I hope that goes for their mother too," Leonardo said as he gave her a short kiss on the lips.

Sherry started to close the door but reopened it. "It docs," she said. Leonardo started to respond, but Sherry had already closed the door.

The next day Sherry and the kids went to early church services and arrived home just as Leonardo drove up in a rented Ford Mustang. Sherry teased him about the big step down from the limousine. Leonardo spent the rest of the day getting to know the kids. They played Monopoly until Cinnamon arrived to babysit while Sherry and Leonardo continued their "get acquainted" weekend at the hotel.

On Monday morning, Sherry dropped the kids off at school and headed straight to the motel. She chuckled when she thought about what she would say when Crystal questioned her about what she and Leonardo did for four days. *I'll tell her I was just helping him get to know me better.* The thought of Crystal's reply, *Shame on you, you hussy,* made her smile. Later that day, Leonardo was content playing games with Sherry and the kids until Sherry announced that she had to help them with their homework. Leonardo reminded her that Tuesday would be the last night they would be able to have some "privacy." Reluctantly, he headed for the motel. Tuesday after the kids went to school, Sherry and Leonardo ate a light lunch and enjoyed just riding around talking and getting to know more about each other. She had assured him that Cinnamon would be over when the kids got home from school, and they could spend his last night at the hotel in "privacy."

Crystal had spent Monday and Tuesday cleaning the house in preparation for Thanksgiving. She'd thought about giving Sherry a call, but she knew her friend was enjoying Leonardo's visit, so she gave them their space. She'd always relied on Eric to help her, but lately he'd either forgotten how to do some things or he would take a long time doing the things that he used to do in no time at all. Crystal didn't push him. She was grateful for the little things that he still managed to do.

Crystal only spoke with Sherry briefly on Tuesday. She called to tease her about being too busy to call an old friend, and to remind her that they were supposed to start cooking the Thanksgiving dinner on Wednesday.

"Remember girl," Crystal said, playfully giving Sherry some motherly advice, "in a relationship, the stove and refrigerator are just as important as the bed."

"Okay 'Mom,' I'll remember that," Sherry said laughing. "I don't have time to talk to you right now. Meet you in the kitchen tomorrow night, bye."

On Thanksgiving Eve Leonardo checked out of the hotel and went to stay with Eric and Crystal. Eric was glad to see him but pretended to be angry about not seeing him sooner. They traded insults as usual and retired to the den laughing and slapping each other on the back. Sherry came over early to help Crystal with the preparations for the holiday feast. As the two women cooked, they could hear Eric and Leonardo laughing and talking while drinking beer and watching television. Crystal, pretending to be upset, teased Sherry by reminding her that she hadn't seen her since they shopped for groceries on Saturday. She also mentioned that Sherry was glowing a lot more than usual.

"Girl, I don't want to believe you paid a babysitter so you could lie up in a hotel with Leonardo for four straight days. You're more than a brazen hussy," Crystal teased, pretending to be outraged. Sherry just stood grinning as if she were posing for a Colgate toothpaste billboard.

"Please, spare me the gory details." Crystal said. She knew Sherry really wanted to tell her everything.

"I'll give you the "411" as soon as Leonardo goes back to L.A.," Sherry said, still grinning from ear to ear.

As they went about making pies and cakes and preparing the dressing for the turkey, Crystal let Sherry know that she was aware of Leonardo's many trips back and forth into the kitchen on the pretense that he was getting he and Eric another beer or getting them some water when he was really watching Sherry. Crystal said she was also aware of how many times Sherry left the kitchen on the pretense of having to use the bathroom but she was really in the den making "goo-goo eyes" at Leonardo. Finally, Crystal told Sherry that everything in the kitchen was under control so she might as well join the guys in the den. Sherry didn't bother to deny any of Crystal's accusations. She quickly discarded her apron and headed for the den. Eric joined Crystal in the kitchen, leaving Sherry and Leonardo alone.

Crystal winked at Eric and said, "Isn't love grand?"

Grabbing Crystal around her waist, he replied, "I don't know baby, let's go upstairs and find out."

"Sorry, 'Mandingo,'" Crystal laughed, "I don't have time for a quickie."

Pulling away, she handed Eric a knife. "Here, work off that urge by peeling those potatoes."

On Thanksgiving Day, Crystal was up at the crack of dawn putting the turkey in the oven and making last-minute preparations. By noon, she and Eric had talked to the guys in L.A and Anna in New York. Although she and Eric talked to them every other week, Crystal couldn't remember a holiday that her children didn't call home. Crystal's godson Tony would be spending the day with his family, but he never forgot to call either.

Sherry and her kids arrived around two o'clock. While she went straight into the kitchen to assist Crystal, the children waited in the den for Eric and Leonardo to come down. Sherry joked saying that she hoped they wouldn't run Leonardo away by wanting him to play Monopoly with them every minute of the day.

By three o'clock, the table was eloquently set like a picture in a House Beautiful magazine. Crystal was ready to receive her other guests. It would be the first time Adelia and Ricardo had seen Eric and Crystal since the cruise, although the two women had chatted a few times on the phone. Adelia and Ricardo arrived around three-thirty. After introducing them, Crystal and Sherry began bringing out the food. The table displayed the traditional turkey and dressing, cranberry sauce, candied sweet potatoes, mustard and turnip greens, potato salad, ham, and of course Crystal's homemade yeast rolls. While the menu was basically the same every year, Sherry's kids bragged about Auntie Crystal's ability to prepare different variations of each dish. After everyone had been seated, Crystal blessed the food and gave thanks for the friends and family she was surrounded by. Eric usually said grace, but for some reason he insisted that Crystal do it. They engaged in very little conversation during dinner, allowing eating to be the main activity. Every now and then someone would compliment Crystal on the taste of a particular dish. She didn't hesitate to give due credit to the help she received from Sherry.

There were apple and pumpkin pies, as well as chocolate and coconut cake for dessert. It was during this time that the conversations became prevalent. The children took their desserts and retired to the den, but not before they tried to get Leonardo to come play Monopoly with them. Sherry gave them a look that said, That's enough. Now go play by yourselves and let the grown folks have some time together.

For an hour, the three couples sat laughing and talking. Ricardo and Adelia bragged that despite celebrating their tenth wedding anniversary on the cruise, they were still just as much in love as they were the day they got married. Eric boasted about how his marriage was better than ever as he winked at Crystal. She smiled, deciding not to add anything to that statement although she certainly did agree with it. She wasn't sure how far Eric would take it. Adelia seemed to dominate the conversation, complimenting Sherry on what a handsome couple she and Leonardo were and also complimenting Crystal on her cooking and the lovely home she and Eric had. When Ricardo could get a word in, he told one of his corny jokes which Adelia still didn't think was funny, so she didn't laugh. Eric bragged about what a great stand-up comedian his buddy Leonardo was. He coaxed Leonardo into telling a joke. Leonardo was always ready to seize the opportunity to play off of Eric.

"Okay, but this is no joke. Eric's son Jay was sent home from school because he didn't know the answer to one of his homework questions. Eric was called to come up to the school. When the teacher asked Jay who signed the Declaration of Independence and Jay said he didn't know, Eric snatched off his belt and grabbed Jay and told him, boy if you signed that thing, you'd better tell us."

Everybody laughed, including Adelia, who surprised everyone by laughing the loudest. Crystal laughed, too, as she attempted to come to Eric's defense.

"Eric was just playing dumb," she said.

"I wasn't playing," Eric protested without cracking a smile.

Leonardo jumped at the opportunity and said, "Nope, he wasn't playing." This really made everybody laugh, except Crystal. While the rest of her guests thought Eric was joking along with Leonardo, Crystal sensed a serious tone in Eric's voice. She regretted having made her remark. Eric was actually admitting he was really dumb. She managed to force a half smile. She was glad when Adelia changed the subject. When Adelia asked Sherry if she and Leonardo were planning on getting married, Sherry just smiled at Leonardo who smiled back at her. Crystal looked at Sherry, awaiting her answer with a raised brow, but neither Sherry nor Leonardo responded. Eric broke the silence.

"Why should he buy the cow when he can get the milk free?"

Crystal shot Eric a look of embarrassment, while everyone except Leonardo sat not knowing what to say or do. Finally, Leonardo laughed.

"But I want to have my cow and eat her too." The guys all laughed. Adelia saw that the other women weren't laughing, so she just sat with a blank expression.

Obviously, Crystal didn't think either of the two jokes were funny and neither did Sherry, who pushed back from the table and stood up. Her expression was an indication of how upset she was.

"Excuse me, Crystal. This "COW" really hates to leave, but I promised to take the baby CALVES Christmas shopping tomorrow." Sherry glared at Leonardo as she called the children to gather their things up. Leonardo tried in vain to convince Sherry it was just a joke as she hustled the kids out, slamming the door behind her. Leonardo apologized to Crystal and the others, grabbed his coat and rushed out after Sherry. Adelia tried to continue the conversation with Crystal and Eric but realized that the mood had changed. After a few more awkward minutes, Ricardo made an excuse about having to get up early in the morning, too. The couple thanked Crystal and Eric for their hospitality as they attempted to make a graceful exit. In a way, Crystal was glad they were leaving. She did not want to confront Eric until after they had gone.

Crystal remained relatively calm, although deep inside she felt the urge to burst into tears. At first she didn't say anything to Eric. She began clearing the table and putting up the food while waiting for him to volunteer an explanation or an apology. Eric put the dishes in the dishwasher and tried to make conversation as if nothing had happened. Finally Crystal could no longer hold her peace.

"Eric, why would you insult Sherry in front of our guests? How could you do that?"

"How did I insult her?" Eric stared at Crystal. He really didn't think he had said anything out of the way.

"Honey, please don't do that." Crystal stared back at him in disbelief.

"Do what?" Eric said in earnest.

"You know what." Crystal's voice became louder as she became angrier.

"Whatever I said, it was just a joke."

"Oh, now you want me to believe you don't remember what you said" Crystal shot back.

"I said a lot of things, I can't remember them all."

"Right, and some of them you should have forgotten to say."

Eric grabbed Crystal around her waist. "Come on honey let's not spoil a perfect day."

"Stop it Eric, and don't go trying to shift the blame on me. This is certainly not the way I'd planned for this day to end."

Eric shrugged his shoulders. "Okay, I'm going in the den. The Bulls might still be playing. I hope they beat Detroit."

Alone in the kitchen, Crystal's thoughts went back to the so-called joke Eric and Leonardo had made. It'll serve him right if Sherry doesn't open the door for him, she thought. She wondered how Leonardo expected to get to first base with Sherry making those kinds of jokes. Crystal stopped for a moment and realized that according to the way he and Sherry had been acting, he'd already gotten to first base. In fact, he had probably crossed home plate.

Crystal was finishing the clean-up when the bell rang. She opened the door for a dejected Leonardo. He followed her back into the kitchen informing her that he'd rang Sherry's bell, but she wouldn't answer the door.

"In fact, she must have told the kids not to answer," he said, looking like a sick puppy. "I sat in the car for a few minutes hoping she would have a change of heart and open the door so I could come in and apologize. I hoped she would look out the window and see me sitting there and feel sorry for me, but she didn't. You know something Crystal? I am really in love with Sherry. I would never deliberately say anything to offend her. It was just a joke."

"Well you did offend her—and so did Eric. You and Eric can joke like that with each other, but that is not the way to joke with someone you're supposed to be in love with. Eric has always teased Sherry, but he has never insinuated that she was a cow."

"I'll admit I was surprised when he said that, and I was just trying to smooth things over. I knew he was joking, but right away I saw how Sherry was taking it. When people get older they change. Sometimes they say things without really thinking."

"Well I'm not ready for a change. I'm happy with the way our lives are," Crystal responded. For an instant, Crystal thought she might tell Leonardo what had happened in Vegas and the gradual changes she had been noticing in Eric. She even thought about telling him about Dr. Winter's diagnosis, but she quickly decided against it. For the last time, she vowed not to think about it again, especially what happened in Vegas. She wondered why the incident she had pushed so far in the back of her mind kept emerging. When Leonardo said he was going to have a talk with Eric, Crystal said "good luck," and followed him into the den. The television was on, but Eric was sound asleep as he snored loudly.

"Okay, you can go ahead and talk with him, but I'm tired. I'm going to lie down. If he complains to you about the bedroom door being locked, tell him to try one of the other four bedrooms. Both of you have a good night." As Crystal started to exit, Leonardo stopped her, begging her.

"Please Crystal, won't you at least call Sherry and ask her to let me in so I can explain?"
Crystal turned and looked at him. For a moment her heart went out to him. He seemed genuinely sorry. But after giving it another thought, she replied, "Nope," and headed up the stairs.

The next day, Crystal intended to sleep late. She had spent three days in the kitchen preparing Thanksgiving dinner, so she deserved to stay in bed as long as she wanted to. But the unrelenting banging on the door caused her eyes to open against her will. The clock on the dresser told her it was only eight. "Crystal, open this door!" She heard an angry Eric shouting. Without answering, Crystal slid out of bed, unlocked the door and jumped back in bed. Eric didn't hear her unlock the door, so he continued to bang and shout.

"Come on in, it's not locked," she shouted back.

Eric eased the door open and with a sheepish grin on his face sat down on the side of the bed. "Good morning, sleepy head. Me and Leonardo made breakfast. Come on downstairs."

Crystal turned away, covering her head with a pillow. Playfully, Eric snatched the pillow, but Crystal grabbed another one and covered her head with it. Eric knew Crystal was extremely ticklish, so he eased one hand under the covers and grabbed her foot and began to tickle the bottom. Crystal screamed, laughing and kicking and begging Eric to stop. Leonardo came rushing in singing the Mighty Mouse song, "Here I come to save the day." Seeing Eric tickling Crystal's foot, he grabbed the other foot and began tickling it. Finally, Crystal kicked loose and leaped out of bed.

"Okay, okay. You win. I'm up. Give me a few minutes to brush my teeth, and I'll be down."

"Don't be long or I'll feed your share to the dog," Eric said as he pushed Leonardo toward the door.

"What dog, we don't even own a dog," Crystal said, taking the bait.

Pointing at Leonardo, Eric said, "You didn't see that dog's plate at dinner yesterday?"

"I thought your mama was coming to dinner, and I didn't want to leave here hungry," Leonardo fired back.

"Go, just go you two," Crystal laughed as she pushed them out and closed the door.

As Crystal was getting dressed, she thought, Maybe Sherry and I have taken the guys too seriously. After all, they are always signifying and joking around with each other. They love doing that. Maybe I should explain this to Sherry. Sherry really doesn't know Leonardo that well. She'll just have to get used to them because that's the way they are.

Crystal decided that after breakfast she would call Sherry and speak on Leonardo's behalf. She also made a mental note to call Adelia and Ricardo and apologize for Eric's and Leonardo's behavior. On second thought, maybe she would just call them and thank them for coming over. They did say they enjoyed it—the dinner that is. She laughed as she remembered the look on Adelia's face when Leonardo literally agreed that Sherry was a cow. Crystal stopped laughing and looked at herself in the mirror. "Girl you've lost your mind. That was not funny," she said aloud. Then she laughed again.

After breakfast, Leonardo urged Crystal to call Sherry while he and Eric cleaned the kitchen. After seeing the mess the two men had made, Crystal agreed they should do the cleanup. She went into the den to call Sherry. Leonardo was crushed when Crystal came back and broke the news that Sherry still wasn't answering the phone.

"Well don't you have a private number or a certain ring that will let her know it's you?" he asked.

"I'm afraid not," she replied.

"Okay then, let's all get in the car and go over there," he suggested.

"You two go, I'm going to watch *All My Children*" Eric announced.

"Damn your children, man. Can't you see I've got a crisis here?"

"You can talk about me, but don't be damning my children," Eric joked, balling up his fists and taking a swing at Leonardo.

"Calm down, you two," Crystal said, "Sherry isn't answering because she's not home. She took the kids shopping, remember? They probably won't be back until after three. Today is the busiest shopping day of the year." Crystal suggested that Leonardo sit down and watch all Eric's children with him. She chuckled at her ability to keep the joke running. Leonardo did not laugh. He needed to talk to Sherry. Crystal thought it funny to see the "funny man" not being funny anymore. Leonardo explained that his heart was heavy, and Crystal was not being a good friend by making light of the situation. Eric ordered them both to be quiet or leave the room so he could finish watching *All My Children*. This made Leonardo laugh and sit down and watch TV—for the moment.

Crystal spent the rest of the afternoon grading papers. The semester was almost over, and she looked forward to spending the holidays in L.A. with the boys. It was four o'clock when Crystal decided to bring out a few of the leftovers for dinner. She usually saved the Thanksgiving leftovers for the following Sunday, but since they had a guest who would be gone by Sunday, she felt it would be nice to share it with him before he left. When Leonardo appeared in the kitchen, she knew exactly what he wanted.

"I'm busy right now," she said. "Call her yourself. She should be home by now."

A short time later, a jubilant Leonardo came rushing back into the kitchen. He picked Crystal up and swung her around.

"She answered the phone! She said I could come over. She's willing to listen to my apology. Don't hold dinner and don't wait up for me."

"You'd better take the extra key because she's not going to let you sleep over; I don't care if you apologize on both hands and both knees." Crystal placed the Thanksgiving leftovers back in the refrigerator and fried some salmon croquets and made some coleslaw. After dinner, they watched television. After watching the news, Crystal decided she and Eric would call it a night. Since Leonardo had a key, he could get in without disturbing them. As she and Eric headed up the stairs, Crystal smiled as she thought to herself, I guess Sherry did accept Leonardo's apology. I hope she feeds him before sending him back here.

The next day, Crystal awoke to realize she and Eric had overslept. It was almost ten o'clock. She had planned to fix Leonardo breakfast before he left for the airport. His flight was scheduled to depart at noon. When she checked his room, she was surprised he was already up. She thought, He even made the bed. She urged Eric to get up and have a bite to eat with Leonardo. She wondered why the smell of coffee had not reached her bedroom. Surely if Leonardo was preparing his own breakfast he would have put the coffee on. Crystal was coming down the stairs when the phone rang. It was Sherry. She was calling to let Crystal know that Leonardo had spent the night—on the sofa, and was on his way back to their house.

"I was just getting ready to call the police and alert them of a missing love-sick puppy," Crystal teased. She told Sherry she was glad everything was okay between them and made Sherry promise to tell her everything over coffee and rolls. Leonardo entered just as Crystal was putting the coffee on.

"You were wrong, Crystal. Both hands and knees did do the trick," he said, gleefully swinging Crystal around as Eric entered.

"Hey, put my Crystal down," Eric said, balling up his fists, pretending to K.O. Leonardo.

The two men pretended to engage in a fist-a-cuff, snarling and calling each other names until Crystal ordered them to break it up before they break something. Since Leonardo had to return the rental car, he didn't need a ride to the airport. He gulped down some coffee, grabbed a roll and headed out; but not before he'd hugged Crystal and his buddy Eric and thanked them for their hospitality, their friendship, and their love. He winked when he thanked Crystal for sharing her best friend with him. Crystal was glad Sherry hadn't wanted to discuss the Thanksgiving Day fiasco. She felt it really was a joke and that Sherry should let it go. She also thought Sherry would probably put most of the blame on Eric.

As usual, Crystal and Eric enjoyed the Christmas holidays in L.A. Leonardo called to apologize for not visiting them during that time because he was always busy performing his comedy routine for the various holiday parties and festivities. He even invited Crystal and Eric to come out to one of his performances, but Crystal declined saying they just wanted to spend the time relaxing with the family. Eric seemed okay, just moving around a bit slower than usual. Sometimes he would sit quietly staring into space. He did show a few signs of the confusion relating to dementia. Not wanting to admit Eric had dementia, Crystal ignored the signs and attributed anything new or unusual to the fact that Eric was getting older.

After celebrating the New Year, Crystal and Eric returned home to face the rest of a predicted long and cold winter. Although Sherry had accepted Leonardo's apology, she didn't talk about the relationship with the same excitement she had shown before. In fact, Crystal could hardly get her to talk about Leonardo at all. She also noticed Sherry had lost some of the "glow" they had teased each other about. Crystal hoped Sherry would put the incident behind her. She felt it wasn't that big of a deal to cause a permanent breakup.

Eric still talked with Leonardo a couple of times a month. He told Crystal that Leonardo was thinking about coming back in April, and he hoped this time the two of them could at least go fishing or hunting together. Crystal laughed as she explained to Eric. "I don't mean to burst your bubble. I know that you and Leonardo have a great relationship built on years of working and playing together; kind of like a father and son. But now that Leonardo is in love and doing some serious courting, fishing and hunting with you is not high on his priority list."

Five
Dementia—Stage One Progresses

IT SEEMED TO TAKE LONGER THAN USUAL FOR SPRING TO COME AROUND. Because she had to work, Crystal had not been affected by the harsh winter, but it kept Eric indoors most of the time. Eric didn't care; he was enjoying the fact that he didn't have to go out in the weather. Again, Crystal suggested a variety of activities Eric could get involved in, including joining a health club, but he rejected them all saying he just wanted to sit back and enjoy his retirement.

Eric had worked all his life from the time he was ten years old, delivering newspapers in Mississippi. He worked at his uncle's funeral home during high school and spent three years working in the army. As soon as he was discharged, he went right to work at the steel mill and after nineteen years there, quit and went to work at CTA for twenty-five years. He felt he'd earned the right to sit down and do nothing for the rest of his life.

He told Crystal that as soon as school was out for the summer they would start traveling again. This time they would go to Florida and perhaps Hawaii and maybe plan another cruise for next year. He seemed to be satisfied watching soap operas during the day and whatever sports was on at night—and sleeping. He was going to bed early, but he would wake up after a few hours. He had a hard time going back to sleep. Sometimes he would just lie awake until the wee hours of the morning. Crystal called Dr. Winter and asked if he would phone Walgreen's and prescribe something to help Eric sleep. The next day she picked up the prescription and in a few days Eric's sleep habits were a little better. At least he was getting more sleep during the night.

In March, Eric and Crystal went for their regular spring checkup. When Dr. Winter asked Eric if he'd experienced any recent headaches, Eric responded no, adding that he never felt better. He even challenged the doctor to a round of golf again. Dr. Winter just laughed it off. He figured Eric was joking and probably had never even been on a golf course. Crystal confirmed both. "Eric isn't having any problems, has never played golf, is getting plenty of rest, and has a healthy appetite."

Dr. Winter also gave Crystal a clean bill of health and told them he would see them both in four months, unless something came up and they needed to come in before that time. Neither of them mentioned Eric's previous health concerns nor Dr. Winter's suggestion that Eric see a neurologist. Dr. Winter knew that in time Crystal would see the effects of her error in judgment. She would then have to consider making the necessary adjustments while living with the consequences. He also knew that sooner or later, she would have to accept the fact that Eric had already entered the first of several stages of a permanent, debilitating, and irreversible condition. He just hoped it wouldn't be too late for either of them—especially for the sake of Crystal's own mental and physical well-being.

Leonardo returned in late April as promised. He stayed with Crystal and Eric instead of at a hotel. He and Eric went to one White Sox baseball game, but there was no fishing or hunting because Leonardo spent most of his time in pursuit of Sherry's affection. Leonardo stayed a week. Before he left, he admitted to Crystal that he had a few loose ends to tie up. After that, he said he hoped Sherry would agree to marry him. Crystal wondered about the "loose ends" but didn't ask and didn't mention the conversation to Sherry. She continued to pray that Leonardo wouldn't break Sherry's heart.

At the end of May, Crystal took advantage of a much-needed vacation, deciding not to teach summer school. She and Eric spent ten days in Florida, visiting with Crystal's aunt who took them to Disney World in Orlando and to a prestigious horse race at Gulfstream Park race track in Miami. Crystal had a great time, but Eric seemed to enjoy it even more. He'd always liked to watch horse racing and even had a friend in Chicago who owned a couple of horses. He and Crystal had often gone to watch his friend's horses run and, on several occasions, had bet on them and won. When his friend died, Eric's enthusiasm for the sport waned. It had been several years since he had gone to the racetrack, but he always watched the Triple Crown races on television. They consisted of the Kentucky Derby, in Louisville; the Preakness, in Maryland; and the Belmont Stakes, in New York. Crystal decided they would attend some horse races when they got back to Chicago.

Sherry performed her usual duties whenever Crystal and Eric went out of town. She didn't sound envious anymore when Crystal discussed her travels, but Crystal did notice Sherry would be in a kind of melancholy mood. Crystal also noticed her friend was no longer constantly talking about Leonardo. When she questioned her, Sherry avoided a lengthy conversation saying only that they were still talking, but he was quite busy with his career. She also said that he had mentioned he had some loose ends to tie up. Crystal started to tell her that Leonardo had told her the same thing, but Sherry changed the subject and Crystal felt she'd better not press the issue.

Crystal and Eric spent the rest of the summer enjoying picnics and barbecues with relatives and friends. They also attended the regular summer festivities at their clubhouse. Sometimes Sherry would go with them but most of the time she would make excuses. Crystal knew Sherry would rather stay at home hoping Leonardo would call. Besides, she would complain about the men who would be trying to hit on her. Eric would tease her and tell her she should take one of them up on his offer. Crystal reminded him that Sherry was engaged to Leonardo—well sort of, so she wasn't interested in dating other men. Occasionally, Eric would mention going on a cruise, but for reasons she couldn't explain Crystal didn't think it was a trip they should plan just yet. Of course she still felt their Caribbean cruise was simply fantastic, an indescribably, wonderfully romantic, and memorable experience. Then why wouldn't I want to do it again? Crystal asked herself this question but failed to have an answer.

It was early fall when Crystal noticed Eric seemed to become listless and withdrawn. As the weeks slowly dragged toward the holidays, Crystal didn't feel the gay anticipation she usually felt. When she came home from work, Eric seemed to be in his own little world. Their romantic moments seemed to be dwindling. She and Sherry weren't spending as much "Me" time together any more. Crystal figured it might be because Sherry and Leonardo were courting, hard and heavy. She started to call her children, just to have somebody to talk to but decided they would hear something in her voice and ask what was bothering her. Crystal decided to start making plans for a theatrical extravaganza for next spring, hoping that it would lift her spirits. She was beginning to miss the fun and laughter she and Eric shared when he first retired.

Leonardo didn't come for Thanksgiving, and Sherry's "glow" seemed to be fading. Crystal voiced her concern, but Sherry just faked a smile and changed the subject. Crystal didn't invite Ricardo and Adelia over for dinner. She sent them a card saying she would see them after the holidays. She and Sherry spent a quiet Thanksgiving with Eric and the kids. After dinner, Eric agreed to play Monopoly with the kids, and they happily retired to the den. Sherry helped Crystal put away the food and clean the kitchen. Crystal decided it was time Sherry talked to her about Leonardo.

"Okay, this is as good a time as any to tell me what's going on between you and Leonardo."

It was if Sherry was waiting for Crystal to ask her that question. Tears swelled in Sherry's eyes, and for a moment she didn't say anything. Crystal went to her and put her arm around her.

"I knew something was wrong," Crystal told her. "You need to talk about it."

"I don't know what happened," Sherry began. "All of a sudden he just stopped calling. He used to call me at least three times a week. When he didn't call me for several days, I called him but didn't get an answer. It's been almost two weeks since I've heard from him."

"Maybe he's sick. Eric knows how to get in touch with him. I'll ask Eric to call around and ..."

"No," Sherry said, "I don't need you or Eric to intercede for me. It's obvious he doesn't want to talk to me. He got what he was after. Besides, a 'cow' with three calves needs a lot of feed." Sherry allowed the tears to flow now.

"Stop it, girl! First of all, you forgave Leonardo and Eric for that. You agreed they were joking. You were supposed to let that go. And second, I believe Leonardo really loves you and your kids. Now I don't know why he hasn't called, but it isn't because he was just after the sex. Something must have happened. He'll probably have a reasonable explanation." She started to tell Sherry what Leonardo had said about tying up some loose ends but decided it might make the situation even worse. She really didn't want Sherry to think he would confide in her instead of his friend Eric. "Come on now, stop crying. He'll probably call you tonight and clear up the whole thing."

"I hope you're right. You know, I'm beginning to regret this long-distance relationship. What if something has happened to him? I can't even go to him." At that moment, Crystal realized how deeply Sherry had fallen for Leonardo.

"You really love the guy."

"I guess I didn't realize it myself until recently. I even prepared the children."

"Prepared them for what?"

"I asked them if they thought Leonardo would make a good father. When they all said yes, jumping up and down with joy, I told them I thought he was going to propose and give me a ring. Then they asked if I was going to accept it, and of course I told them I would."

"You told them before you told me?" Crystal teased. Crystal figured that would cause Sherry to smile, and it did. I have Leonardo's phone number. I'll call him myself tomorrow. He'd better have a good reason for upsetting my friend, Crystal thought to herself. Suddenly, they heard loud talking and crying coming from the den. They both went to see what was going on. Sherry's youngest son, Clyde, was crying while Carolyne and Johnny were loudly accusing Eric of cheating. Eric was denying it, although several one hundred dollar bills were sticking out from under the arm he had resting on the table. Crystal moved his arm, exposing the Monopoly money.

"See, I told you he stole some of my money," Clyde cried.

"Eric, you ought to be ashamed. Why do you cheat these kids?" Crystal asked.

"To win," Eric said emphatically, displaying a sly Jack Nicholson grin.

"Okay kids, it's time to go home anyway," Sherry said.

"Stop crying Clyde. He's going to be punished for stealing your money," Crystal snarled, while giving Eric a mean look.

"I'm glad you and the kids spent this day with us," Crystal said as she walked Sherry and the kids to the door. "And I'm glad you decided to confide in me," she added.

"I'll be glad when you decide to do the same," Sherry said as she exited without waiting for a response.

Crystal knew exactly what Sherry meant, and she was glad she didn't have to respond. Later that night, while she was undressing for bed, Crystal asked Eric if he had spoken with Leonardo recently.

"Yes, I talked to him, but I don't remember what day it was," Eric said.

"What did he say?"

"He said, hey buddy, how are you? What's been going on?"

"Okay Eric, you know what I mean. Did he mention Sherry?"

"No, why would he call me to ask about Sherry when he can call her?"

"Right," Crystal said smiling. She didn't want to let on that she was concerned about Leonardo's reason for not calling Sherry. She decided she would call Jay the next day and have him find out what was going on.

The next day, Crystal spoke briefly with Sherry. She didn't mention that she had called Jay. She knew Sherry and the kids were about to leave for their annual day-after-Thanksgiving shopping spree. She also knew that Sherry was still upset about Leonardo. She didn't hear from Jay until Sunday afternoon.

"Hey Mom, I caught up with Leonardo. He's fine. He's been working at this club in San Diego for the last two weeks."

"Did he say why he hadn't called Sherry?"

"He said Sherry had dumped him. Who is this guy she moved into her house?" Jay questioned.

"What guy? There's no guy living in her house," Crystal said, raising her voice.

"That's what Dad told Leonardo."

"What? You're lying!"

"Mom, why would I lie?"

"It's a figure of speech, Jay. I didn't mean you weren't telling the truth. I don't know why Eric would tell him something like that. It isn't true."

"Well, when he gets back in town next week, somebody better tell him. He's not taking it too well. I've gotta go, Mom. Love you."

Crystal was still holding the phone when Jay hung up. She couldn't believe her ears. Finally, she hung up and went straight into the den where Eric was watching the Bears football game.

"Honey, why did you tell Leonardo a man was living with Sherry?"

"I didn't tell Leonardo anything," he said defensively.

"Leonardo said you did."

"Well he's a lie. I didn't know she had a man living with her."

"She doesn't have a man living with her!" Crystal was almost shouting. Suddenly she realized what had happened. Eric must have overheard her telling one her club members that a mutual friend named Terry had moved her boyfriend in and Eric thought she'd said Sherry. But why didn't Eric just admit his mistake? If he did tell Leonardo that, how could he have forgotten?" Crystal knew she had to straighten things out and in a hurry. She called Jay back but got his answering machine. She left a message, explaining what had happened and urged Jay to get back in touch with Leonardo and explain it to him. She also told Jay to tell Leonardo to call Sherry ASAP. Next she called Sherry. When she answered the phone, Crystal could tell Sherry had been crying.

"Am I glad you're home. Don't go anywhere, I'll be right over. I've got something to tell you, so you can stop sitting around looking like three rainy days and a hurricane." When Crystal arrived at Sherry's house, she wasn't prepared for her friend's startling appearance. Sherry's face and eyes were swollen from what must have been hours of crying. Her hair was uncombed, and she was wearing an old faded duster. Crystal thought to herself, She must have gotten that thing from the Good Will on purpose. I don't ever remember seeing anything resembling that in her entire wardrobe. "Girl, have you looked in the mirror? You look like somebody sent for you but you couldn't come. Are you depressed?"

For a moment Sherry just stood silent. Suddenly she blurted out, "Do I look depressed?"

"Actually, you really do." Sherry began to cry uncontrollably. Crystal hugged her as she apologized. "Honey, I'm sorry. I didn't mean to add insult to injury. In fact, I have news that will lift your spirits and cure your blues. First, I'll remind you that you're always telling me that you don't pay Eric any mind. Well, I want you to practice what you preach because I just found out that Eric made a mistake. He overheard me talking about Terry allowing her boyfriend to move in, and he thought I said Sherry instead of Terry. He told Leonardo you had moved your boyfriend in with you."

"But why didn't Leonardo call me to find out the truth? Why didn't he return any of my calls?"

"Jay said Leonardo didn't fare well with the news, but he's trying to reach Leonardo as we speak. Leonardo has been traveling doing his stand-up in different venues in and out of L. A. He'll probably call you as soon as Jay talks to him. Please don't be mad at Eric."

Sherry hesitated to respond for a moment, then she said, "Crystal, I am your friend and I know you don't want to hear this, but I really think you know what's wrong with Eric."

"And I know you don't believe me, but I am not in denial. Eric is fine. I'm with him every day. I only mention certain things about him in conversation because you are my friend. Now fix yourself up in case Leonardo can see you when he calls," Crystal added trying to bring a smile to Sherry's face. "I've got to get on back now; Eric will be wondering where I am."

After that, Sherry and Leonardo's relationship began to escalate once again. No one mentioned the misinformation Eric had given to Leonardo. Sherry did ask Leonardo about the "loose ends" he had mentioned but he brushed her off saying he would tell her everything she needed to know in time.

Crystal and Eric spent Christmas and New Year's in L.A. again. She told Sherry it was their best Christmas ever. Maybe it was because Eric seemed like his old self again, and she was able to relax. Crystal began the new year with a prayer thanking God for keeping her family safe and healthy, especially her beloved husband.

Sherry was disappointed that she didn't receive an engagement ring on Valentine's Day, and Crystal didn't mention it for fear something had happened and Sherry didn't want to talk about it. In fact, Crystal realized that for the first time since they'd met, Eric didn't even acknowledge Valentine's Day. She tried not to let it bother her, but it did.

June marked the second anniversary of Eric's retirement celebration. Since the whole affair had been videotaped, Crystal thought it a good idea to watch the tape with Eric. She and Eric laughed at Leonardo. They both agreed that he made the party the huge success that it was. Eric said he was glad they had taped it. He hoped it would be something his grandchildren would be able to enjoy long after he was gone. Crystal didn't like for him to talk like that. She knew death was inevitable, but she wasn't ready to think about life without him.

Leonardo invited Sherry to visit him in L.A. while her kids spent two weeks at summer camp. Sherry told Crystal she was thinking about accepting Leonardo's invitation. She had never been to California and was excited about the thought of going. Crystal knew Sherry was asking her advice; should she or shouldn't she go? Since she thought it was a good idea for Sherry to get away, Crystal encouraged her to follow her heart. The two of them had fun shopping for the trip. Crystal was as excited as Sherry.

When it was time to leave, Crystal drove Sherry to the airport. During the ride, Sherry joked about this being the first time she was the one leaving instead of Crystal. As if waiting for this discussion but not really wanting to be the one to bring it up, Crystal confided that she was really going to miss her. She hinted that Eric had not been himself lately. He was forgetting how to do simple things like using the T.V. remote. Sherry tried to make light of it. "Girl, that is scary. Surfing with the remote is real proof of a man's dominance," she laughed.

Sherry remembered what happened between she and Crystal when she commented on Eric's health, so she decided not to expound on the subject. She agreed when Crystal said it was just part of the aging process. She even admitted she too was forgetting things hoping it would ease Crystal's mind. She would be gone for a week and didn't want her friend to worry all alone. At the airport, they hugged.

"You have a good time and don't worry; I'll check the mail and water the plants."

Sherry paused for a moment, trying to read Crystal's thoughts. "I'll call you from L.A."

"Whenever you get time," Crystal teased.

"I'll make time" Sherry assured her.

Crystal watered the plants and checked the mail as she promised, and Sherry called twice during the week as she had promised. It was during that week that Eric complained several times of experiencing severe headaches. Crystal also noticed he was not sleeping well again at night, despite the medication he was taking.

When Crystal drove Sherry home from the airport, she decided to go in and sit a while so Sherry could talk about her trip. It was obvious she'd had a great time because she couldn't stop smiling when she talked about it. The "glow" was back and for the next few days, that's all she talked about.

Sherry's children were due back on Sunday so she spent Friday morning drinking coffee and eating homemade rolls with Crystal. She finally got around to asking about Eric. Crystal told her Eric was his usual self—maybe not quite as amorous, but other than his forgetfulness, a few nagging headaches and not being able to sleep all night, he was fine. Sherry took a long hard look at her friend.

"After naming all those problems, how could you say he's fine? Crystal, it's obvious, you are in denial about something. What's really going on with Eric?" Trying to ward off an oncoming argument, but also firm with her assertion, Crystal responded.

"I am not in denial about anything. Now back to your trip to L.A. Tell me more."

Sherry couldn't understand why Crystal was so adamant about denying that Eric wasn't in the best of health. This really bothered her, but she decided to allow her friend to change the subject. Besides, she couldn't keep her good news to herself any longer. She was excited as she blurted out that Leonardo had all but proposed to her. He'd talked about moving back to Chicago since Sherry had made it clear she couldn't uproot her kids and move to L. A., although the weather there was very tempting. Crystal suggested that another year of courtship would be beneficial for both of them.

"Okay, mother," Sherry teased, "I get the message. You want me to be sure, and I am. So come on, share my enthusiasm."

"Only if you promise to get married in this house," Crystal said, a big grin covering her face.

Suddenly Eric entered the kitchen, startling the two women as usual. They never could hear him coming. He was dressed only in his "under-drawers" as Sherry called them. She covered her eyes and mouth while trying unsuccessfully to stifle a laugh.

"Eric, don't you see Sherry? You need to go put on some clothes."

"I'm in my house. Sherry needs to be in her house."

"Come on Eric, please don't start," Crystal said, her voice sounding a bit irritated.

"He's right, Crystal. I'll let myself out, call you later," Sherry said as she headed for the door.

"Eric, why would you come down here in your underwear?"

"Because it's MY house, and I should be able to walk around MY house in whatever I want. I didn't know Sherry was here. I was trying to find something to wear without much luck. I kept calling you, but you wouldn't answer so I came down to get you to come up and help me pick out something." He laughed as he pulled Crystal into his arms singing the words to an old song by Diana Ross and the Supremes, "Come see about your baby."

Pushing him away, Crystal threw up both hands and mumbled, mostly to herself, "Since you're not going anywhere, what difference does it make what you have on." As she followed Eric up the stairs, she thought, I created this monster. I guess I'll just have to live with it. She still couldn't believe what he had done. In all the years they had lived there, Eric had never come downstairs in his underwear—never.

The following weekend something happened that should have been a red flag for Crystal. It was after eight o'clock, but it was still light outside. She and Eric were returning home from a friend's cookout. Crystal was discussing what a wonderful time they'd had and how good the food was. When Eric didn't respond, Crystal continued talking, commenting about how nice it was to see some of their old friends again. Eric was still unresponsive. This didn't bother Crystal since she hadn't asked him a question. She figured he was watching the road and allowing her to do the talking. Suddenly Eric drove the car over the curb and down the sidewalk. Crystal let out a scream as she tried to grab the steering wheel. She screamed for Eric to stop, telling him he was on the sidewalk.

The car rolled over the grass, hit a tricycle, tore through a rose bush, crushed an empty baby stroller, and barely missed a tree. Crystal managed to put her foot on the brakes as she shifted the gears into park. All the time, she had thought they would surely be thrown through the windshield. She was still yelling and asking Eric what was wrong with him. She even questioned his sobriety. When he calmly assured her he was not drunk and asked her why she was getting so upset, Crystal nearly lost it.

"That's it," she yelled, "Your driving days are over." Move! Get out and get over here in the passenger seat!"

"You don't have to yell, I can hear you," he yelled back. Eric got out and walked around to the passenger side. Crystal slid into the driver's seat. She put the car in gear and drove back onto the street, then pulled over to the curb and turned the motor off. For a moment, she just sat staring at Eric who sat staring into space. Crystal didn't want to admit it, but she was scared. A group of people appeared, inspecting the damages. A man came over to the car and asked if they were all right, explaining that he was the owner of the house, the rose bush, and the crushed stroller. Crystal said they were okay. She reached into her purse and took out paper and pen and wrote down her name, address, and phone number. She assured the man she would pay for the damages. The man said okay but before he could say anything else, she started the car and pulled off. She drove the rest of the way in silence.

At home, Eric went right up to bed. Crystal slept on the sofa in the den.

The next day, neither Crystal nor Eric spoke of the incident. She decided she wouldn't mention it to Sherry either. Whenever the man called her with the cost of the damages, she would write him a check, mail it, and that would be that. Crystal made up her mind, from now on, she was the designated driver—at least until Eric had his eyes checked. Hold it! That's it, she thought, maybe he was telling the truth, maybe he didn't see the curb. Maybe he needs glasses. That was the reason for his slowing down, his inability to do the things he normally was able to do. She'd caught him trying to read the newspaper upside down. She hadn't given it much thought, but that must be it! He can't see. He needs glasses.

The next morning, Crystal called the University of Chicago Hospital and made an appointment to have Eric's eyes checked. Through a friend, she'd heard the clinic had an excellent eye doctor. Crystal was so happy she had made this revelation. She called Sherry, who managed to hide the fact that she was not that enthused. Eric may need glasses and if he does, then by all means he needs to get some but she felt there was more to it than Crystal was willing to admit.

After an extensive examination, Dr. Williams, the optometrist, confirmed it: glasses might indeed help Eric's vision—temporarily. But much to Crystal's dismay, Eric had little or no vision in his left eye and very little in his right eye. Eric had glaucoma, a disease that would eventually render him blind. When Crystal asked the doctor if he was sure about his diagnosis, he looked at her a moment before answering.

"Mrs. Haywood," he said, obviously choosing his words carefully, "Mr. Haywood's eye exam substantiates my diagnosis. There are no cataracts present. If you like, I can show you his x-rays or, if you like, you can go elsewhere for a second opinion. I'll give him a prescription for some glasses that might help him see better in his right eye, but they won't do much to help the left eye. I'm sorry."

Crystal didn't speak for a moment. "Okay," she said, heaving a sigh, "we'll take the prescription." Crystal had thought about getting a second opinion but realized, as Dr. Williams said, it would be a waste of time and money. Besides, he came highly recommended and deep down inside, she had the feeling that his diagnosis was correct. By the end of the following week, Eric had his new glasses and Crystal was able to see an immediate improvement in his ability to function and complete some tasks. He told her he could see much better. But when Crystal told Sherry that Eric had his glasses and his vision had improved, Sherry did not hear the jubilation she had heard when Crystal first revealed that Eric needed glasses. Maybe that's because obtaining the glasses did not solve the underlying problem, Sherry thought. The one Crystal was in denial about.

A few days later, Sherry called and asked Crystal if she would go shopping with her. As usual, they took time out for a bite to eat at a nearby restaurant. While eating, Sherry was aware that Crystal appeared deep in thought. She didn't want to probe but couldn't help steering the conversation toward getting Crystal to confide in her. She asked her if she was ready to go back to work. When Crystal nonchalantly said she guessed so, Sherry decided it was time to remove the kid gloves and come right out and voice her concerns.

"Alright Crystal, what's wrong?"

"Nothing," Crystal said, not looking directly at her friend.

"We've been friends too long. I can tell when something is bothering you." Sherry knew she was treading on thin ice, but she continued anyway. "Crystal, I've said it before and I'm saying it again. You are in denial about something. What is it?"

Knowing Sherry was not going to let it go this time, Crystal denied she was in denial about anything but admitted that she was concerned about Eric's eyesight. Without telling Sherry exactly what had happened, she said Eric couldn't see how to drive anymore.

"What about his new glasses? You said he was seeing much better."

"He is but ..." Crystal was determined not to go into details. "He just doesn't see that well when he is driving."

"That means you have to do all the driving," Sherry stated. "

At least for now," Crystal said. "What do you mean for now?" Sherry asked. Crystal didn't speak. She didn't know how she could answer without telling Sherry the whole story, which for reasons she couldn't explain, she wasn't quite ready to discuss.

Sherry said, "You used to be so open with me. You used to tell me everything. You told me about your childhood; how you were a "daddy's girl"; how your father got custody of you after the divorce; how you always wanted a sister; how you feel I am the sister you never had. But right now, I don't feel like a sister or even your best friend. I feel you're holding something back. What is it? Please talk to me. What's wrong?"

"If something was wrong, I would certainly tell my best friend, wouldn't I?" Crystal said, hoping Sherry would finally be convinced and stop badgering her. She had a lot on her mind and just wasn't ready to share her problems. Sherry just sat looking at her.

"You're really in deep denial," Sherry said, shaking her head. "Now, what's been going on lately between you and Leonardo?" Crystal asked, hoping she could finally change the subject.

Sherry calmly replied, "You know something? You're a master at changing the subject. When you tell me what's going on with you and Eric, I'll tell you what's going on between me and Leonardo." Checking her watch, Sherry added, "Where did the time go? It's after three. Let's get out of here." As they gathered their packages and headed out, Crystal said, "You're a pretty good master of changing the subject yourself." They both laughed, but Sherry knew it wasn't a laughing matter, and Crystal had a feeling this conversation was far from over.

Upon arriving at home, Crystal was greeted by a panic-stricken Eric. "Baby, don't take your coat off," he said. "You need to take me to the emergency room. I was cleaning out my ear with a hairpin and it went all the way in and I can't get it out." Crystal dropped her packages and examined Eric's ear.

"I don't see anything in your ear," she said.

"I told you, it went inside. Take me to the emergency room, they'll get it out," Eric pleaded.

A half an hour later, Crystal was sitting in the emergency room when Sherry came rushing in. Crystal had called her to let her know what was happening. She had told Sherry it wasn't necessary for her to come, but there she was like a true blue friend.

"I wasn't going to let you sit here by yourself. I know how long these things take. And why are you sitting out here? Shouldn't you be in the examining room with Eric?"

"I told you it wasn't necessary for you to come, but I knew you would. I was waiting out here so I could send you back home."

Sherry smiled, "I figured you would need me."

"Like you said, this could take a long time. Now go on home, we'll be alright," Crystal insisted.

As Sherry watched her friend walk toward the examining area, she thought, Crystal, I know you are going through a lot right now. I just wish there was some way I could help you. Crystal disappeared behind the double doors, but Sherry just stood for a while before she turned and headed for home. Several hours later, Crystal and Eric returned home from the emergency room.

"Why are you so angry with me?" Eric asked almost child-like.

"Because I knew there wasn't anything in your ear. We wasted three and a half hours," Crystal said, trying not to display the anger she really felt.

"Please don't be mad at me, honey. It felt like something was in there." The x-ray had shown there was nothing in Eric's ear although his pressure was a bit elevated. The doctor said that could have been caused by Eric's fear that he had really pushed something into his ear. Crystal was beginning to worry about Eric. Maybe she could no longer leave him at home alone. She expressed her thoughts to him.

"I am not a child. You can go to work and anywhere else you want to go. I can take care of myself," Eric responded. Crystal detected a bit of animosity in his voice. There seemed to be a lot of that lately. He had rarely, if ever, talked to her in that way. She shrugged it off, blaming the summer heat and the fact that Eric needed to get out more. She knew she would be going back to work in September. That gave her a little over a month to work out a plan.

Since Eric was always up early anyway, maybe she could get up a little earlier herself. They could resume taking their walks; she could fix his breakfast and leave something already prepared for his lunch. Like always, they'd eat dinner together when she got home. It was a little extra work for her but what the heck—it would solve her problem. When she related this to Eric, he grabbed her playfully.

"As Jay would say, 'sounds like a plan to me'. Now how about a snack? I'm hungry enough to eat a family of five and wait for the distant relatives to come to the funeral—and eat them too. What do you say?"

"I say you need more than a snack," Crystal said laughing.

Eric sounded like his old self. She couldn't understand it. He was one way one minute and another way a few minutes later. This really puzzled her. She looked at him. He still looked good for a man his age. He wasn't even seventy yet. She thought, There's nothing wrong with him. So what if he forgets a little. Younger people forget things too. But something else was bothering Crystal. Eric was no longer trying to chase her. In fact, it had been a while since they'd made love or even talked about sex. His blood pressure medication is probably interfering with his sex drive, she thought. I'll make an appointment with Dr. Winter. Maybe he can change the prescription or prescribe a lower dosage. That should do it. He'll be just fine. Crystal smiled at the thought. If and when his health starts to fail, I'll take care of him—and that's a promise.

The next morning Crystal called and made an appointment for Eric to see Dr. Winter. She didn't know that Sherry was on her own phone putting in a call to Jay. Sherry explained her concerns about Eric and the stress she felt Crystal was under. She suggested Jay come home—just for the weekend. If he couldn't come, she told him to at least call his mother. Maybe she would tell him what's going on. Sherry begged Jay not to tell Crystal she had called him. He promised he wouldn't. When she'd hung up, Sherry heaved a sigh. She felt she had done the right thing.

The next day Crystal was up early. She decided to prepare Eric's favorites for breakfast: eggs, hash browns, sausage, and pancakes. Eric beamed like a college student on spring break and planted a long and passionate kiss right on Crystal's lips.

"Whoa there, down boy. You haven't kissed me like that in months," she said.

"Come back to bed, and I'll do something else I haven't done in months," Eric threatened jokingly. Crystal was both surprised and happy to see Eric back in the groove, but she told him to wait until later because Mike, the young man across the street, was coming to cut their grass.

"Why can't I cut my own grass? In fact, after eating a breakfast like that, I need to cut the grass, wash the windows, and clean the gutters."

Crystal had to think fast to come up with a response. "I know you can still do all of that, but I want you to use every ounce of that energy on me."

Eric grabbed her playfully, "Well what are we waiting for?"

"Hold on there King Fish, Mike will be ringing the bell any minute."

"So, this won't take but a minute," he teased.

Crystal laughed, as the door bell rang. "Saved by the bell," she said.

"Damn, hurry up and get rid of that kid," Eric said, "I'll be upstairs waiting."

The bell rang again. "Okay, okay, I'm coming," Crystal called out. "Hold your horses." Crystal opened the door expecting to see Mike, but it was Sherry.

"I had to ring twice. By any chance could I have been interrupting something?"

Crystal laughed. "Yes, but I'm glad you did. Come on in, girl." Before the two could sit down, the bell rang again. Crystal told Sherry to pour herself a cup of coffee while she talked to Mike about cutting the grass. The telephone rang as Crystal was going to answer the door.

"I'll get it," Sherry yelled. It was Jay. Sherry whispered a reminder that he was not to let on that she had called him. Crystal returned, and Sherry handed her the phone. Sherry pretended not to listen as she poured herself a cup of coffee, but she could pretty much tell what Jay was saying by what Crystal was saying. When Crystal hung up, Sherry nonchalantly asked her what was causing her puzzling expression.

"Jay is coming home, but I have my doubts about his reason for making the trip."

"Maybe he's homesick," Sherry said, hoping she sounded more innocent than she felt. Or maybe he's finally found 'Miss Right' and he's bringing her home to surprise you and Eric."

"Oh, that would make Eric so happy. In fact, he'd die on the ground if that were true, but I know my son, that's not what this visit is about."

"Then what do you think it's about?" Sherry asked, not looking at Crystal for fear she'd suspect she knew something.

"He said he was coming for business. I don't know, but I intend to find out. He'll be here next Thursday."

Sherry had expected Jay to come much sooner and realized that was the same day Leonardo would be arriving. Crystal saw the look on Sherry's face.

"What?" she asked.

"That's the same day Leonardo is supposed to come," Sherry said.

"I wonder why Eric didn't mention it," Crystal said, voicing her thoughts. "Maybe Leonardo forgot to tell him," she added.

"I don't think so. Leonardo said he and Eric made plans to go fishing," Sherry informed her.

Crystal was puzzled. "Did Leonardo say where he was staying?"

"Yes, he said he was staying here with you and Eric. I don't know why Eric didn't say anything to you about it."

"Maybe for the same reason you didn't tell me Leonardo was coming—until now."

"I was about to tell you but with the doorbell ringing and then the telephone, I didn't get the chance," Sherry said. "Besides," she added, "Leonardo talked to Eric before he told me so I thought you knew."

Tired of going around in circles, Crystal finally said, "I'm the housekeeper and maid around here, but it seems that everybody knows when guests are arriving—except me."

"Don't put me in that 'everybody' group," Sherry said, defensively.

The phone rang again. This time Sherry was glad. She wanted the conversation to end before Crystal sensed that she already knew Jay was coming. Sherry could tell by Crystal's responses she was not pleased with the caller. Crystal reached for a pen and paper and began to write down a name and address. Sherry heard her say a doctor somebody. She didn't understand the name, but she knew it wasn't Dr. Winter. When Crystal hung up, she had a puzzling expression on her face. Before Sherry could ask, Crystal revealed she had made an appointment for Eric to see Dr. Winter. The phone call was from Dr. Winter's nurse who said Dr. Winter had an out-of-town emergency and had switched Eric's appointment to a colleague, Dr. Hussein.

"So why is this other doctor located in a different office?"

"I don't know. Maybe I should have told her to reschedule Eric's appointment. We don't have an emergency." Crystal suddenly reminded Sherry that the appointment was on the same day Jay was coming. Sherry told her not to worry because if she needed her to, she would pick Jay up from the airport. "Maybe you won't have to. I'll just call the nurse back and have her reschedule Eric's appointment."

"I'm just saying, if you need me to, I will," Sherry reiterated, hoping that it would encourage Crystal to keep the appointment.

Without warning, Eric appeared in the kitchen doorway. He was wearing a pair of Crystal's bikini panties—nothing more. He was just as surprised to see Sherry as the two women were to see him—dressed as he was. He put his hand over his private parts as he apologized and said he didn't know Crystal had company. Sherry covered her mouth to stifle a laugh, but Crystal was far from seeing anything funny.

"Eric, what the hell is going on with you? Those are my panties you have on. And don't you see Sherry in here?" Eric defended himself.

"I've been waiting upstairs for you for a long time. I just came down to see what was taking you so long. I didn't know these were yours." He looked down at the panties.

Unable to hide her embarrassment, Crystal told Eric to go back upstairs and wait for her. After Eric had left, Sherry finally released her laughter. She told Crystal she would let herself out. Crystal walked Sherry to the door anyway since Eric had already gone back upstairs.

"Sherry, I wish you wouldn't laugh at his antics," Crystal said, unable to suppress her emotions.

"Why not? You should be laughing too. He really did look funny in your panties."

"Like I said, it wasn't funny and I'm not laughing."

At the door, Sherry turned to Crystal and said, "Seriously, I'm trying to get you to laugh because, as your friend, I know you, and I know you must be going through hell seeing Eric—like that. He made you curse. That's not like you at all. It's obvious, Crystal, something is going on with Eric. As your best friend—please, don't cancel that appointment." Not waiting for a response, Sherry hurried to her car. She didn't have to look back to know that Crystal was still standing at the door, pondering over what she had just said.

The next few days were pretty ordinary, with nothing unusual happening. Crystal began to be more observant, checking to see where Eric was and what he was up to. She was tempted several times to cancel Eric's appointment with Dr. Hussein, but Sherry's words kept echoing in her mind.

Thursday morning was hot and humid. The weather man had promised the temperature would be in the upper nineties—the highest since August had begun. Crystal was glad Dr. Hussein's office was nice and cool. After waiting only ten minutes, his nurse—a small, neat young girl of Asian descent—called Eric's name and motioned them into the examining room. The nurse weighed Eric and took his temperature and blood pressure, which were both normal. She said the doctor would be in shortly and left. A light bulb went off in Crystal's head when she noticed a medical plaque hanging on the wall with Dr. Hussein's name on it. He was a neurologist. Crystal felt anger swelling up inside and thought maybe she and Eric should get up and leave. Dr. Winter had deliberately tricked them into seeing a Neurologist. But before she could put her thought into action, the door opened and in walked a very handsome, medium-built man of foreign descent—she wasn't sure if he was from Iran, Iraq, or Jordan, but she knew he was from the Middle East.

Extending his hand, he introduced himself and called them by their last name adding a question mark. Eric was in a playful mood and said, "Yes, but I'm Crystal and she's Eric." The doctor smiled, and then cleared his throat, becoming serious. He began to ask Eric some questions.

"Are any of your parents living?"

Crystal answered, "Both our parents are deceased." Dr. Hussein continued to direct his questions to Eric.

"Were either of your parents diagnosed with Alzheimer's disease or dementia?"

Again Crystal answered, "No, why?"

He explained that Dr. Winter had sent over Eric's test results, as well as his medical history, and felt the prognosis should be discussed at length. He asked Eric how he was feeling. When Eric said great, he asked if he was still experiencing headaches. Eric said no. Crystal started to tell the doctor that Eric had complained of headaches several times within the last three weeks but decided not to mention it. She didn't want to say or do anything that would aid in causing Dr. Winter's diagnosis to materialize. In her mind, she believed it would directly interfere with her daily prayer for God to remove any and all forms of such a debilitating disease from Eric's brain. She did tell the doctor that originally she had made an appointment with Dr. Winter to have Eric's blood pressure medication changed because she thought it might be interfering with his sex drive. Dr. Hussein informed her she should be more concerned with what the EEG and the MRI showed. Suddenly and without warning, Crystal went on the defensive.

"Don't you think you should run some more tests before you make any diagnosis or prognosis?" Dr. Hussein paused. He knew he was faced with a delicate situation. Dr. Winter had warned him that Crystal was not ready to accept the truth—Eric was in the early stages of dementia. After a moment, he quietly and simply made a statement.

"More tests would only be a waste of time, as well as money, since the records Dr. Winter sent over clearly show that Eric has suffered a series of mini-strokes, possibly while asleep or even while he was awake."

"But wouldn't he have known he was having a stroke if he was awake?" She asked.

"Not necessarily," Dr. Hussein replied. "Sometimes mini-strokes are disguised as severe headaches without showing any severe aftereffects." He placed Eric's EEG pictures on the wall and explained the light and dark areas, even though Dr. Winter had stated he'd already shown them the test results that aided in his decision to refer Eric to a neurologist.

"The dark areas at the base of Eric's brain depict normality, but the light gray areas confirm that abnormal activity has occurred. A stroke is considered abnormal activity. A stroke occurs when there is a rupture or an obstruction of a blood vessel in the brain." When Crystal asked how the abnormality could be treated, Dr. Hussein replied with candor.

"At the present time, it can't be treated nor reversed. It is similar to when a glass is broken and shatters into many small pieces. It cannot be put back together again." Without hesitating, he went on to say, "Because of this, Eric can be diagnosed as being in the early stages of dementia."

Crystal felt as if the doctor had taken his fist and punched her hard in the abdomen. She had to catch her breath. She repeated the word as if asking a question. Then she did ask one. "You mean like in Alzheimer's?" Dr. Hussein nodded yes. Crystal looked at the doctor for a moment, then she stood up and said she did not believe her husband had either Alzheimer's or dementia. She said Eric might forget every now and then, but everybody does that. She went on an emotional tirade, describing Eric's impeccable work record while driving a CTA train for over twenty years, never being absent or late. She rattled on about all of his commendations and how active he was now, even at his age. She also mentioned his sexual prowess. She accused Dr. Winter of making a terrible mistake and that he might have sent over the wrong test results. She ended her tirade with, "My husband is as normal as any other sixty-seven-year-old man. He has a great sense of humor and he loves to clown around a lot. You saw that for yourself."

Undaunted by Crystal's emotional tirade, Dr. Hussein went on to say, "Dementia is a progressive disease, marked by a deterioration of cognitive functions. It occurs over time and may not be displayed every day nor detected right away. But there are early tell-tale signs of forgetfulness and disorientation. Because of your husband's sense of humor, you and other family members could easily think most of the antics are pranks or jokes. Some of you may simply accept them as signs of aging."

Crystal sat motionless as Dr. Hussein continued.

"Since Eric is in the early stages, there is a medication that will help to slow down the progression. I can see him on a regular basis and monitor his progress." Crystal still said nothing. Dr. Hussein never took his eyes from her. "I would suggest that you join a support group. I can put you in touch with one that meets monthly."

Suddenly Crystal stood up. "Thank you for your time, doctor. Get your cap, honey, let's go." Ignoring Crystal's command, Dr. Hussein asked Eric if he had any questions. Crystal quickly answered no for Eric. Dr. Hussein reminded Crystal that he was their second opinion but they could seek a third one. He told Eric he could write a prescription if he'd like. Crystal spoke for him. "No, he wouldn't like."

Dr. Hussein had to agree with Dr. Winter. It was obvious: Crystal was in a severe state of denial. He wished he could convince her to accept the diagnosis and determine her options, but Crystal was unrelenting. When Dr. Hussein suggested seeing Eric again in three weeks, Crystal informed him that Eric's next appointment would be his regular appointment with Dr. Winter.

On the drive home, it was all Crystal could do to fight back the tears. She tried not to think about what Dr. Hussein had said. She talked about the plans they'd been making for their vacation, hoping Eric wouldn't think about what the doctor had said either.

They returned home to find Jay and Sherry setting the table with a carry-out meal from a nearby fast-food restaurant. When Crystal told Jay she had planned to take him out to eat, he jokingly said he'd rather eat at home with his favorite mom and dad. Jay didn't let on that Sherry had filled him in on some of her fears and what little she knew about Eric's health. When Crystal asked about Leonardo, Sherry told her his plane wouldn't be in until later that evening. Crystal apologized for causing her to make two trips to the airport. Sherry explained that she wouldn't be picking Leonardo up since he had decided to rent a car. Jay noticed Eric sitting quietly, staring into space. "Hey man, make some noise. I'm home and I'm looking for some excitement."

Eric perked up, turning his blank stare into a smile. "I'll show you some excitement," he said. "Bow your heads everybody. Good bread, good meat, good Lord, let's eat!" Then he grabbed a chicken leg in one hand and a thigh in the other and started biting into them like a hungry hound.

"Now that's more like my dad, and he's poetic too." Jay smiled broadly.

Sherry waited until everyone had finished eating before she asked, "So how did it go with the new doctor?" Crystal shot her a look that said, You're getting in my business again.

Remembering that Crystal did not know that Sherry had filled him in on as much as she knew about the new doctor, Jay tried to look surprised.

"You changed doctors? I thought you always went to Dr. Winter."

Crystal explained that Dr. Winter was out of town, so Eric had to see one of his colleagues.

"Your father is fine, and he won't have to see that doctor again."

Sherry shot Crystal a surprised look. Surely Crystal didn't expect her to believe that. Then Crystal asked Jay what kind of business had brought him home so suddenly. That's when Sherry realized Crystal had not been honest about the new doctor. She was skillfully changing the subject as only she could do. Sherry didn't know how she would revert back to the subject of the new doctor, nor did she think it a good idea—at this time. Maybe Jay can get some information out of her after I leave, she thought. After all, that was the real purpose for his visit. When Eric said he hoped Jay had come home to find a wife, Jay teased Eric, telling him to get off his back.

Sherry laughed. "I'm glad you're home, Jay. Maybe now your father can get off my back—for the moment anyway."

Crystal gave Jay a sly wink. "Eric isn't the only one on Sherry's back. I hope I'm not the only one noticing that certain glow."

"It's about time she decided to accept some affection from the opposite sex," Eric said.

"Hey, I don't blame Leonardo for easing on in. If she didn't have so many kids, I would have beaten him to the punch," Jay joked. Sherry laughed and shook her head.

"You guys are talking about me like I've left the room. Jay you're much too young for me, and besides, Eric would have a stroke. He wants you to get married more than anything. But ... to a woman who has been married twice and with three almost-grown kids? I don't think so."

Crystal was glad no one noticed her uneasiness when Sherry teased about Eric having a stroke. When Crystal commented about how fast Leonardo was moving in on Sherry, Eric perked up again and joined the conversation. "He's got to be fast, he has to travel two thousand miles just to go on a date."

Crystal smiled, looking at Eric and thinking to herself, Now does that sound like somebody suffering from any kind of dementia?

As Crystal cleared the table, she suggested they take in a movie. Jay hesitated for a moment, then asked Sherry if she was up to it. Sherry declined.

"Leonardo is coming in, and I would like to spend some time with him—that is if you don't mind," she said jokingly. "Besides Jay, you need to spend time alone with Eric and Crystal."

"That's right, but isn't Leonardo staying here too?"

"No ... uh ... he decided he didn't want to impose on your mom and dad, especially since you were coming home. He booked a room at the Ramada," Sherry said before Crystal could answer.

Crystal gave Sherry a "knowing" look. "Is Cinnamon babysitting for you tonight?"

Sherry smiled as she replied, "I would never leave my kids home alone."

Crystal smiled back. "Will Cinnamon be spending the night?"

Sherry knew exactly where this was going. She continued smiling as she answered, "No, she won't."

Jay laughed. "You two act like a couple of secret agents speaking in codes. Now either cut that out or cut me and Dad in." They all laughed.

Sherry was glad she had called Jay. Crystal and Eric seemed more relaxed and happy with him home. Finally, Sherry said she had to go. Jay and Eric settled in the den to watch television while Crystal walked Sherry to the door.

After watching television for a while, Crystal was aware of the way Jay watched their every move. She had to almost pull him out of the house to the movies. He said he just wanted to stay at home with them and watch TV, but when Eric kept asking Jay when he was going to get married, Jay teased him admitting a movie might be more peaceful. They chose to see Three Men and a Baby. Eric and Jay enjoyed it, but Crystal enjoyed it more. She always took in a movie with Sherry, but it had been a while since she had gone with Eric.

Jay thought the evening went well, but when he and Crystal were alone, he questioned her about Eric's health. He admitted Eric had always hounded him about his marital plans, but now it had become an obsession with him. He also mentioned that Eric seemed to have developed a habit of repeating himself and asking about the same thing more than just a few times. Crystal laughed and said, "Keep on living. When you get to be his age, you'll end up doing the same thing." When they returned from the movies, Crystal began making plans for the next day.

"Slow down a minute, Mom. I want to spend some time with the two of you. Since I won't be leaving until Sunday, I've got plenty of time to hang out with you." When Crystal mentioned that she thought he'd come home to take care of some business, Jay laughed. "You are my business."

Crystal was happy about that, but she still wondered if Eric had said something crazy during one of his bimonthly telephone conversations with Jay, something that might have caused Jay to worry about them. Then she

157

thought, Oh well, whatever the reason, I'm happy when any of my children come home.

Later that night, Eric was lying in bed watching Crystal undress and slip into her nightgown. Suddenly he said, "Honey, I was thinking about what that new doctor said. Why is this happening to me? I never did anything to anyone. I didn't misuse my body. I tried to set a good example for my kids. I never did or said anything to deliberately hurt anyone. What did I do wrong?" He began to cry.

In all the years they'd been married, there had only been one time she had seen him cry—years ago, when his friend who owned the horses died. They had been childhood friends. In fact, he had been Eric's best man when they had gotten married.

Crystal sat down on the side of the bed. "Stop beating up on yourself. You haven't done anything wrong, and there's nothing wrong with you. Everybody forgets now and then. Honey, doctors don't know everything. You'll be alright. You just need to stay busy and keep your mind active."

"But what if the doctor is right? What if I do have the disease? You remember my Aunt Bee? She used to do crazy stuff all the time. What if it runs in my family? What if I start to do crazy stuff?"

"You won't," Crystal insisted.

"But what if I do?"

Crystal looked at him for a moment. He looked so pitiful; she had to hold back her own tears. If he saw her crying, it might make him cry even more; and she didn't want Jay to come in and find them both bawling like babies. "Then we'll fight it," she said. "If you do come down with—dementia, there's a medication you can take. Dr. Winter can write you a prescription and don't forget, we've always got our faith. You still believe in God don't you?"

"You know I do," Eric replied almost childlike.

"Then we'll pray. God is a healer. He knows we've still got a lot of living to do, and we're going to do it together. You don't have dementia and you're not going to get it."

"I'm so lucky to have you," Eric said. "What would I do without you?"

Crystal looked at him, not with pity now but with all the love in her heart. "You'll never know the answer to that," she said as she turned out the light and slid in bed beside him. He snuggled up to her like a little boy. She rubbed his head until she heard him snoring softly. She closed her eyes, but she couldn't go to sleep—not just yet, not before she prayed.

On Saturday, Sherry and Leonardo popped in for breakfast. Leonardo confirmed his fishing date with Eric for the following Monday.

Crystal smiled as she said, "Sherry, you've got that glow again."

Hoping Crystal would get her drift, Sherry said, "I want to see your glow come back."

Still smiling, Crystal said, "I don't know why you can't see it—it's still there, it never left."

After Sherry and Leonardo had gone, Jay suggested that they spend a quiet evening at home, playing Monopoly or dominos. Crystal opted for Monopoly since she felt it would be an easier game for Eric because it wouldn't take a lot of thinking. Crystal didn't know it, but Jay wanted to watch Eric's cognitive actions and responses. He'd had an extensive conversation with Sherry, but he hadn't gotten much information from Crystal, who kept saying everything was fine. Jay tried, but he found little if any unusual actions from Eric. Finally, he thought Sherry might be overreacting and Crystal was right; Dad was fine. Whatever was wrong—if anything—probably was part of the aging process.

On Sunday morning Crystal was glad she didn't have to coax Jay into attending church with them. She was extremely happy when he said he was glad to have the opportunity to worship with his parents again. He said it felt like old times. When it was time for Jay to leave, Eric said, "I really hate to see you go, son. Did you find a wife?"

Of course the question didn't surprise Jay. He'd been expecting it. It had become a ritual. Jay laughed as he said, "No, but I'll be back. My friend Al is hooking me up with a blind date."

"What do you want with a blind woman?" Eric asked.

"Eric, you know what a blind date is," Crystal said laughing.

"Yes I do, he's going on a date with a blind woman. I don't have anything against blind people, but if he intends to start a family, he needs a woman who can see what she's doing."

"He's joking isn't he, Mom?" Jay asked, laughing.

"Yes he is," Crystal said, laughing too, but not knowing if Eric really was joking.

The sound of Al's horn outside brought the conversation to an abrupt halt. As they walked Jay to the door, Crystal chided him for not allowing them to drive him to the airport.

"Al wants to give me the 411 on the young lady he's going to hook me up with. Besides Mom, I didn't want you dealing with the traffic since you have to do the driving until Dad gets used to his new glasses." Crystal didn't tell Jay that glasses or no glasses, Eric's driving days were over. Jay hugged Eric and Crystal and said he would see them in L.A. for the holidays. As Jay was getting into the car, Eric called out to him.

"Hurry back! A blind bride beats no bride at all."

Crystal laughed but deep down inside, she had a strong feeling of apprehension that she couldn't explain. Crystal decided she and Eric would turn in early. Leonardo had called and said he would be picking Eric up at four o'clock the next morning for their fishing trip. They had two favorite lakes in which they liked to fish: a lake in Canada, and a small lake somewhere between Wisconsin and Minnesota. Since Leonardo wanted to fish and get back to Sherry, he chose the latter; it took the least amount of time to get there and back. Crystal knew she would have to get up with Eric and help him get ready. Sure enough, the next morning Leonardo pulled into the driveway at four o'clock on the dot. Crystal had awakened at three and helped Eric get dressed. Since they would be gone almost twenty- four hours, she'd prepared a fairly big lunch to take with them, the night before. Crystal watched as the two men drove away, hoping as she always seemed to be hoping lately, that everything would be okay. She crawled back into bed, too sleepy to stay up and worry.

By the time Eric and Leonardo reached their favorite fishing spot and baited their rods, the sun was coming up. Eric slung his rod to one side and entangled Leonardo's line with his. Leonardo swore at Eric as he began to untangle the lines. When he had finally straightened them out, he showed Eric how to work the reel and bait the rod. He teased Eric about his inability to remember how to fish. Eric responded with a few choice words of his own and reminded Leonardo that he was the one who taught his "dumb ass" how to fish.

They sat down together on the pier and waited for their first bite. Leonardo knew it might be a while before they would catch anything, so he engaged Eric in small talk. Sherry had shared her fear that something was going on with Eric, but she didn't know what and her friend Crystal wasn't talking. She said she feared Eric was getting-senile. Leonardo disputed this, saying he had seen Eric the day before and he was as sharp and witty as ever. Still, Sherry made Leonardo promise to be mindful of the things Eric said and did. He promised, but he felt he knew his friend and there was no need to worry.

"Do you remember the first time we met?" Leonardo knew this would be a good question to test Eric's memory with.

"Hell yes, I remember! It was twenty years ago. I was driving on the Congress line and when I saw they had assigned a young fart-face to be my conductor, I started to turn in my resignation. Then when we went to lunch and you told one of your dirty jokes, I knew you were a chip off my old block." They both laughed.

Leonardo looked at his friend and felt really glad he had kept his promise to take him fishing. Eric remembered quite a bit, especially the parties he and Crystal used to throw. Leonardo remembered them too, admitting he had spent more time at Eric's house than his own. He reminded Eric how, at first, their co-workers at CTA thought Eric was his father or at least a close relative. Leonardo continued to reminisce.

"Man, we've been friends a long time," Leonardo said.

"We won't be friends much longer if this pole doesn't get to shaking pretty soon," Eric warned. Leonard laughed. "You can laugh if you want to, but I'm serious, I'm going home and you can take your tired ass on back where you came from."

"Relax and give the fish a chance to wake up and look around for some breakfast. Besides, we've only been waiting an hour. I know your ass is old, but you've still got enough time left to sit here and catch a fish."

"Go to hell," Eric said, pretending to be angry.

"I can't go to your house when you're not home," Leonardo joked.

"Then drop dead," Eric said."

"And look like you?" Leonardo shot back.

"It would be an improvement," Eric laughed.

"Yeah, for a monkey," Leonardo ended, feeling like he'd won that exchange.

They both laughed. It was just like old times. Leonardo turned the conversation toward his relationship with Sherry.

"You know something? I remember seeing Sherry and Herbert a number of times at your house. I even remember the guys at work talking about him going down south and coming back with a wife young enough to be his daughter."

"You mean granddaughter," Eric cut in.

"I remembered Sherry," Leonardo continued, "but I never paid her much attention. Maybe it was because she was married."

"That never stopped you with other women," Eric reminded him.

"You really like her, don't you?"

"You think I keep coming back and forth from L.A. to Chicago just to see your monkey ass?"

"Yes," Eric joked.

"Not unless you start wearing a wig, a bra, and some lipstick. And even then, you'd be one ugly transvestite."

"What about those hand-me-down kids?" Eric asked, missing his chance to get in a retort.

"Those kids are part of the package," Leonardo admitted.

"Yeah, I guess they are," Eric agreed. "But I just can't see you with a wife and three ready-made kids. All I've gotta say is, what a man won't do for love." They sat, neither saying anything for a while. Leonardo was more convinced than ever that Crystal was right—Eric was fine. He had to admit that Eric wasn't the same as he was ten or twenty years ago, but he was fine. He also had to admit he'd missed those good times he'd shared with his friend. Leonardo closed his eyes for what seemed like only a moment, but he had actually been asleep for almost an hour. Suddenly Eric's rod began to move up and down. "I got one! I got one," Eric yelled.

Leonardo awoke to see Eric drop his fishing rod and lean down, reaching into the water, trying to grab the fish with his hands. Before Leonardo could tell Eric to pick up his rod and reel in his catch, Eric tumbled into the lake. Knowing Eric could not swim, Leonardo quickly jumped in after him. Eric had panicked and swallowed quite a bit of water. After pulling Eric out the lake and pumping out most of the water he had swallowed, Leonardo began to scold him. "That was a dumb ass thing to do. Why would you jump in the lake knowing you can't swim?"

"I wasn't trying to swim, couldn't you see I was fishing, you jackass?" Leonardo stared at his friend for a moment. Eric picked up the empty rod and sadly looking down at it said, "I tried to get him, but he got away." Leonardo thought about what Sherry had said and in that instant felt she might be right; there was definitely something going on with his buddy. He looked at Eric's wet clothes and realized his own were just as wet. "Come on man, let's get you home before you kill yourself or we both catch pneumonia and die anyway." He made it sound like a joke, but he was dead serious.

Crystal was surprised to see the men back so soon and even more surprised to see their clothes were very damp. Plus, they didn't have any fish. She urged them to come in and change into some dry clothes while

Leonardo explain what had happened. Crystal praised Leonardo, telling him how grateful she was that he was able to pull Eric from the lake. The thought of Eric almost drowning really upset her. She told Leonardo that she was never going to let Eric go fishing again or even go near the water. Leonardo noticed the sheer panic on Crystal's face as she spoke. When she saw Leonardo's expression, she calmed down, reminding him that it had been a while since the two of them had gone fishing and maybe Eric just forgot how to do it. Leonardo had to admit that it had been a while, but Eric was an excellent fisherman. In fact, he reminded her that it had been Eric who had taught him to fish. He cautioned her that there might be more going on with Eric besides forgetfulness due to old age.

"Eric is under the care of a doctor and certain tests are being made. Stop worrying, he's fine," Crystal insisted.

Leonardo didn't notice as Crystal managed to shift the conversation to his relationship with Sherry. Because Crystal and Sherry were such close friends, Leonardo thought it a good idea to reveal his feelings for Sherry and her children. He knew that Crystal would tell Sherry about their conversation and possibly enhance his chances of getting her to marry him and move to L. A. He had a feeling that Crystal was definitely in his corner. He said he would be leaving on Wednesday, but he would stop by and say goodbye to his buddy before he left. Crystal asked him to remind Sherry to call her after he left. Leonardo smiled and said, "That's when she'll have time to talk to you—after I leave."

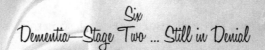

Six
Dementia—Stage Two ... Still in Denial

It was almost the end of summer. A year had passed with only small changes in Eric's behavior. Crystal was still ignoring some of Eric's antics since he seemed perfectly normal most of the time.

Sherry didn't visit as much since her kids were getting older and more demanding of her time, and of course she and Leonardo were doing some really serious courting now. He would visit her, and she would travel to L.A. to visit him. In July, around her birthday, Leonardo sent for Sherry and the kids exposing them to Disneyland and Knott's Berry Farm for the first time, hoping to sway them toward making that big move to L.A. It was on this occasion that Leonardo surprised Sherry with a diamond engagement ring. She could hardly wait to get back home and show Crystal. Crystal shared her friend's excitement but questioned her about Leonardo's reluctance to move back to Chicago. Sherry admitted she planned to work on that, reminding Crystal of her suggestion about not rushing into anything for at least another year. Crystal wondered what line of work Leonardo planned on doing once he made the move. She started to ask Sherry then, decided not to pry since she would definitely bring the subject up at a later date.

At least once each month, Leonardo would call and talk to both Crystal and Eric. He always joked around with Eric, but when he talked with Crystal he was always serious and more concerned about Eric's health. Of course she always said, "Everything's fine." She would tell him to be sure and tell the children the same thing and that there was nothing to worry about. Most of the time when they called, Eric was able to hold a normal conversation. When she thought he was having a bad day, she would say he was sleeping and she didn't want to disturb him.

Crystal had opted to work summer school, something she hadn't done too often in the past. This year she felt it was necessary in order to give herself a break from the household chores that Eric seldom helped her with anymore. She always kept very neat and clean surroundings—with his help of course. But lately she had to do most of the cleaning by herself. He would try but just couldn't quite get things right. If he helped with the dishes, he would always end up dropping and breaking something. It would frustrate him, and she would fight hard not to show her own frustration.

One day after work, Crystal called Sherry and asked her to come over. When Sherry arrived, they decided to sit in the back on the patio. It was early evening but still it was a beautiful day, not cool but not too hot. Sherry admitted they hadn't spent much time together lately and expressed how delighted she had been when Crystal called and asked her to come over. When Sherry asked how things had been going, Crystal's answer was the same as always when she didn't want to talk about her problems—everything was fine. Sherry knew Crystal was about to change the subject so she changed it for her by asking about her drama classes and her students. Crystal liked talking about her work and her students. She told Sherry she had given them an assignment over the weekend. She'd put them into groups of four and told them to write a scene and be prepared to act it out. Sherry said she thought that was a fun idea and asked if there was a particular subject they had to write about. Crystal paused for a moment before she answered. She hoped Sherry wouldn't get the wrong idea.

"I told them to write a scene about a family member's reaction to caring for an ailing older loved one."

Sherry looked at Crystal suspiciously and asked, "Any reason why you chose that particular subject?"

"I just want to get the younger generation's take on the subject, that's all."

"Uh huh," Sherry said while giving Crystal a look that said, Yeah girl, tell me anything. "Well you're looking better, I mean you don't look stressed out about anything," Sherry said hoping to lead her into a more personal conversation. Crystal did not take the bait and remained silent. "How's Eric? Does he still chase you around the house?" Sherry teased.

Feeling Sherry was not going to rest until they talked about this, Crystal replied, "No, his memory is getting—kind of bad. I guess he doesn't even think about sex anymore. Since we don't snuggle up like we used to, it doesn't get ..." Crystal hesitated as if she was searching for the right word or phrase.

"It? Oh, so now you're too embarrassed to discuss sex with me?" Sherry queried.

"No, but I am embarrassed to admit that I want to do it and he doesn't."

"A few months ago it was sex after breakfast, sex after lunch, and sex twice after dinner," Sherry laughed.

"Stop exaggerating, it was only once after dinner." Crystal said, laughing too.

"You know something? It's really good to see you laughing again. It's like ... old times," Sherry lamented. Sherry spoke more seriously, hoping her friend would know exactly what she was inferring. "I don't know if you realized it but lately it seemed that most of your laughter had been forced. It was as if you were miles away and you were just laughing because I laughed."

"Sorry, I've probably been thinking about my trip to L.A. for the holidays." Sherry knew her friend was up to her old trick again—changing the subject. "You know we'll be staying in the hotel again," Crystal continued.

"Good, maybe staying in a hotel might wake up Eric's 'it,'" Sherry said, signifying.

"Girl, I don't think "it" would wake up if we called in three paramedics with two defibrillators." Sherry laughed so hard she had to hold her stomach.

"Oh oh, sounds like you're about to declare celibacy."

"I might as well." Crystal told her. "I don't know what else to do."

"You'll think of something," Sherry laughed. "At least you've got a man lying beside you every night," Sherry said, her voice sounding a bit melancholy.

"Well you need to have one lying beside you," Eric said as he joined the two startled women.

"Honey, you need to stop sneaking up on us when we're girl-talking."

"I wasn't sneaking. I heard you two out here talking and I decided to come out and get some fresh air too."

"Come on honey, you never sit out here. You claim that this time of year the mosquitoes eat you up," Crystal reminded him.

Admiring Eric's attire, Sherry said, "Eric, you're looking mighty spiffy today. Should I compliment Crystal on that?"

"You'd do it anyway even if I told you I dressed myself."

"That's because I wouldn't believe you," Sherry snapped back jokingly.

"Would you believe me if I said you'd better run on home, because your house is on fire and your kids are trapped inside?"

"Eric that's a terrible thing to say, even if you are joking."

"I'm not joking. I heard it on the news."

"When?" Crystal asked.

"Just now," Eric replied with a straight face.

"Honey, that is nothing to joke about."

Sherry was visibly upset. "I know you are joking, but that's the cruelest joke you've ever made. I'm leaving just in case it's not a joke." Sherry stormed off in tears. She didn't bother to go through the house. She ran through the yard and around to the front. Crystal ran after her trying to apologize. Getting into the car, Sherry said, "You need to stop apologizing for Eric. Come out of denial, Crystal, and get him some help."

Crystal watched Sherry drive away before heading back to the patio. She was furious and intended to find out why Eric would play such a cruel joke on Sherry, but he had gone inside. She found him sitting in the den watching television as if nothing had happened. Crystal lit into him. "I can't believe you're deliberately trying to hurt Sherry's feelings. You and I both know you didn't hear anything like that on the news. You know you are wrong."

Eric stared at her in disbelief, "What did I do? You're always accusing me of something I didn't do." Now it was Crystal's turn to stare at him in disbelief. She could no longer hold back the tears when she asked him what was happening to him. His expression was that of a stranger's.

"Those crocodile tears don't move me, but I heard that the more you cry the less you pee," Eric said laughing.

Crystal knew she was about to lose it, so she stormed off into the kitchen. She sat wondering if Eric really wasn't aware of the things he said and did. After a while, she decided to prepare dinner. When she'd finished, she went back into the den and asked him if he wanted something to eat. Eric smiled as he got up and grabbed her playfully. "I sure do, and I want you to eat with me." Crystal pulled away and headed back into the kitchen with Eric following close behind asking her what she'd prepared for dinner. He's acting like nothing happened. Is this part of what Dr. Winter said he would be going through? Please God, help us. Hard as she tried, Crystal couldn't stop thinking about some of the things she had buried in the back of her mind. She continued to tell herself Eric was going to be okay and according to a phrase she had read somewhere, "This too shall pass."

The next afternoon Crystal and Eric were seated in the waiting room of Dr. Winter's office. Crystal beckoned to the nurse, pulling her aside and speaking almost in a whisper. "Could I speak with Dr. Winter—alone—before he sees Eric?" The nurse nodded. A few minutes later, Crystal and Dr. Winter were alone in the examining room.

"From what you've told me, I would say Eric has entered stage two of the dementia." Dr. Winter said.

"Stage two, what happened to stage one?" Crystal asked, already knowing the answer.

"He was in stage one when you refused to accept Dr. Hussein's diagnosis. You thought his forgetfulness was due to his age."

"How many stages are there?" she queried.

"It depends on the individual and other health issues. Are you ready to discuss what lies ahead? Like Dr. Hussein said, there's medication. There's also a senior day care facility and a support group you can become involved with. Eventually, you might think about a skilled nursing home."

"Skilled or unskilled, a nursing home is not an option, and I'm not interested in a support group," she said defiantly. "We'll take the prescription for that medication you said would slow everything down, but that's all we need for now."

"Well, it's up to you," he said. "I can't force you to accept help. In the mean time, it's my job to keep both of you physically healthy. Now let's bring Eric in here so I can check him out."

Crystal had been trying to get in touch with Sherry to no avail. Her line was either busy or the answering machine would pick up. Whenever one of the kids answered, they said Sherry was either gone or in the shower. Despite the numerous messages she'd left, Crystal had not received a single return call. So, she decided to pay her friend a visit. Crystal thought for a moment that Sherry wasn't going to answer the door either. She had seen her car in the garage so she figured she was home. Finally, Sherry came to the door.

"Hi, I came to see you since you won't come to see me or return any of my calls. May I come in?" Sherry let her in and asked if she'd like something to drink, some coffee maybe or some juice. Crystal said that what she really wanted was for Sherry to accept her apology on behalf of Eric. She begged her friend to have a little more patience and compassion. She said she didn't have a lot of time because the bus would be bringing Eric home from St. Albee's Senior Day Care Center. With her apology, Crystal suggested that maybe Eric displayed a little bit of meanness while joshing with her because he was sitting around all day doing nothing. She said she hoped his participation in the Senior Day Care program would help. She admitted that Sherry could have had an accident rushing home to see about her kids. She also admitted that it was an awful joke for Eric to play. While Sherry was more than willing to accept Crystal's apology, she wanted to know if her friend was ready to face up to her husband's condition and if she was also ready to stop denying the obvious. Crystal tried to explain saying Eric would act normal one minute and the next he would be like a stranger, accusing people of all sorts of nefarious deeds, including taking his money and his clothes. She admitted she had not disclosed Eric's real medical challenge to her or anybody else for that matter. Tears began to form in the corner of Crystal's eyes, but she managed to hold them back. I'm "truly sorry," she said.

Sherry knew Crystal's apology was sincere. She might not know exactly what Crystal was going through, but she knew she loved her and Eric and she was willing to do whatever she could to help them. "I accept the apology, and you should know by now that I'll be there for you no matter how mean Eric becomes," Sherry said, fighting back her own tears.

"I am truly grateful for your friendship. I need it now more than ever," Crystal admitted.

"I'll always be your friend," Sherry assured her, "I just want you to accept the things you can't change."

"I'm trying, but it's not that easy," Crystal confessed.

"I know, that's why it's always good to talk to a friend."

"From now on, I will," Crystal promised. Sherry stood at the door, watching her friend as she hurried off. Silently she said a prayer for Crystal and Eric.

An hour later, Crystal was in the kitchen thinking about what Sherry had said. She was glad they had made up. She prayed they would never fall out with each other again. Her thoughts were interrupted by the sound of a horn beeping. Realizing it must be the bus bringing Eric home from the senior day care, she went to let him in. When she opened the door, Eric stormed in angrily pushing by her.

"I'm not going back to that damn nursery school anymore," he said almost yelling. "They took me to the fucking zoo. What made them think I wanted to go to the fucking zoo?" Eric had often used cuss words. In fact, he and Leonardo used them all the time. He and his CTA buddies used what is referred to as "mild" cuss words like shit, damn, hell, and piss. But he'd never used any of those words while talking to Crystal, especially the "f" word. Crystal let him know how surprised she was that he was using such language.

"I hope you didn't use that kind of language when speaking to the priests and nuns at the center," she said as she headed back into the kitchen. Eric followed her grumbling, still very angry. When Crystal asked if he was hungry, he replied, "Hell yes, I'm hungry! All I had was a fucking hot dog and some punch that tasted like liquid cat shit."

Crystal turned to Eric, "Look, I don't know what's gotten into you, but you can't come in here yelling and cussing at me like that. You've always respected me and I'm not going to allow you to start disrespecting me now. Those people at the center were only trying to be nice and kind to you." It never occurred to her that this was a symptom of the dementia. She was angry, and she had to let him know it. He sat silently while she dished up his dinner. She didn't say anything either, but she was deep in thought. I haven't been this angry with him since he retired, she thought. She hoped that seeing how angry he had made her, he wouldn't cuss anymore. She made a vow to try to control her own temper.

They ate in silence for a while. Crystal kept her head down, not wanting to look at him. She knew if she looked at him he would have that hurt puppy-dog-like expression and she would feel sorry for him. But Eric did look at her and finally he said, "I'm sorry I hurt your feelings, but they pissed me off at that nursery and I'm not going back." Crystal didn't respond. "If they call, don't answer the phone." Crystal looked up at him. She was determined she was not going to get upset again.

Quietly she said, "It's not a nursery school, it's a senior day care, and how will I be able to tell it's them when the phone rings?"

"Just don't answer the phone at all," he warned.

"I can't do that; the kids might call and think something is wrong." They continued to eat in silence. Finally Eric asked, "When are we going to L.A.?" Crystal started not to answer but then she felt Eric was really trying to smooth things over, and she was willing to do that. She was willing to do anything to bring some normality back into their existence.

"In December, for the holidays," Crystal replied.

Suddenly Eric stood up. "I'd better go start packing."

Crystal stopped eating and stared at him. "I said we're going in December, this is September. We've got plenty of time. Sit back down and finish eating."

"Okay, but we'd better start packing as soon as we finish eating," Eric said, sitting back down. Crystal hesitated for a moment.

"We will," she said, trying to remain calm, "Finish eating your dinner."

There was very little conversation between them for the rest of the evening. Eric forgot about packing. He watched television while Crystal wrote checks for their bills. That night, as Eric's snoring kept her awake,

Crystal wondered how long it would be before she would reach her breaking point. How long would it be before God stopped testing her faith? She knew she had to stay calm. She also knew she almost lost it when Eric came home using the "f" word. She closed her eyes and asked God to give her the patience she finally realized she was going to need—and must have.

It was eight forty-five when Crystal pulled into the parking lot of Thorne Ridge College. Although she was beginning to feel the stress of dealing with Eric, her spirits were always lifted when she arrived at the school. Crystal only taught theater courses but was well-known throughout the school by both students and faculty members, mostly because of the great productions she and her students presented at the end of each spring semester. As she made her way to her classroom, several of her students walked with her. They were excited about the assignment and argued over who should go first. By nine o'clock all of the students had arrived, and after settling them down, Crystal began the class.

"I assigned you into groups of fours and asked you to write and act out a three-minute scene dealing with how family members react to the task of having to care for an ailing older member of their family. You were to make it real and believable, memorize and rehearse the dialogue. Are there any questions?" Sasha, a talented and popular student raised her hand.

"Professor Haywood, did you say we could write the dialogue the way we talk?"

"Of course, they are your characters; you know how you want them to talk. It's your creation. Who wants to go first?" Several of the students raised their hands yelling, "We want to go first." Crystal decided she would choose a group.

"Okay, Sasha, why don't you and your group go first. Set up your stage and give us a brief synopsis."

Sasha and her group arranged four chairs in the front of the room and each took a seat. Sasha asked Crystal to act as stage manager and record the time since they were not to go over three minutes. Sasha began with the synopsis. "This scene takes place in Sidney and Cora's apartment. They are having a conversation with their friends Sharon and Rick." She pointed at each student as she gave their character names and their roles. Sasha took the role of Cora.

Crystal began to count. "In five, four, three, two ..." Without having to say one, Crystal nodded and the students began.

THE SCENE:

CORA

Sharon, I'm glad you and Rick decided to stop by. Can I get you some more wine?

SHARON

I've had enough, and Rick has had too much.

SIDNEY

Oh, oh Rick, I see Sharon has you under her itty, bitty finger.

RICK

Yeah Sidney, we can't offend these women. Remember, they are the ones who get to choose our nursing home.

SHARON

(Laughing) That's right, Ricky baby, and don't you forget it.

                    RICK

See what I mean, man?

                    SIDNEY

Hell, I'm not worried. Even if I get that"all timer's" disease, my baby here will take good care of me, won't you baby?

                    CORA

(shaking her head)Uh uh, plan A ain't gonna work. You'd better go to fucking plan B because I'm not gonna be chasing your diaper-wearing ass up and down the street, while you're talking crazy about you're on your way to visit your mama in Mississippi and she's been dead for ten years. I'm not having you smear brown shit all over my white walls and my white furniture in my white kitchen, talking about you're finger painting. No, no ...

∞

Crystal had been trying to interrupt by saying "cut," but the student's laughter drowned her out. "Stop it! I said cut!" Crystal shouted, visibly upset. Sasha stopped in the middle of her sentence. Crystal could hardly control her shaking voice.

"At the beginning of the semester, you were given a syllabus, which stated this acting class would allow you to write short scenes. But I also explained that having access to pen and paper shouldn't give you the license to use unnecessary expletives. I believe in free speech, and I certainly did give you permission to write in your own words, but I had hoped you would have some respect for me and the fact that I've already let it be known how I feel about pornography, as well as profanity!" Crystal hesitated a minute, trying to regain her composure. In a softer but stern voice, she continued. "Sasha, clean up your scene and the rest of you do the same if necessary. All of you take the remainder of this class period to rehearse your scenes. I need a break. Be prepared to continue this assignment on Wednesday."

As she gathered her things and prepared to leave, Crystal overheard Sasha saying, "Didn't she say we could say anything we wanted to?" When most of the students agreed saying, "She sure did." Sasha asked, "Then why are her drawers in a bunch?"

Crystal started to answer that question but didn't trust her emotions. Before Crystal exited, slamming the door behind her, she heard another student remark. "I had her playwriting class last semester, and she wasn't all uptight like that. I don't know what's wrong with her, but I know she's changed."

Crystal walked aimlessly through the nearby park. Finally, she stopped and sat down on a bench. She closed her eyes as the words of Sasha and her group echoed in her head. Am I no longer a respected and admired professor? She thought as tears began to form beneath the lids of her closed eyes. When she opened her eyes, the tears streamed down her cheeks. Have I really changed? Was I more lenient last semester? Is the situation at home affecting my attitude toward my students ... my work? Is the stress taking its toll on me? She hadn't realized it, but evidently her students thought so. She had always let her students know how she felt about the use of unnecessary profanity. They knew better. She had taught them they did not have to use that kind of language to get a point across. There were times when she allowed it in her playwriting class when developing a certain kind of character, but she had warned them against using profanity to produce shock or humor.

Crystal sat thinking as the tears on her cheeks began to dry. Her thoughts were interrupted as an elderly couple slowly approached. The man seemed to be older, his steps not as steady as the woman's. As the pair passed Crystal, the man stumbled and was about to fall. The woman grabbed his arm, preventing him from falling. The two just stood for a moment. The woman held the old man's arm until he regained his composure. Crystal thought she heard the woman say, "Don't worry, honey, I've got you. You can depend on me." After a while, the old man straightened up and the pair continued their journey, holding hands. Crystal thought she noticed them quickening their steps as if the old man had received a burst of new energy from the old woman. Crystal's tears had dried, and a smile slowly inched its way across her mouth. She stood up and began to walk back toward the campus with an urgent new sense of determination.

Another Thanksgiving Day passed without incident. Sherry and the kids came over for dinner as usual. Sherry said Leonardo had several gigs and would not be able to make it. Eric was noticeably quiet while Crystal and Sherry made small talk. The children couldn't wait to go into the den and play with the new game they had brought. They expressed their desire for Eric to come and play with them. Crystal instructed Eric not to cheat again. She made a mental note to inform her own children that in the future, they needed to come home for Thanksgiving. After all, Thanksgiving was and should be a family day.

Sherry thought Crystal showed signs of stress, but she didn't dare verbalize her concern—not today, not right now. She vowed she would spend more time with her friend. She wanted to help Crystal, but she wanted her to ask for help. She didn't want to feel as though she was intruding and definitely didn't want to cause another angry verbal confrontation.

With Christmas only four days away, Sherry drove Eric and Crystal to the airport for their trip to L.A. Sherry had been glad when Crystal called her to come over and help her pack. Crystal hadn't talked much about Eric's health, but Sherry had noticed two things: Eric's looks and mannerisms had changed and Crystal was starting to show signs of extreme stress. It had always been in the back of Sherry's mind, but now she was really beginning to think Eric might have Alzheimer's. Her grandmother, back in Little Rock, was said to be senile but was later diagnosed as having Alzheimer's after she was found walking around outside butt-naked.

At the airport the two hugged, each wishing the other a merry Christmas. Sherry thought she saw a tear in the corner of Crystal's eye. She also thought Crystal held her extra tight. To Crystal's surprise, Sherry also gave Eric a hug, something she had never done before. Eric smiled.

Crystal and Eric both slept most of the three hours and fifty-five minutes of the flight. Crystal was ready to see her children and grandson and maybe get a little last-minute shopping in. She'd much rather shop in the warmth of L.A., than in the cold and snowy weather of Chicago. Although she loved seeing a white Christmas, she just didn't want to be out in one.

Arriving at LAX, they walked leisurely through the terminal. Lately, Crystal had become aware of Eric's decrease in pace and had no problem adjusting her steps to accommodate his. As they were approaching the escalator leading down to the baggage claim area, Crystal went ahead of Eric. Once on the moving stairs, she turned to look back at him. Eric made a misstep and suddenly he was falling head first toward her. She panicked but was able to use her body to keep him from falling all the way to the bottom of the stairs. He hit his head on the railing and cracked one of the lenses of his glasses, causing a small cut under his eye. When they'd reached the bottom, Crystal grabbed Eric by his arm, making sure he didn't fall again.

Several people rushed over to see if Eric was okay. Someone offered to call an ambulance, but Crystal refused saying he was fine and had only suffered a minor injury. Relieved that Eric had not been seriously hurt, Crystal was happy when they arrived in "The Valley" aboard the "Fly-Away" bus. They were greeted by their eldest son, Mark, who expressed his joy and excitement that they would be spending another Christmas with him and his family.

On Christmas Eve, after two days of shopping with her daughter-in-law Latisha, and helping to prepare Christmas dinner, Crystal was ready to relax. She and Latisha, had always had a good relationship despite the cultural difference; Latisha was a very attractive woman of Mexican descent with hair to her waist. She had a quiet demeanor, but at times she could be quite feisty.

Crystal and Eric had settled down in the suite Mark had reserved for them. Eric seemed happy and content watching television. He hadn't complained about the cut under his eye, but Crystal had placed a small bandage over it as a precaution against infection. At ten o'clock, mark poked his head in to check on them.

"We're fine, son. We are about to go to bed so we'll be fresh for the big day."

"Okay, I'll be working the front desk until six in the morning. If you need anything, just call me."

"We're fine. See you in the morning, son."

Hours later, Crystal was asleep on the living room sofa when the telephone awakened her. It was Mark. Crystal asked him the time. When he said it was two in the morning, she asked him why he was calling at that time of night. Mark told her she needed to come and get Eric, who had wandered out to the front desk. Crystal jumped up and rushed down the hall to the front desk. Eric was standing there in his underwear. She knew he had been wearing pajamas when he went to bed. Obviously, he had taken them off and put his underwear back on. Crystal wondered why he hadn't put on all of his clothes, but she was thinking rationally and from looking at him, she figured Eric's thoughts had been far from rational. She couldn't understand how he had gotten past her. Hadn't that been the reason why I'd gone to sleep on the sofa, near the door? I could hear him if he attempted to go out. When Crystal verbalized her thoughts, Mark questioned her.

"You mean you anticipated Dad would try to sneak out and go wandering around?"

In defense, Crystal replied, "He was probably looking for the bathroom."

"Wouldn't it be in the same place it was in when he used it before going to bed," Mark joked. "He told me he was looking for you."

Crystal decided to agree since she just wanted to get Eric back in the room and into bed. "He probably was looking for me to help him find the bathroom," she said jokingly, despite not being in a joking mood. "Come on, honey. Let's go back to our room. See you in the morning, son."

"Yeah, and by the way, Merry Christmas."

"That's right, it is Christmas. Merry Christmas, son."

Crystal took Eric by the hand and led him back down the hall. As they entered their suite, Eric apologized, saying that if he'd caused any trouble he was sorry. He insisted that he'd been looking for her. Trying not to become angry, Crystal told him he couldn't have been looking for her since he had passed right by her when he snuck out. Hard as she tried, she couldn't stop thinking about their trip to Vegas. It was *déjà vu*.

Crystal nearly freaked out when they entered the bedroom The mattress had not only been removed from the bed but was standing against the wall on the opposite side of the room. The bed itself had been moved and so had the nightstand. The lampshade was on one side of the room, while the lamp sat on the floor on the other side. The bed covers were strewn about.

"Eric, look what you've done to this room," she shouted.

"I didn't do anything to this room," he yelled back.

Making a real effort to calm down, she said, "Then who did it?"

"I didn't," Eric replied defiantly.

Crystal went to the telephone and dialed the front desk urging Mark to come immediately. She was in tears when Mark arrived. He stood staring at the bedroom for a moment. Eric sat on the sofa looking quite innocent. Mark waited for an explanation, but Crystal gave none as she started to put the room back together. Mark began to help her as he laughed.

"Dad did this? Boy he's strong. This is some heavy stuff."

"I don't think it's so funny," Crystal said. "He could have hurt himself."

"Has he ever done this before?"

"No, this is the first time," Crystal replied, no longer able to conceal her frustration.

Mark was still laughing when he said, "I've got to get back to the desk. Maybe he should lie down with his clothes on, that way if he comes out again, I can keep him in the office with me. You know, you could also tie him in bed."

"I told you, it's not funny."

"Okay Mom, don't get upset."

"And why shouldn't I?" Crystal snapped.

Mark had started out but turned back smiling as he said, "Because, it's Christmas!"

"Bah humbug," Eric said laughing.

Crystal helped Eric into his pajamas and into the bed. She went back to the sofa, but this time, she put the extra lock on and moved the end table in front of the door. Now let him try to get out, she thought before she finally drifted off.

Crystal awoke hours later, grateful that Eric was still asleep and in bed and had allowed her to sleep without another incident. He's probably tired from being up half the night moving furniture, she thought. She helped him shower and dress. He watched television while she showered and dressed. Crystal thought about the way young mothers of today use the TV as a babysitter. It was certainly a big help to her—most of the time.

At ten o'clock, coffee, juice, and sweet rolls arrived. Mark had prearranged this continental breakfast for them. Crystal drank most of the coffee, but she let Eric eat the rolls and drink the juice. She figured he probably awoke with an appetite after playing "Bekin Movers."

At noon, she and Eric went to Mark's apartment. She called it an apartment because of the unique way he had put two suites together to accommodate his family. Eric sat in the living room with their four-year-old grandson, Isaiah, while Crystal helped Latisha with last-minute preparations for Christmas dinner. Mark was still asleep. He had awakened Isaiah to come see what Santa had brought before he laid down. After working all night, he needed to take a short nap so he could enjoy the rest of the day. Isaiah was glad when grandpa agreed to play with him and his new toys.

"What did Santa bring you, Grandpa?" Isaiah asked.

"Nothing." Eric replied. "The jackass didn't bring me a damn thing."

"You must have been bad, Grandpa."

"Yeah, I guess I was," Eric said.

"Well you can play with some of my toys, Grandpa. Next year you'd better be good so you can get your own."

"Okay," Eric said, smiling as he picked up a red fire truck. "I'll be damn good so I can get one of these."

At three o'clock, Shaun and Jay arrived. Isaiah met them at the door. As Jay lifted Isaiah high in the air, he asked, "What's up little guy? What did Santa bring you for Christmas?"

"He brought me lots of toys, but the jackass didn't bring grandpa a damn thing."

Shaun, Mark, and Jay roared with laughter, but Crystal didn't think it was funny and neither did Latisha. "That's because he's been naughty," Crystal said, giving Eric a "shame-on-you" look. "He shouldn't call Santa names and use bad words."

"And you shouldn't either," Latisha admonished Isaiah, in her thick Mexican accent, "because he won't bring you anything next year."

They all sat down to enjoy dinner as a family. Anna had called earlier to express regret that she and Abraham could not join them. She had decided to spend the holidays with Abraham's family in New Jersey, but promised to spend Christmas with them next year. Mark said it was the best dinner he'd eaten since last Christmas.

"Dinner is always good when your mother help me cook," Latisha said.

Shaun made everyone laugh as he poked fun at Latisha. "Mom, if you hadn't been in the kitchen, Latisha would have stuffed the turkey with tacos, burritos, and enchiladas." Latisha was used to Shaun joking about her cooking and laughed too. Crystal suggested that since they loved her cooking so much, they should all move back to Chicago. They could eat her cooking seven days a week.

"Hey, I was thinking about doing just that," Shaun said.

"Stop lying dude, you know you wouldn't be able to pimp year-round in Chi Town," Jay responded.

"Pimping ain't easy, but somebody's gotta do it," Shaun fired back.

Everyone laughed. Crystal felt relaxed and happy around her children. She glanced at Eric, who laughed a little but didn't say much. When Jay asked why he was so quiet, Mark answered.

"He's probably sneaking a nod. He was up half the night."

"Doing what," Jay asked.

"He hasn't been sleeping well lately," Crystal answered quickly.

"Hey, how come everybody is answering for him? Can't he talk?" Jay looked at Crystal waiting for an answer. Crystal was hoping someone would change the subject.

"I don't know about the other nights, but last night he dreamed he worked for a moving company," Mark said laughing.

Crystal shot Mark a warning look. Latisha saved the day when she suggested they stop talking and open their presents. Shaun agreed, saying it was about time. Crystal gave Latisha a grateful look as she silently mouthed the words, "Thank you." She knew Mark had probably informed Latisha about Eric's escapade.

Later, after all the presents had been opened, Mark helped Latisha gather up the torn wrapping paper. Shaun said he hated to leave, but he had a "hot" date. He thanked everybody for his gifts, kissed Crystal and hugged Eric. As he headed out the door, he grabbed Isaiah's red truck, pretending to take it with him. Isaiah noticed and ran after him snatching the toy back. Crystal laughed, that is, until Isaiah said, "Ask Santa to bring you your own damn toys." She was glad Isaiah loved to play with his uncles. She was also glad that Eric had developed a relationship with Isaiah, but she wished Eric wouldn't teach the boy to cuss. "Isaiah, stop using those words," Latisha said. She was smiling, but everyone knew she was serious. She took Isaiah aside and explained why he shouldn't repeat the bad words he'd heard Grandpa say.

Eric settled down to watch television, while Crystal and Jay cleaned off the table and carried the leftover food into the kitchen. When Crystal questioned Jay about why he didn't have a date, Jay said he just wanted to spend the holidays with his family.

"I guess that means no wedding bells soon," Crystal said, regretting having said it and hoping Jay took it as a joke. He didn't. Jay was surprised that his mother had brought up the conversation since she knew how much he hated it when Eric harped on the subject.

"Mom, it was you and Dad who taught us that marriage was a serious contract between two people who loved each other."

"I know Jay, but your father and I aren't getting any younger."

"Mom, it isn't about you or Dad, it's about me; and I haven't met anyone that I want to make such a commitment to. I'm only twenty-six. Shaun is almost twenty nine. He's the one you and Dad should be working on."

"Are you talking about the player?" Crystal asked, laughing.

"Yeah, you're right," Jay said, laughing too. "He ain't thinking about anything as serious as marriage."

"When you do decide to take that big step," Crystal said, "promise me you'll come back home."

"What? You expect me to bring my beautiful, fragile, used-to-warm-weather bride-to-be home with me, to get married and live in Chicago's frigid, snowy, icy cold climate? When I get married, the wedding will be in L.A., and me and my wife will live in L.A."

"Like I said, son, your father is getting up in age and..."

Jay interrupted, "Dad isn't going anywhere. He's in good health, so stop using his age for an excuse to keep harassing me. I think it's time to have some of Latisha's homemade eggnog. You think Dad wants some?"

Crystal looked back into the living room where Eric sat snoring. "Nope, it'll just be you and me for now."

"Mom, I'm glad you and Dad came. You always make our holidays happy and joyful, and I know I speak for the others too."

"As selfish as it may sound, we do it more for ourselves than for the rest of you." Crystal had wished the holidays would never end so she wouldn't have to return to a predictable January in Chicago. It seemed that nothing really exciting ever happened during the first three months of the year.

It was early April 1989, and Crystal was already looking forward to May when classes would be over. She had made up her mind she wouldn't work summer school. She refused to admit it, but Eric's behavior was becoming more erratic. There hadn't been anymore episodes like the one in the hotel at Christmas, and his projected progression was developing slowly, but she just never knew what to expect from one day to the next. She continued to pray as she realized her faith was as strong as ever. Some days and for weeks even, Eric was fine. Then boom, he would say or do something that left Crystal both perplexed and bewildered. Sherry had started stopping by more often, but Crystal knew she had her own family to see about and of course she was getting more deeply involved with Leonardo. It had always been Crystal's desire to give rather than to receive. She wanted to be needed, not be the one in need. She never wanted to impose on anyone, especially her friends. Her vow "in sickness and in health" became more sacred than ever. She didn't even want the children to feel they were obligated to her or their father. Lately, whenever they called, she would make up an excuse why Eric couldn't come to the phone, especially when he was having one of his "challenging" days.

One day Crystal returned home from work a little bit later than usual. She entered the house thinking how nice it would be to just sit and soak in a tub of hot, scented, soapy bubbles. She had rehearsed her students most of the day for the big end-of-semester production. She wasn't prepared to deal with any of Eric's erratic behavior. She called out to him letting him know she was home. He met her smiling as he kissed her and returned to the den. She was glad he was in a good mood. She could hear the television in the den. Jeopardy was still on, so she headed there to relax for a few minutes before preparing their evening meal. She stopped in the doorway, seeing four folding chairs, two chairs Eric must have dragged in from the kitchen, along with two chairs from the dining room; eight chairs in all, situated in a half circle in front of the television.

"Why are all of these chairs sitting in front of the TV?" she asked, fearing she wasn't going to like the answer.

"Some of your friends came by to watch television with you. They tried to wait, but you took too long, so they left."

"Eric," Crystal was trying to control her voice. She didn't want to sound as irritable as she was. "There's no one here but you," she said.

"I told you, they left," Eric said.

As anger slowly arose, Crystal started snatching up the chairs, dragging them back where they belonged. Eric tried to help as best he could. "The next time they come over, at least make them put things back like they found them," Crystal said, slamming the folding chairs against the wall.

"I told them you were going to be mad."

"You're darn right I'm mad," Crystal yelled. "After working all day, I've got to come home and pick up after them."

"I told them," Eric said again.

"And I told you about opening the door. Next time don't let them in."

"I didn't. I don't know how they got in here."

Crystal stood looking at him. She thought, Something must be wrong with me. Why am I having this conversation with him? I'm talking as if I believe some people have really been here. Finally she said, "Come on, let's go eat." Crystal didn't say anything else to Eric, but she thought to herself, At least he remembered not to open the door for anyone. He didn't know how they got in, but he knew he hadn't let them in. She couldn't help it, she had to smile at that one.

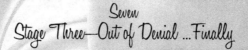

Seven

Stage Three—Out of Denial ...Finally

A FEW WEEKS LATER, Crystal was asleep on the sofa when a loud noise from the kitchen awakened her. Fearing the worse, she rushed toward the kitchen wondering what Eric had gotten into now. She found Eric sitting at the table while Sherry was sweeping up pieces of a broken plate. Sherry apologized for waking her, explaining that Eric was drying the dishes and one of the plates slipped out of his hands.

"How did you get in here?" Crystal asked.

"Eric let me in. I figured you must have gotten up pretty early and was still tired, since it was only eleven o'clock and already you were taking a nap. Obviously you didn't even hear the bell. Eric cautioned me not to disturb you. He was in here trying to fix himself a snack, so I made him a sandwich and gave him some of the potato salad in the refrigerator." Now he is opening the door and letting people in, Crystal thought. She gave Eric a look he recognized.

"I'll go watch television, so you ladies can chat," Eric said, wanting to get away from the "look." "Thanks, Sherry, for my sandwich."

"You're welcome."

As Eric hurried out, Sherry turned to Crystal. "Well, summer is almost here. Are you planning on working straight through?"

"At first I said I wasn't going to do summer school, but then I changed my mind. Besides, I don't think we'll be going out of town this year," Crystal admitted.

"So, have you thought about getting some help with Eric?" Sherry asked, hoping it wouldn't cause Crystal to get upset.

"I don't know if it's necessary right now. You see how he can do for himself. He's fine."

"You know, you could have a homemaker come in five days a week. The state will pay part, and you'll have to pay part. It would be cheaper than a nursing home." Sherry knew right away she had said the wrong thing, but she figured this was the only way to get Crystal to talk about Eric.

"Have you lost your mind? I'm not putting my husband in a nursing home," Crystal said in a voice louder than she'd intended. "Why would you even suggest something like that? You know my position on that."

"You never know what you might have to do," Sherry said, remaining calm.

"I know I won't have to do that," Crystal countered in a voice that said end of discussion.

Eric had gone into the den to watch television, but he was having a hard time trying to get the remote to work. Finally he gave up and threw the remote at the TV. Sherry and Crystal started toward the den as Eric returned to the kitchen and sat down at the table. Crystal and Sherry were surprised. Crystal thought maybe he was still hungry but before she could ask him, he said, "Hi Sherry, how are the kids?" The two women exchanged looks. Crystal opened her mouth to say something, but Sherry raised her hand, shaking her head.

"Hi Eric, the kids are okay. Thanks for asking," Sherry replied. For a while, no one said anything else. "Crystal, it's getting late, I'd better go before the kids get back from the skating rink," Sherry said, breaking the silence.

"You got kids?" Eric asked.

"You know I have kids," Sherry said, her voice soft and composed.

"How would I know you have kids?" Eric asked.

Crystal couldn't keep quiet any longer. "Honey, you just asked her about the kids a minute ago, and she told you they were okay."

"I did? Oh ... I meant to ask about her husband, how is he?"

"Eric, that is nothing to joke about. You know Herbert is dead," Crystal said.

"He is? I'm sorry, when did he die?" Crystal became visibly irritated. "Eric, Herbert has been ..."

"It's okay Crystal," Sherry said showing the patience of Job.

"Eric, Herbert has been dead for over three years."

"He has? Well, let me know about the funeral arrangements. He was my best friend, you know."

"Yes, I know, and I'll let you know about the funeral."

Sherry turned to Crystal and said, "I really have to go. Come walk me to the door."

"Okay," Crystal said as she started to walk Sherry to the door.

"So long," Eric said, "Be sure and tell Herbert to stop by and see me sometime."

"I will," Sherry said, over her shoulder.

"Why did you do that?" Crystal asked when they had reached the door.

"Because that's what I have to do, and you need to do it too."

"I don't think I can," Crystal said.

"You can as soon as you stop denying that anything is wrong. You'll have to do it if you want to keep the peace and maintain your sanity. You don't want any help. You chose to deal with it by yourself, so deal with it. And please, try to stay calm. Stop getting so angry with him. I'll call you later."

Crystal closed the door and leaned back against it. She knew her friend was telling her the truth. She sighed as if exhausted and headed back into the kitchen. She started to ask Eric how he could have forgotten that Herbert had died, but she didn't want to engage in another confusing conversation, especially when Eric grabbed her by the arm and said, "Come on, let's finish watching that movie we were looking at before your friend barged in on us." With another sigh, Crystal went into the den to watch the movie with Eric.

Several weeks later, Crystal pulled into the driveway returning home from the college. As she got out of the car, she saw her neighbor Mrs. Robertson peeking out the window. It wasn't that Crystal didn't want to be a good neighbor, she just didn't believe in visiting with them. The garage was attached to the house, so once she'd let the door down, she entered the house from inside the garage. The only time she came in contact with a neighbor was when she would leave the car in the driveway, and then it was just a wave or a "Hi, how are you?" During the years they were raising their children, she and Eric were busy working and socializing with their friends, relatives, and club members. Their children knew just about everybody in the neighborhood, but Crystal hardly knew any of the adults. Eric was friendlier with the men folk because he was out cutting the grass in the summer and shoveling the snow in the winter. They never really socialized with Dorothy and Eddie Robertson, their next-door neighbors.

Crystal called out to Eric as she entered the foyer. "Honey, I'm home. Sorry I'm late. I left the car in the driveway in case you want to eat out tonight." When Eric didn't respond, Crystal called to him again and again no response. She went through the house checking each room and calling out his name. Hearing nothing, she feared the worse and ran back out to the foyer. As she opened the door, Eric and Mrs. Robertson were standing there. Eric had on his underwear and a pair of Crystal's pantyhose. An unfamiliar oversized towel draped his upper torso.

"Hi, Mr. Haywood locked himself out," Mrs. Robertson said. She was a nice looking, medium-built woman. Her face did not reveal her seventy odd years, although her hair was nearly white. She smiled broadly, but Crystal felt this only reinforced her suspicions: Mrs. Robertson was a nosy neighbor.

"I offered him some of my husband's clothes, but he said he had plenty of his own. He said he made it a rule: Never wear anyone else's clothes." She was aware of the look on Crystal's face as she stared at Eric's attire, including her pantyhose. Crystal was unsuccessful at trying to hide her embarrassment.

"Thank you. I'm sorry if he disturbed you."

"No, no, he wasn't no problem at all." When Mrs. Robertson tried to explain, Crystal pulled Eric inside, snatched the towel off, almost throwing it at her.

"Here's your towel and thanks again." Crystal closed the door without hearing Mrs. Robertson's final words and immediately lashed out at Eric.

"Why did you go outside in the first place? I've told you not to even open the door. And why did you take your clothes off? I helped you get dressed before I left. How long were you over to her house? How could you embarrass me like this?"

"Which question do you want me to answer first?" Eric said with a smile.

"I'm not in the mood for your jokes Eric," Crystal said, almost in tears.

"I knew you were going to be mad," he said. "I was just looking for you."

"Why is it you're always looking for me? You knew I was at work." Now Eric was looking like a little boy being chastised for sneaking into the cookie jar without permission. Crystal hated it when he did that. She lowered her voice and tried to remove some of the animosity.

"Honey, we talked about this. You said you could stay by yourself and you'd be okay."

"I am okay," he said. Crystal looked at him. He wasn't okay. He was standing there in his underwear and her pink pantyhose. There was nothing okay about that. She shook her head and heaved a sigh.

"Come on upstairs and put some clothes on." Moments later, as Crystal was helping him get dressed, Eric peered at himself in the mirror.

"You must have a hell of a cleaning bill." Crystal was afraid to ask why, so she just waited for him to tell her. Eric pointed at himself in the mirror.

"Because that son-of-a-bitch wears my clothes too. See, he's got them on right now."

"Eric will you stop using that profanity? That's you in the mirror," she yelled, "that's you!"

"No, that's not ... it's him," Eric insisted angrily, yelling back at her. "He's wearing my clothes!" Crystal threw up her hands in frustration.

"Okay, I'll tell him to stay out of your closet. Come on, let's go eat."

A few hours later, Crystal pulled into the garage. They had eaten at a nearby Chinese restaurant. They both loved Chinese food. Eric had said he wasn't quite sure, but he thought he'd had a snack at Mrs. Robertson's. Crystal thought, If he did, it must have been crackers and milk because at the restaurant he ate as if he hadn't eaten all week. She'd ordered extra shrimp fried rice to go, in case Eric wanted to eat some more later on. They had just settled down in the den to watch Wheel of Fortune when the doorbell rang. Crystal wondered who could be visiting them since Sherry usually called before she stopped by and so did all of Eric's buddies. It's probably Tony. He seldom called before coming. He's probably checking on us and looking for a good home-cooked meal. He could eat the shrimp fried rice, but he's allergic to shellfish. He'll just have to make him a ham sandwich and call it a night. When she opened the door, Mrs. Robertson was standing there holding a miniature, freshly baked peach cobbler.

"Hi, Mrs. Haywood. Mr. Haywood said he loved peach cobbler and that you don't know how to bake one. So, I baked one especially for him." She eagerly awaited the invitation to enter.

Crystal didn't know whether to take the pie, thank Mrs. Robertson and close the door, or ask her to come in. She really didn't want to do either. She had not made it a habit of popping in and out of her neighbor's house, and she certainly hoped Mrs. Robertson didn't intend to make it a habit of popping in on her. Crystal decided to take the pie.

"Mr. Haywood is resting. We ate out, and he decided to turn in early," she said without asking Mrs. Robertson to come in.

"Oh, that's okay. I really wanted to talk with you," Mrs. Robertson said as she stepped inside, squeezing past Crystal. "That is ... if I'm not interrupting anything."

Not wanting her to see Eric in the den watching television, Crystal led Mrs. Robertson into the kitchen.

"I was just making myself a cup of tea, Crystal lied. She knew it was rude, but she didn't ask Mrs. Robertson to have any because she was hoping she wouldn't stay.

"Oh, I'd like some tea myself. Thank you, Mrs. Haywood ... or can I call you Crystal? Mr. Haywood told me your first name is Crystal. All these years and I never knew your name is Crystal."

"Yes ... I guess you can call me Crystal ... Mrs. Robertson. And would you like to call Mr. Haywood Eric? That's his first name you know." Crystal meant to be sarcastic, but it went right over Mrs. Robertson's head.

"Yes of course, I'd like that if you don't mind."

"No, I don't mind at all ... Mrs. Robertson." She purposely emphasized "Mrs. Robertson," but if Crystal was trying to get Mrs. Robertson to say her first name, it didn't work.

"Crystal, I know what you're going through. I mean with Eric. I came over to offer my help. You know I used to be a nurse. I did private duty too, but now I'm retired and I'm home all day. If you want, I could come over and stay with Eric while you go to work. I could take him for a walk sometimes too. Like I said, I'm a retired nurse."

"Oh, I didn't know you were a nurse. In fact, I don't know what any of my neighbor's do ... or did for a living." Crystal was purposely being sarcastic, but again it went right over Mrs. Robertson's head.

"Well, Mr. Brown across the street is a police officer and Mr. Smith is a pharmacist and his wife is a ..."

"That's very nice of you, Mrs. Robertson," Crystal said interrupting, "knowing all that about your neighbors, but Eric was just trying to get the mail. The wind must have blown the door shut." Crystal wasn't ready to seek help and certainly not from a neighbor as nosy as Mrs. Robertson.

"Please Mrs. Hay ... I mean Crystal, there's no need to be embarrassed. Alzheimer's isn't an easy thing to deal with. You need help."

"My husband doesn't have Alzheimer's." Crystal tried to sound nonchalant and casual, but it didn't quite come out that way.

"Alzheimer's, dementia, it's the same thing. I recognize the symptoms. I told you, I used to be a nurse. Since I live next door, I could come right over and ..." Crystal interrupted her again.

"Really Mrs. Robertson, I appreciate your concern. I'm not trying to be rude, but I don't need any help. And even if I did need help, my son Shaun is moving back here from L.A., probably next week. He'll be a big help to me," Crystal lied.

Crystal knew Shaun had been saying he was moving back home for quite some time. Jay had warned Crystal not to believe him because Shaun was always joking. She hadn't been totally honest with Shaun about Eric's health. She just told him Eric was forgetting a lot but that the doctor said it was due to his age. She hadn't mentioned that dreadful word "dementia." She knew he would tell the others, and they would all come running back home acting like it was doomsday. She didn't want them to do that since she was sure—well almost sure—that Eric didn't have dementia. Lately, Shaun had sounded very serious about making the move. Of course she had to admit he hadn't said when. She wished it would be soon-like tomorrow.

Without warning, Eric entered. "Honey, I thought you were coming back into the den to watch television with me. Oh, I didn't know you had company." For once Crystal was glad Eric was interrupting, even though it did prove she lied about him being in bed.

"Hi Eric, remember me, your neighbor? Your wife said I could call her Crystal and I could call you Eric. She said you were resting. I hope I didn't disturb you. Look, I brought you your very own peach cobbler. You remember you told me you loved peach cobbler but Crystal didn't know how to make one. You can have some right now, it's still hot. It just came out of the oven." Eric looked at the cobbler.

"Okay, but I'm too full to eat it right now. Honey, since you have company, I'll wait upstairs for you. Goodnight, Mrs. Neighbor and thanks for the cake."

"Yes ... it's Robertson ... and it's a ... cobbler," she stammered.

"Go on, honey. I'll be right up," Crystal said as she turned and looked at Mrs. Robertson.

"Well, I guess that's my cue. I should be getting on home. Everything here seems ... normal."

"Yes, we're fine—and normal. Thanks. And goodnight, Mrs. Robertson." Crystal literally pushed Mrs. Robertson out into the foyer and opened the door.

"Goodnight, Crystal. Enjoy the ..." Crystal closed the door before Mrs. Robertson could say cobbler.

During the next few weeks, Crystal noticed that Eric was sleeping less and less during the night. This caused her to get less sleep herself since she kept waking up to see what he was into. She put the double locks on all the doors in case he decided to go for his early morning walk—alone. She thought, If he isn't sleeping at night, he must be sleeping during the day. She didn't know if this was good or bad.

Eric kept going in and out of reality as Crystal tried to handle every new episode. She wouldn't admit it to herself, but it was beginning to take a toll. It was almost the end of the semester. Crystal didn't know if it would be better to stay at home with Eric or teach summer school so she could enjoy a little freedom and a little peace of mind. She couldn't believe her own thoughts. This was her husband, the love of her life. Do I really think that getting away and not being home all day with him is freedom and peace of mind? Finally she made her decision: Dementia or no dementia, she would work summer school. Suddenly, Crystal realized she had allowed the word "dementia" to enter into her thoughts.

Several days later, Crystal and Sherry were sitting in the living room flipping through photo albums. "Look," Crystal said showing Sherry a picture, "Here's Jay when he was eight months old. I was giving him a bath in the kitchen sink."

"Aw, he was so cute. I hope you didn't wash him with dish liquid," Sherry laughed.

"And here's the three of them on Easter. They were the only kids in the neighborhood wearing tailor-made suits; and look at Anna. She was so thrilled to have a dress with a coat made of the same material to match it."

"Did you have her outfit made too?" Sherry asked.

"No, it came from a friend of mine's boutique. She gave me a great discount, but it was still expensive."

"You sure spent a lot of money on those kids."

"Oh look, here's a picture of me and Eric dancing at the Greenville Club."

"And there I am with Herbert that same night," Sherry squealed. "I still have that dress. Crystal, I never knew you had these pictures."

"I thought I showed them to you before I put them in the album."

"No you didn't," Sherry said.

"Look, I think I'll take this one and put it in a frame. I can hang it right up there over the fireplace," Crystal said as she stared at the picture a moment. She was thinking back to the night the picture was taken. Eric and I were having so much fun, clowning around and dancing like we were Ginger Rogers and Fred Astaire. Eric had swung me out, my dress swirling around me. He'd pulled me back to him and thrown me backwards, down toward the floor. Everyone had applauded us.

"When are you going to get someone to help you with Eric?" Sherry said, bringing Crystal back to the present.

Crystal hesitated a moment, then said, "I've been thinking about asking my neighbor Mrs. Robertson to come over and sit for a few hours." In a roundabout way, without giving all the details, Crystal related the incident concerning Mrs. Robertson, so Sherry would know who she was.

"Good, I think that's a great idea," she said, showing her delight. "But you need her for more than a few hours. You really need some time for yourself. I mean time to just go and hang out at the mall, take in a movie. It's called, "ME" time.

They suddenly stopped talking. Listening, they heard a shuffling sound approaching. They turned to see Eric standing in the doorway. He entered, barely able to walk. He had put his legs into the arms of one of Crystal's sweaters.

"Honey, I think these pants are way too little for me," he said despairingly.

"Eric, that's not your pants!" Crystal screamed, "That's my hundred and fifty dollar cashmere sweater. You're going to ruin it!"

"Calm down," Sherry said quietly, hoping Crystal would emulate her. It didn't work.

"You can be calm; it's not your sweater!" Crystal yelled.

Eric yelled too. "Well how did I know? It was in my damn room!"

Crystal yelled even louder, "It's my damn room too! Can't you tell a sweater from a pair of pants?"

"They both have two legs!" Eric shot back.

"Come on Crystal, can't you see he's fighting aggression with aggression?" Sherry said, almost pleading with her. Eric grabbed a nearby chair and picked it up and threw it across the room. It went crashing into the wall.

"Stop it Eric," Crystal cried. "Are you crazy?"

"No, you're crazy. I don't see why you're getting so mad about a damn sweater."

"Come on, Crystal," Sherry said. "He didn't know it wasn't his pants." Eric looked down at his legs as if he were disappointed that the sweater was not his pants. He shuffled over and turned the chair upright and sat down on it. For a minute, Crystal and Sherry watched him trying to get his legs out of the arms of the sweater. He was really trying hard. Sherry started to go help him but Crystal pulled her back.

"Let me help you, honey," she said, her voice so gentle she even surprised Sherry. Eric tried to lift his legs so Crystal could pull the sweater off. "I'm sorry I yelled at you," Crystal said, lifting Eric's leg and gently removing the sweater's arms.

"Can I stay down here with you and your friend?" Eric said, almost childlike.

"Only if you go upstairs and put on some pants," Crystal said. Eric looked down at himself and laughed.

"Will you come help me find some?"

"Go on and help him, Crystal, I'll let myself out."

"You don't have to go." Crystal said," hoping Sherry would stay.

"Oh yes she does," Eric said.

"You must have plans for her," Sherry teased.

"Yep, I've got big plans. But first, she's got to find me some pants."

Sherry laughed as she nudged Crystal, and whispered, "Laugh!"

Crystal didn't laugh, but she did force a smile. As Sherry let herself out and closed the door behind her, she thought, Did Crystal just come out of denial or was it just my imagination?

The first week in June began the summer semester. Crystal seemed refreshed even though she'd only had ten days off. Halitosis is better than no breath at all, she thought as she pulled into the parking lot of the college. As usual, a few students recognized her and walked to the entrance with her. Before going to class, she stopped at the main office to check her mailbox.

"Good morning, Mrs. Haywood," Rene, the student clerk said, greeting her. "How was your weekend?"

"It was good," Crystal replied, "How about yours?"

"Boring, I had a lot of homework, but I guess that's what summer school is all about, right?"

Rene spoke while chewing down on a wad of gum after every other word. Crystal had often wondered who trained her.

"Oh Rene, I meant to tell you Friday that I have a housekeeper. I gave her the office number in case of an emergency. She probably won't be calling, but if she does, stick the messages in my box. I'll check them at lunchtime and again on my way out."

The phone rang and Crystal went back to checking her mail. She was surprised when Rene said, Crystal ... I mean Mrs. Haywood, it's for you," and handed her the phone. Crystal already knew who it was. "Hello ... yes, Mrs. Robertson ... what? Come home? What do you mean he won't let you? ... Well, don't worry about it. I'll help him with his bath when I get home. And please, when you call here, don't ask for Crystal, okay? ... goodbye."

"Was that the lady who takes care of your husband?" Rene asked. Crystal hesitated as she thought, I only told the president of the college and the professor I share my office with that I was getting someone to stay with Eric. I didn't think my personal business would be shared with the office clerk. "Yes," Crystal replied, "her name is Mrs. Robertson."

"Okay so whenever she calls, I'll let you know right away."

"Just take the message. You can let me know right away only when it's an emergency," Crystal said. She hoped she didn't sound as irritated as she was becoming.

"Yes ma'am, I gotcha," Rene said. As Crystal headed to her classroom, she made a mental note to inform Rene that "gotcha" wasn't exactly the appropriate professional response for college office personnel.

Crystal's morning went pretty smooth. Since the students didn't have to work on a major production during summer school, she only taught them acting, oral interpretation, and voice and diction. During the lunch break, she went to the office to check her mailbox. Since Rene hadn't gotten in touch with her, she figured there had not been an emergency at home. She was grateful for that. Crystal entered the office and went straight to her mailbox.

"Oh, Mrs. Haywood, Mrs. Robertson called three times. First she said Mr. Haywood wouldn't let her put him on the potty. Then she called back to say he went by himself. Not too long ago she called and said he accused her of taking his money and that he was acting like he wanted to fight her.

I was getting ready to notify you since that sounded like it was going to be an emergency."

"Thank you, Rene. I only have one more class, and I'll be leaving. If she calls back, tell her I'll be home shortly."

"Gotcha," Rene said. Crystal stood looking at Rene a moment. She started to say something, but thought, It probably wouldn't do any good since it's obvious no one has instructed Rene on office protocol, which also raises the question, Who selected her?

The rest of Crystal's day at the college went well, but as she entered her front door, she couldn't help wondering what to expect. Although Mrs. Robertson had been taking care of Eric more than a week now, Crystal had her doubts about her ability to really handle him, especially after she called the school three times in one day.

"Hello, I'm home," she called out as she entered.

"We're in the kitchen," Mrs. Robertson called back.

Entering the kitchen, Crystal asked, "How's everything?"

"Fine. Eric was just finishing his snack." Crystal leaned down and kissed Eric on top of his slightly balding head.

"Hi, honey. How do you feel?"

"Fine," he said as he chewed the last bite.

"Well I'd better be getting on," Mrs. Robertson said as she headed toward the foyer.

"Okay, thanks. See you tomorrow," Crystal said, walking Mrs. Robertson to the door. As she was passing, Crystal glanced into the den. She stopped dead in her tracks. There was a huge hole in the wall. It was big enough for at least one of them to crawl right into. Shocked, Crystal asked, "What happened in here?" Mrs. Robertson turned around, knowing what

Crystal was referring to.

"I called and told that lady at the school to tell you that Eric was trying to fight me. I didn't have no choice; I had to push him off of me. He bumped into the wall."

"Are you okay?" Crystal asked her.

"Yes, I'm fine." Crystal turned and rushed back into the kitchen to check Eric for any visible bruises.

"Are you okay, honey? Does anything hurt you?"

"No," Eric replied.

Crystal went back to inspect the hole.

"I'll pay to have that repaired," Mrs. Robertson offered.

"No ... that's okay. I'll take care of it. Uh ... one little ... bump caused that?" Mrs. Robertson nodded her head and shrugged her shoulders as Crystal still stood staring at the hole.

"Goodnight," Mrs. Robertson said as she proceeded to leave.

"Okay ... see you tomorrow." Crystal said slowly, as she continued to survey the hole. That night when Sherry called, Crystal related the events of the day. When she told her about the hole in the wall, Sherry burst into laughter. Crystal didn't think it was funny and shared her feelings; maybe she shouldn't allow Mrs. Robertson to continue.

"Listen Crystal, you opted to teach summer school. You admitted that Eric could no longer be left alone, so who else is on your list of potential caregivers?"

"If you saw the size of that hole, you would say Eric couldn't be in much more danger if he were left alone." Sherry advised Crystal to sit down and have a talk with Mrs. Robertson in order to devise some safety rules. Crystal had a better idea. She would call and talk to Shaun. Maybe he would consider moving back home soon—like tomorrow. Sherry told Crystal that since she knew that wasn't going to happen, she should try and work with Mrs. Robertson as she'd suggested.

Crystal managed to get through the summer without any more major incidents. Although the hole in the wall had cost her a hundred and twenty-five dollars, she was grateful that no one had been hurt. She was also grateful Eric had gotten used to Mrs. Robertson. Crystal smiled as she thought, He probably thinks she's his mother and she'll knock the crap out of him if he doesn't behave. Crystal wanted to call Sherry and tell her Eric's "so-called dementia" seemed to be in a holding pattern. But she didn't want to personify the word just yet.

Since she had two weeks off before the fall semester began, Crystal decided to let Mrs. Robertson have the first week, but she needed the second week for herself. Sherry suggested they go on a much-needed shopping spree and movie-going escapade, capping it off with dining at their favorite café. Crystal had begun to wonder if her life would ever return to normal. She yearned for the closeness she and Eric once shared, and the "me" time she and Sherry used to have. Sometimes she would go into the bathroom and cry, but she was careful not to let him see her do it.

Crystal didn't attend church as often as she used to, but her faith remained strong. Whenever she and Eric did go, Pastor Williams would "extend the invitation," or as some church folks say, "open the doors of the church," Eric would always get up to join. She just couldn't make him understand that he didn't need to keep joining since he was already a member. Crystal was glad she had allowed Mrs. Robertson to continue helping her with Eric. She finally admitted to herself that she really needed the help.

In October, when the kids called her on her birthday, Crystal hinted to each of them how nice it would be for them to spend Christmas in Chicago, especially since it might be a "white one." Of course she didn't tell them it might be a cold one too, but they already knew that. The meteorologists predicted an early winter, with record-breaking, below-zero temperatures. She hoped her kids would all come home for Christmas since it was too much of a challenge to travel with Eric. Crystal hadn't exactly been up front with them about their father's health. When Crystal called Shaun trying to entice him to move back home, she didn't explain the real reason. She told him that Eric had a friend in the trucking business who would be willing to give him a job once he got his CDL license. She told him those drivers made good money. With Shaun home and Mrs. Robertson next door, Crystal felt caring for Eric would be a lot easier. Sherry didn't pop in as often as she used to. Since her kids were getting older and becoming more involved in school academics, and sports, Sherry gave them her full support. Crystal was glad, but she missed the time she and Sherry used to spend together.

The week before Thanksgiving, Crystal and Sherry were discussing how to make this year's dinner different and more exciting. Sherry suggested that Crystal invite her friends Adellia and Ricardo Mendoza again. Crystal said no to that idea. She didn't trust what Eric might do or say this time to really embarrass her, but she did want to invite Mrs. Robertson and her husband. She never thought the day would come when she would actually invite one of her neighbors over for a social visit. Mrs. Robertson was in and out all the time now, acting like she was part of the family. Crystal had to laugh when she realized she didn't even know Mr. Robertson's first name. In fact, she had just recently learned that Mrs. Robertson's first name was Dorothy. Sherry reminded Crystal to ask Dorothy to bake one of her peach cobblers for Thanksgiving.

As usual, the Saturday before Thanksgiving, Crystal and Sherry were at the grocery store bright and early. Sherry shared Crystal's upbeat holiday spirit. The two laughed and talked while they shopped. It had been a long time since Sherry had seen her friend so carefree and happy. She wondered what had brought about this sudden transition. Crystal herself hadn't realized how relaxed she had become. Maybe it was because she was beginning to realize that Eric's condition was irreversible, and God had sent Dorothy to provide the help she needed.

Eric had started to depend on Crystal and Dorothy to do many of the things he was now unable to do for himself. Crystal was surprised one night when Eric suggested they make love. He tried, but he couldn't. Crystal told herself it was because of the medication he was on. She was convinced that once he got off of it, he would be able to perform again. So she withheld Eric's blood pressure medication for several days but nothing changed, and he didn't mention sex again. Although she was disappointed, she knew it might be dangerous to keep him off the medication any longer. She didn't discuss this with Sherry—she felt it was too personal. Sherry would have been surprised to know Crystal felt this way since they had always been able to discuss anything and everything, including their most intimate sexual fantasies. In fact, on the many occasions they talked about sex, Crystal would take charge of the conversation. Sherry would laugh and accuse her of being an "old pro." When they used to do "girls' night out," whenever someone would ask if they were related, Sherry would say Crystal was her aunt or her mother. Crystal didn't mind because deep down inside, they both felt that kind of closeness.

They were in the check-out line when Crystal looked at her watch and realized they had been shopping for almost two hours. She didn't want Dorothy to stay much longer. She tried not to ask her to come over at all on the weekend, but she knew she just couldn't leave Eric alone anymore. Crystal dropped Sherry off, helping her with her groceries before heading home. She had assured Sherry that Dorothy and Eric would be waiting to help her with her bags.

Crystal pulled into the garage and started to unload her groceries. Suddenly the door leading into the house opened. She figured it was Dorothy coming to help her without being asked. When she turned around, to her surprise, there stood Shaun. Crystal squealed with delight as she ran and threw her arms around him, releasing a flood of joyful tears as she thought, God has truly answered my prayers.

"Hallelujah, praise the Lord," she exclaimed.

"Hey, take it easy, Mom. Somebody might think you're glad to see me," Shaun laughed. Eric and Dorothy stood in the doorway smiling. After everyone had helped bring in the groceries, Crystal sat down, bombarding Shaun with a barrage of questions.

"Why didn't you tell me you were coming? Did you move all your stuff? How did you get here from the airport? Did your brothers know you were moving back?"

"Relax Mom, I wanted to surprise you and Dad. I'm here to stay. Yes I moved all my stuff back. We drove all the way from L.A., and it took almost three days." Crystal started to ask who was the "we" but figured that was part of the surprise, and he was about to tell her. She hoped it was that Jay and Mark, or at least one of them, had come too. "And yes, I told my brothers I was moving back but I haven't spoken to Anna yet,"

Shaun continued. "And last but not least, I got married just before I left L.A." Shaun waited for that last part to sink in.

After a moment Crystal said, "Married? You mean as in a wife?" Shaun nodded.

"Where is she? Who is she? What's her name?"

"Her name is Marie, Mom, and right now she's with her mother, who doesn't live too far from here. She's everything you'd want in a daughter-in-law."

"Did you hear that, Eric? Shaun is married."

"Yep, I heard him and all I've got to say is, I sure hope it rubs off on his little brother." Still stunned by Shaun's news, Crystal thanked Dorothy for staying with Eric. She told her she would let her know if she needed her in the future now that Shaun was home and had brought his wife. While helping Crystal put away the groceries, Shaun explained what prompted him to get married without the fanfare he knew Crystal was hoping for. Eric sat quietly listening.

Shaun pointed out that marriage was the furthest thing from his mind. He and Marie had been dating with no plans for the future. He knew she was originally from Chicago and that her mother still lived here. Marie often talked about her mother and how her mother had kept after her to move back home. When Marie informed Shaun that she might have to move back to help her mother take care of her aunt, he realized he had fallen in love with her. He suggested they get married and move back together. "So here we are. That's my story and I'm sticking to it," Shaun said laughing. Eric clapped loudly and said, "Now if we could just get your brother Jay to do the same thing, I can live happily ever after."

Crystal was ecstatic. She told Shaun she couldn't wait for them to move their stuff in. Shaun hated to burst Crystal's bubble, but that's exactly what he did when he informed her that they would be staying with Marie's mother. Crystal couldn't hide her disappointment.

"You know there's plenty of room here," she said. "Marie's mother's house is probably not as big as this one."

"I know Mom, but she does have three bedrooms and that's where my wife wants to stay, at least for now. But I promise you I'll be here whenever you need me."

"I need you to stay here," Crystal said, pouting.

"Come on, Mom. We really don't need to stay with either of our parents. Dad taught us that every tub needs to stand on its own bottom. We intend to get our own place as soon as I start working."

"Okay, I'm still glad to have you home. I would love for you to bring Marie and her mother over for Thanksgiving, but I would like to meet them before then."

"Alright, I'll bring them by tomorrow after she and her mother come from church."

Crystal smiled, hoping it would somehow shield her disappointment. Dorothy would have to continue to help her with Eric. Explaining that he needed to get back to help Marie unpack their belongings, Shaun hugged Crystal and Eric. Crystal watched him drive off. He could have stayed a little longer, she thought, But he's home and not two thousand miles away, and that's what counts. Crystal immediately called Sherry with the good news. Sherry was just as happy as Crystal.

"God is good," she told Crystal. "What a wonderful Thanksgiving we're going to have."

"Yes, and I think I'll take you up on your suggestion that I invite

Adelia and Ricardo."

"Good, but you'd better put in that extra leaf to your dining room table."

"And you'd better get over here Wednesday and help me cook," Crystal said threateningly.

"Wednesday?" Sherry said laughing. "You mean Tuesday. Are you sure we bought enough food?"

"I'll check to make sure; if not, we'll just go buy some more. Did you say Leonardo was coming?"

"No I didn't. He can't come. He's accepting all gigs, saving up for our wedding." Crystal wondered if Leonardo had finished tying up the "loose ends."

"And when will that be if I'm not getting too nosy?"

"Well, I can't move to L.A. until Johnny graduates and Leonardo can't move here unless he can find work here," Sherry concluded.

"Well something's got to give, and soon, because I want to plan a wedding!" Crystal said threateningly.

"So do I," Sherry said, laughing.

The next afternoon, as promised, Shaun brought Marie over to meet them. He said her mother couldn't come, but she accepted the invitation to Thanksgiving Day dinner. Crystal liked Marie the moment she walked in. She's as pretty as a picture, Crystal thought, And so charming and well spoken. Crystal also thought she looked a bit Asian but decided not to inquire—at least not just yet. At first Marie was shy, but after Crystal put her at ease, within an hour they were chatting as if they had known each other forever. Marie passed the test with Eric too because he was unusually friendly, putting to rest any thoughts Crystal might have had that he would say or do something embarrassing.

It was obvious that Shaun and Marie were very much in love. Crystal made it a point to let Marie know that she and Shaun were welcome to stay with her. Marie thanked her but reiterated what Shaun had said: They needed their own space. She also thanked Crystal for inviting them over for Thanksgiving. She said her mother looked forward to meeting them. Eric told Shaun he did fine, picking such a pretty and intelligent girl.

"Like the words in that song." Shaun began singing. "I want a girl just like the girl that married dear old dad."

"I just hope you'll be as good a husband as 'dear old dad,'" Crystal laughed.

"It's good to be appreciated around here," Eric said. Crystal was pleasantly surprised by Eric's comment. She thought, Maybe having Shaun home is bringing Eric back to his old self. She had to agree with Sherry, this was going to be one happy Thanksgiving.

All day Wednesday, Crystal and Sherry were busy in the kitchen. Cinnamon had taken Sherry's kids to the movies so they were able to get an early start. Eric stayed pretty much out of the way, watching his soaps and taking an occasional nap. He seemed to sense the festive mood in the air and his attitude was unusually pleasant. Another thing Crystal had noticed, he hadn't said anything mean to Sherry. She prayed it wasn't "the lull before the storm." Crystal told Sherry about her suspicion that Marie might be part Asian.

"Maybe we should add an oriental dish to the menu," Sherry said.

Crystal shook her head, "No girl, she's got enough black in her; the traditional turkey and dressing will do just fine."

Thanksgiving morning Crystal was up bright and early. She decided to let Eric sleep a little longer, while she showered and dressed. At nine o' clock, she got Eric up and laid out his clothes. He wanted to sit in the tub, but she was able to convince him to take a shower instead. It was much easier for her, especially since lately once he got in the tub, it took quite an effort to get him out. By ten o' clock Eric was all spruced up. Crystal looked at him admirably as she thought, In spite of his age and the fact that he seems to be losing weight, he's still as handsome as ever.

After breakfast Eric settled down in the den to watch Macy's Thanksgiving Day parade, while Crystal began setting the table with a centerpiece of fresh flowers and her best china and stemware. Between noon and a quarter to one, Jay, Mark, and Anna called. They always tried to get their greetings in before the dinner hour. They expressed their joy over Shaun's marriage and his move back home, and the fact that Crystal and Eric were having a happy Thanksgiving.

Sherry and the kids arrived shortly after one o'clock. Crystal commented on how much the kids seemed to have grown. At thirteen, Carolyne had blossomed into a beautiful and shapely young lady. Johnny, sixteen, and Clyde, fifteen, were both tall and handsome. Crystal teased Johnny about the little fuzz above his top lip and told Clyde his feet were as big as Eric's. They definitely didn't look like kids anymore. But Sherry was from the "old school." She'd raised them to conduct themselves politely and mannerly. She still believed in sitters, not wanting her teenagers to be home alone too often. As usual, they brought their board games. Sherry went right to work in the kitchen, helping Crystal with last-minute preparations. Sherry confessed that she was happy they were having extra guests this year but wished Leonardo could have come.

"You know what they say, 'Absence makes the heart wander,'

Crystal said jokingly.

"It's 'Absence makes the heart grow fonder,'" Sherry corrected her, pretending indignation.

"Don't be hostile and unfriendly, I was just kidding," Crystal said defensively.

"I know," Sherry said as the two frowned at each other before they burst into laughter. It was moments like this that gave Crystal and Sherry the warm mother-daughter like feeling they both shared.

Shaun, Marie, and Joy, Marie's mother, arrived first. Joy was just as attractive as her daughter. It may be an old cliché, Crystal thought, but they could really pass for sisters. Adelia and Ricardo arrived next with Dorothy and her husband Eddie coming in right behind them. Crystal figured Dorothy had probably been watching out of her window and rushed over to make sure she didn't miss out on anything. Crystal led them into the living room where she introduced everyone. She finally called Dorothy by her first name. She hadn't planned to call her Dorothy, but she didn't have a choice since she had introduced everyone else by his or her first name, including Eddie.

When dinner was ready to be served, Crystal and Sherry led everybody into the dining room to be seated. She beamed with pride when her guests praised her for the beautiful table setting and the delicious-looking entrees. Crystal knew she had outdone herself with a spread fit for a king and a queen. On the menu was roasted turkey with oyster dressing, honey baked ham, and a standing beef rib roast. There was macaroni and cheese with mushrooms and peppers, mustard and turnip greens, sweet potato and marshmallow casserole, creamy potato salad, corn pudding, a green bean and onion ring casserole, and of course as always, her homemade yeast rolls.

A separate dessert table had been set up on the side. On this table sat a chocolate, a coconut and a caramel cake; a sweet potato pie, a mincemeat pie, and a lemon meringue pie; and Dorothy's peach cobbler. If her arms had been longer, Crystal would have pat her own self on the back. When it was time for dessert, Crystal would announce they had a choice of New York, chocolate, or strawberry ice cream or a scoop of each.

Eric sat at the head of the table, while Crystal sat at the other end and blessed the food. Eric stood up and announced he was about to carve the turkey. Shaun took his cue from Crystal's expression.

"Let me do the honor, Dad. After all, as a new head-of-household I need the practice."

Crystal heaved a grateful sigh. She could just see Eric slicing off one of his fingers along with the turkey's breast. Dinner went smoothly and everyone said they really enjoyed the meal. They made small talk, and Adelia must have cautioned Ricardo not to tell any of his corny jokes. Crystal began to relax since Eric seemed to be doing fine with the exception of a few minor challenges, like when he was trying to eat with the wrong end of his fork. She was glad Shaun had sat to Eric's right. She was pleasantly surprised to see that he knew just how to handle his father. He showed patience and understanding that she hadn't realized he had.

When Sherry's kids had finished their dessert, they were eager to retire into the den to play with their games. They told Eric to hurry up and finish his pie so he could join them. They were doubly excited when Shaun said he would play too. Clyde said he was glad that Shaun was going to play so he could stop Eric from cheating. Crystal knew that Shaun was still a kid at heart and was happy he had agreed to join them too. Maybe it was because she also knew Shaun would keep an eye on his father.

Ricardo got up and invited Eddie to follow him into the den, since all the men were leaving the table. He advised the women to do what they did best—gossip. Crystal was overjoyed at how well Eric had behaved in front of all their guests, especially Marie and Joy. When Eric had finished eating his pie, he politely excused himself, while the women were left to enjoy each other.

As usual, Adelia dominated the conversation talking about her and Ricardo's marital bliss. Dorothy tried her hand at monopolizing the conversation, discussing her years as a nurse at Cook County Hospital. Finally, Crystal steered the conversation toward Marie and Joy. Sherry reveled at the tact and diplomacy Crystal displayed. She too was glad Shaun had come home. It had been a long time since she'd seen her friend so relaxed—so stress free. Sherry could tell that Crystal had taken an instant liking to Joy and Marie. Joy related her upbringing as a native Chicagoan. Crystal was surprised they knew some of the same people. The women spent almost an hour laughing and talking, sharing stories and events from their pasts.

When Shaun called out for Eric to hurry up if he wanted to play because they were starting a new game, Crystal said she thought he was already in the den with them. Suddenly Eric appeared in the dining room. "Honey, could you come and help me find the rest of my clothes?" Eric said without showing a shred of embarrassment.

Crystal sat frozen in her chair, embarrassment engulfing her. There Eric stood, in the doorway, stark naked from the waist down. She managed to get out a high pitched, inaudible utterance. In an instant, Shaun was there, quickly leading Eric back into the bathroom to help him put his pants on. For a moment, no one said a word. Sherry quickly steered the ladies back to their discussion by announcing she was engaged to be married. The other guests seemed to accept what Crystal had obviously been denying. They all acted as if they knew Eric was suffering from dementia or, as most people called it, Alzheimer's. They were all too happy to give momentum to Sherry questioning her about the "big day." They continued to laugh and talk, easing the pain of Crystal's embarrassment. Shaun had obviously taken Eric into the den to play the game. Crystal thought, Sherry is such a good friend. I'm grateful she took charge of this obviously very embarrassing situation.

Later that evening, Sherry made Crystal admit it had still been a wonderful Thanksgiving. No one seemed affected by Eric's antic. Joy even thanked Crystal for a wonderful Thanksgiving and hoped they could get together again soon. Before Shaun left, he assured Crystal he would always be there for her and Eric. Crystal knew then that Shaun had accepted his father's fate. Dorothy was the last to leave, insisting on helping Crystal clean up while Eddie and Eric watched TV.

Although their other children didn't come home as Crystal had hoped, Christmas was enjoyable. Eric hadn't done anything unusual since his Thanksgiving Day disrobement. Shaun and Marie stopped by without Joy. They said they were meeting her at Joy's sister's house for dinner. Crystal realized that now that Shaun was married, she would have to share him with Marie's relatives. Sherry stopped by for a few minutes to bring Crystal and Eric their gifts and since she had cooked something for her own Christmas dinner, she brought dinner for them too. Dorothy, Crystal had gotten used to calling Mrs. Robertson by her first name now, brought over gifts, along with a peach cobbler. Crystal had put up a Christmas tree, praying that Eric wouldn't get up during the night and knock it over. She managed to go shopping and buy gifts for everyone. She'd even sent gifts to her kids in L.A. and to Anna and her husband in New York. All of them had called to wish she and Eric a merry Christmas. Eric actually held a pretty good conversation with each of them, but none of them talked very long. Just before New Year's Eve, Crystal received a large package from L.A. and one from New York. In it were presents for she and Eric from Jay, Mark, and Anna. They spent New Year's Eve together just the two of them. At the stroke of midnight, they kissed and wished each other a Happy New Year and opened their gifts. After each of their kids had called wishing them a Happy New Year, Crystal took Eric by the hand and led him upstairs.

After climbing in bed beside Eric, Crystal began to pray aloud.

"Thank you, Lord, for allowing us to witness another year. And thank you for blessing us and keeping us all safe. I ask for your continued blessings. In Jesus' name I pray, amen."

Crystal closed her eyes but opened them when she heard Eric say, "Thank you, God, for this wonderful woman who loves me and takes good care of me, amen." Crystal put her arm around Eric, pulling him closer to her. She closed her eyes again, allowing the tears that had formed to flow freely. She laid there a while thinking about Eric and their future. Before she was finally able to drift off to sleep, Crystal whispered, "Thank you again, Lord."

It was near the end of April and Crystal had managed to survive the winter with the help of Dorothy and Shaun. She hadn't seen much of Marie and Joy, but she had spoken with both of them on the phone. One Saturday, Shaun came over to sit with Eric so Crystal could have some "ME" time with Sherry. Eric was just finishing breakfast when Shaun arrived.

"Hi, Mom. What's up, Dad?" Shaun greeted them.

"Good morning, son. How is Marie?" Crystal asked.

"She's fine. She went shopping with her mother."

"Marie, she's your daughter isn't she?" Eric asked.

"Honey, Marie is his wife. They don't have any children. He came back home to help us, but he brought a wife with him instead."

"Mom, being married hasn't stopped me from helping you," Shaun said defensively.

"I know. I was just messing with you," Crystal said. "I couldn't have made it without your help, especially on weekends."

"I said I'd always be here for you and Dad, and I meant that. You and Sherry take your time and enjoy shopping and the movie. Dad and I will have fun drinking beer and watching the Cub's game."

"That'll be great. You know your father always did love baseball. But I wouldn't give him too much beer." Crystal heard a horn outside honking. "That must be Sherry. See you two boys later and enjoy the game," she said as she hurried out. A few hours later, Shaun and Eric were watching the ball game and drinking beer.

"Man! This is one hell of a game," Shaun said.

"What kind of game is this?" Eric asked.

"What do you mean what kind of game is this? Don't you see the bat in the man's hand? It's a baseball game."

"How do you play that game?" Eric asked. For a moment, Shaun sat staring at Eric. Finally he said, "Just watch the game man. I'll explain it later. And that's your last beer."

"I only had one," Eric said pouting.

"And that one made you forget how to play baseball."

"I didn't forget. I never played that game before."

"Okay, sit back and relax. I'll teach you the game later," Shaun sighed. They continued to watch the game. Suddenly Eric jumped up and started yelling and pointing.

"Hey, tell that kid to get down from there."

"What kid? Get down from where?"

"Stop him! He's going to fall and hurt his self." Eric was really getting excited now. Shaun knew what he had to do.

Pretending to see the kid, Shaun yelled, "Hey kid, get down from there before you hurt yourself. Okay Dad, he's down. Now watch the game."

"I don't know why these kids like to jump up on stuff," Eric said. "He would have hurt his self if I hadn't seen him." At that moment, Shaun's thoughts wandered away from the game. He had begun to realize just what his mother was going through. It had to be hard for her to watch her husband's mind slowly deteriorate. He was glad he had made the decision to come back home. He regretted not having made the move sooner. Why hadn't she told us? If she'd only been honest and had accepted ... but, like he'd previously thought, it hasn't been easy for her to accept. Somehow I have to convince Mom she has to find a way to make it easier on herself.

A few hours later, Crystal returned. "I'm back," she said as she entered. "Boy did I enjoy that outing. How was the game?"

"Fine, the Cubs won. What movie did you see?" Crystal told him they had found a cheap theater that showed old movies that had been released months ago. She and Sherry had missed *Rain Man* so they jumped at the chance to see it. When Shaun asked her how she liked it, she said she thought it was great. When he asked if she could relate because of what Eric was going through, she said "No, autism is different from dementia. Young people are diagnosed with autism. Autism is the inability to relate to others sociably. On the other hand, dementia develops in older people and deals with the deterioration of the brain. Eventually it leads to Alzheimer's disease."

"Wow! It sounds like you've been doing some serious researching. And you know something? This is the first time I've heard you admit that Dad has dementia. Now when are you going to tell the others?"

"I had to get an understanding myself before I could try to explain it to anyone else. And don't you go calling them and telling them that Eric has dementia. I'm not really sure what's wrong with your father. It might not be dementia."

"Come on Mom, you're almost there. Don't start regressing now."

Eric suddenly jumped up shouting, "Watch out for that train!"

Startled, Crystal asked, "What train, Eric?"

"Right there," he yelled. "It almost ran over you."

"Come on Mom, I know you see that train," Shaun said as he drew her attention to his winking eye."

"Eric, you drove a train for over twenty years, so move it. Get it out of here," Crystal said, taking the bait. "You had no business bringing it in here in the first place," she added.

"Good Mom, real good," Shaun said commending her. "Now how about removing the animosity?"

"I'm trying," she said. "Believe me, I'm trying."

"You can try harder. Believe me, you can try harder."

"You think this is funny, don't you?" she asked. "Yes I do, and you need to find the humor in it too."

"I can't laugh when I feel like crying," Crystal said.

"So go ahead and cry, and then laugh right through those tears. It might bring you all the way out of denial." Crystal didn't laugh nor did she cry. She just stood looking at Shaun. Finally she said, "Thanks, son. Enjoy the rest of your weekend, and tell Marie and Joy I asked about them."

"That's okay, Mom. You can put me out, but you don't have to thank me."

"I know, but I do. You're a big help, son." Crystal kissed him, patted him on his head, and pointed him toward the door. At the door he turned and smiled, giving her a hug.

"I love you, Mom."

"I know, and I love you too." Crystal said softly.

With Shaun and Dorothy's help, Crystal was able to work summer school. Being with her students seemed to ease some of the stress she had been experiencing. She even got the chance to spend some ME time with Sherry. She began to open up a bit more to Sherry ... talk more about her personal problems. She still kept telling Sherry that she believed Eric was going to get better. Sherry didn't try to make her accept the inevitable anymore. She was too busy trying to convince Leonardo to move back to Chicago.

Crystal enjoyed her two-week break between summer school and the fall semester. Another year was almost gone. Crystal settled into a routine of going to work, keeping house, and caring for Eric—with the help of Dorothy and Shaun of course. She managed to keep their appointments with Dr. Winter, but she still didn't totally agree with his diagnosis. She felt if she kept just one shred of hope, Eric would soon be back to his old self again.

Their kids in L.A. still called to check on them and so did Anna in New York. Her godson Tony had become involved in the theater arts but managed to call at least once every other week. She fussed at him for letting so much time pass without visiting them. He promised to get them some comp tickets the next time a production came to the theater company he was working with. Before Eric retired, Tony would come around often. She missed his good-natured personality. He and Eric always seemed to enjoy each other's company. Sometimes he acted as though Eric and Crystal were his real parents. Sherry visited Leonardo in L.A, and he came to Chicago for the weekend whenever he could, but she hadn't mentioned marriage again. Crystal felt they would marry—eventually.

Not totally out of denial, Crystal had begun to notice Eric's condition was slowly becoming more obvious. This made it harder for her to celebrate holidays, which used to be her passion—especially Thanksgiving and Christmas. Deep down inside, Crystal wanted Eric to be like he was before and she was determined to hang in there until he was. She felt taking care of Eric was her cross to bear and didn't concern anyone else, especially their children, but then she had to admit Shaun was helping her to bear her cross. Well, she hadn't asked him to do it, he just did it ... on his own ... and she was grateful. It was God. He'd sent Dorothy and Shaun to help her. Crystal smiled whenever she thought about it.

Crystal almost hated to see winter approaching. She knew the cold and snowy weather would further limit Eric's outdoor activities. She tried to think of all the indoor projects she and Dorothy could engage him in that would keep his mind sharp and fresh. She was always thinking about what could be done or used to stimulate his brain. If only there was something—anything, she thought.

They celebrated the holidays quietly. For various reasons, Mark and Jay couldn't come from L.A., and Anna was preparing to audition for a hit

Broadway show. Sherry was disappointed that Leonardo didn't come, so she threw herself into her church festivities. Joy invited Eric and Crystal over for Christmas. They went but didn't stay very long. Joy had invited quite a few guests and Crystal was uneasy about what Eric might say or do. Eric surprised her, remaining calm and congenial throughout the holidays. As winter settled in, they continued their uneventful routine with Crystal working at the college four days a week and Dorothy and Shaun helping out with Eric.

One especially cold weekend, Crystal decided she would try to get Eric to reminisce—talk about old times, the "good old days." She popped some popcorn and made some hot tea with honey and lemon. She spiked her tea with a little vodka. She wasn't a heavy drinker, but lately a little cocktail now and then seemed to help her "chill out."

When they had settled in the den, she showed him some special photographs of the two of them. She pointed to one of her favorites. Eric stared at the picture a moment and then smiled. Crystal smiled back. This was a great idea, she thought. When Eric looked at her, again she thought, Is that a glimmer of lust that I see in his eyes? Then Eric asked, "How old were you when I was born?"

Crystal's spirits plunged. Could he possibly think that I'm his ... mother, she thought with her mouth agape. Crystal heard herself repeating the question aloud. "How old was I when you were born?"

"Yeah," Eric said with the innocence of a five-year-old.

"You think I'm your mother?" Crystal asked.

Eric didn't say anything, but she knew the answer. Crystal sighed as she threw up both hands in dismay. Grabbing the remote she asked, "What do you want to watch?"

In March, glad that winter had finally come to an end, Crystal and Sherry took a "ME" day. They went to one of their favorite restaurants, Hooligan's. "I'm glad Shaun could stay with Eric so we could get out. It's been a while," Sherry said as they finished their lunch and started in on their dessert.

Hooligan's was famous for their strawberry-toffee, whipped cream banana splits. Crystal rarely indulged in sweets, but she just couldn't resist those banana splits and neither could Sherry. They dug in like two little girls, laughing at the whipped cream on Crystal's nose and Sherry's upper lip. When they had finished their dessert, they leaned back in the booth and relaxed.

"Boy, that was delicious," Sherry said. "I need to sit here for a minute. I'm so full I can hardly move."

"Me too," Crystal said. "Besides, it feels so good to be out on such a beautiful day."

"You seem to be spending a lot more time at home with Eric. I thought Shaun and Dorothy were supposed to make it easier for you."

"They are a big help but ... Sherry? When you're alone, do you still ... cry? I mean ..." Crystal hesitated.

"I know what you mean, and yes I do. I've fallen in love with Leonardo, but I still miss Herbert. I can't just erase what Herbert and I had as if it were drawn on a piece of paper. Whether the other person is alive or dead, you still have that longing deep down inside; and the pain—it just doesn't go away that easy. You've been crying a lot lately, haven't you?"

"Yes. Eric seems to be deteriorating before my eyes. Sherry, there's so much I want to say to him."

"Then say it, girl."

"But what if he doesn't know what I'm talking about?"

"Say it anyway." Sherry's heart was aching for her friend. She hated to see Crystal going through so much pain and frustration.

"We'll be celebrating our thirtieth wedding anniversary in May, but he probably won't even remember that we're married."

"You said he comes and goes?"

"Yes he does."

"Well, wait until he comes and remind him that you're his wife before he goes."

"You're trying to make me laugh, aren't you?"

"Yes I am, what's wrong with that? But I'm really serious," Sherry said. She hesitated for a moment. Crystal knew she was thinking of something. "Listen, why don't you throw a party? It's been a long time since you had one. You can invite a few of Eric's close CTA buddies, and God knows you have enough relatives to finish making a party. Girl, celebrate your anniversary. Have it in the backyard. It can be a lawn party. Maybe the kids will even come home."

"Uh huh, you just want an excuse for Leonardo to fly in."

"He already has an excuse, if you get my drift." Sherry said, striking a seductive pose and winking. "But for real Crystal, when a person is suffering from amnesia, they say that placing them in familiar surroundings can help them to remember."

"Sherry, Eric has dementia, not amnesia."

"Well, that's the first time you've said that. I believe you're coming out of denial. Now maybe you'll tell your children."

"It's not the first time I've said that word. And I did tell my children—at least one of them. But you know something? I think you're right. A party might be just what I need to lift Eric's spirits, and mine too. Will you help me?"

"Oh oh, I put my foot in my mouth, didn't I?"

"Please?" Crystal begged, "I think it's worth a try. Besides, you know you love to plan a party."

"Alright, we'd better get busy. May is right around the corner, and your yard is big enough to hold at least seventy-five guests."

"Listen to you, girl. Don't forget we need space for the D.J." Crystal reminded her. They both could feel the excitement building.

"This will be the best lawn party or backyard party or whatever-you-want-to-call-it party the neighborhood has ever seen," Crystal said.

"So let's get out of here, girl. We've got some planning to do. There's the menu, the decorations, and the invitations. Hey, let's have it catered," Sherry squealed with delight.

"Of course," Crystal agreed. "I hope you didn't think I was going to cook for that many people. We'll need to make out a guest list."

"Will there be any children invited?" Sherry asked.

"Only yours and mine," Crystal said. We'll have to put that on the invitation, 'No children.'"

"That sounds kind of harsh," Sherry said.

"I need to make it sound like that; I know my relatives. Their kids will be running all over the place and no one will be watching them, especially their parents. I don't want nothing—and I mean nothing—to spoil this party." Sherry knew they had their work cut out, but she also knew it was going to be fun. If it was one thing she and Crystal knew how to do, it was throw a big unequaled, unforgettable eloquent bash. Sherry felt she had finally thought of something that would lift her friend out of the depths of despair. Crystal felt her friend had suggested something that would finally bring Eric back to his old self and their lives will be back to normal. As they stood up to gather their packages and head for home, Crystal reached over and gave Sherry a hug. "Thank you for being such a good friend."

The 30th Wedding *Eight* Anniversary Party

CRYSTAL AND SHERRY WASTED LITTLE TIME AS THEY PLANNED THE ANNIVERSARY PARTY EVERYONE WOULD BE TALKING ABOUT—at least those who were invited. Crystal agreed with Sherry, she would invite only close friends and relatives. Of course she would have to invite Dorothy and Eddie and Adelia and Ricardo, but the rest of the guests would be people Eric worked with and really knew. She wouldn't even invite her own co-workers. Maybe because she still felt a little leery about what Eric might say or ... No no girl, don't even think about it. She chided herself. He'll be just fine. Like Sherry said, placing him in familiar surroundings with family and friends just might do the trick.

Sherry worked with Crystal as if it were her own party. They chose a popular caterer who everybody in the area raved about. Together they chose the menu, the color scheme, and type of entertainment. Sherry expressed her delight when Crystal informed her that Lady Sax had agreed to be a part of the entertainment. Sherry suggested that Eric's cousin Lonnie could videotape the whole affair. Crystal thought that was an excellent idea. Then whenever Eric became bored or restless, she could play the tape. That would be another way to keep his mind sharp and occupied.

Crystal called her godson Tony to create and design the invitations. He was exceptionally good at that. She wondered why he hadn't started his own greeting card business. Sherry agreed when she saw the invitations. She and Crystal were in awe of not only the design but the unique words he had written. Sherry said she wanted an invitation for a keepsake. Shaun's wife, Marie, offered to make the centerpieces for the tables. Crystal soon found out Marie really had the talent to create the most beautiful floral designs. She thought that would be a good partnership; Tony could create invitations and greeting cards and Marie could provide the decorations and floral designs. Crystal was always thinking of a business or enterprise that her friends or family could go into.

Although the school term was ending the first of May and Crystal had decided not to teach summer school, she still needed to hire someone to help with the cleaning of the house. Dorothy helped a lot, but Crystal didn't want her to do the heavy cleaning like the refrigerator and range or the windows and floors. Crystal felt Dorothy had her hands full with Eric—and sometimes she did too. The party would be outside, but people needed to use the washrooms inside. And then it might rain. Sherry's motto was, "It's better to be safe than sorry," reminding Crystal the party might have to be brought indoors. Crystal didn't mind this because she had a fully furnished and paneled basement, capable of accommodating such a gathering.

After six weeks of planning, the anniversary party was less than forty-eight hours away. Crystal was beginning to feel nervous. She wouldn't dare let Sherry know that she still hadn't told her other children about the possibility that Eric may have dementia. Every night she'd been praying that she wouldn't have to tell them—that she would wake up in the morning and Eric would be his old self again. She kept telling herself that she was no longer in denial, but deep down inside it wasn't the truth. Finally Crystal pushed all negative thoughts to the back of her mind as she threw herself into last-minute preparations. She would deal with telling the children after the party—if it became necessary.

They will all be home. Mark and Jay from L.A., Anna and Abraham from New York, and of course Shaun and Tony are already here, she thought. It will almost be like Eric's retirement party or as Leonardo would put it, like the days when Eric and I were known as the party animals. Leonardo said he wouldn't miss this party if he had to cancel a gig, and he wouldn't do that for anyone—except Eric. Crystal would have loved it if Latisha could come and bring Isaiah. But ... maybe they'll come for Christmas. She and Eric would probably have to pay their airfare, but Crystal wouldn't mind that at all.

On Saturday morning, May 18, 1991, the truck from the furniture rental company arrived at nine o'clock in the morning and began setting up the ten tables and eighty-five folding chairs Crystal had ordered. Again, Sherry was in charge as the chief hostess along with two young ladies from her church who volunteered their services. The trio immediately went to work decorating the tables with tablecloths and the floral center pieces Marie had made, all in Crystal's chosen color scheme. Each table accommodated eight to ten people. When Dorothy peeped out her window and saw all the hustling and bustling in Crystal's yard, she came out to offer her assistance. She told Crystal she had a surprise for her and ran back inside, returning with a freshly backed peach cobbler. She said it wasn't big enough for everyone but she could serve it to her special guests.

Crystal and Sherry exchanged looks. Crystal thanked Dorothy but graciously declined her help. She handed Sherry the cobbler and gave her a look that said, "Put this ... little thing away and don't bring it out until my guests are gone—all of them." Of course Sherry could always read Crystal's expressions. As Dorothy turned to leave, Crystal decided she could be of some help after all, and asked her to go inside and keep Eric busy.

The weatherman had predicted sunshine with temperatures in the upper seventies and no chance of rain. He hadn't lied. Already it had been a beautiful spring morning. By noon, everything was just about ready. Crystal was delighted with the way things were shaping up. She told everyone to go home and get dressed. Since the party started at three, she suggested they come back at two-thirty.

At twelve-thirty Mark, Jay, and Leonardo arrived. They had rented a car so no one would have to drop what they were doing to pick them up from the airport. Crystal hated it when they flew in on the same day of the party and had to leave the next day. But this time they would all be staying at least two or three days. Anna and Abraham drove up at one o'clock. There was so much excitement Crystal could hardly get dressed. She was grateful Dorothy lived next door and called her to come back over. With Dorothy's help, Crystal and Eric were dressed by two o' clock. Crystal looked gorgeous in a powder blue, trimmed-in-navy, two-piece silk dress. Eric wore a navy blue suit, a powder blue shirt and a tie bursting with splashes of powder blue, navy, yellow, and white. Although slightly frail, he couldn't have looked more handsome.

Sherry was back before two o'clock. She too looked gorgeous in her navy blue low-cut, form fitting dress that Crystal had helped her pick out. Crystal thought Sherry and Leonardo would never get through hugging and kissing. "Do you guys need a room?" she teased. As always Crystal was glad there were five bedrooms and all of them were being used as well as three of the five bathrooms. When Jay questioned Crystal about the weight Eric seemed to have dropped, she assured him it wasn't as much as it seemed and Eric was still fitting into his clothes and eating everything in sight. Crystal knew that wasn't true but she didn't want to have this discussion with her children—not now.

The back lawn was beautifully manicured and the huge patio served well as the dance floor with ample space for the D.J. and his equipment. Colorful lights were mounted on the ornate fence and trees as well as beautiful floral designs and other eloquent decorations, all in the powder blue and navy color scheme with accents of yellow and white. Two chrome and wood portable bars had been set up with favorite scotches, bourbons, vodkas, rums, wines, and beers—and of course a variety of chasers and soft drinks. Special bottles of champagne were on ice. The bartenders would be a part of the catering package. Crystal had dug deep into her savings sparing no costs.

At two-fifteen the caterer arrived with her crew and began setting up. She wasn't cheap, but what she did was worth every penny. She set up a long beautifully decorated serving table that would eventually contain what Leonardo described to be the most "delectable looking, delicious tasting variety of eloquently prepared cuisine to ever enter his mouth and touch his palate as it slid across his tongue on its way into the major passage way to his stomach." The menu consisted of chicken drumettes, winglets, Swedish meatballs, roast leg of lamb, potato salad, cole slaw, tuna macaroni salad, green beans, grilled asparagus, corn and pepper salad, and a salmon and green pea salad.

A dessert table contained a variety of cakes, pies, cookies, and brownies and a large strawberry whipped cream sheet cake that read, "Happy 30th

Anniversary Eric and Crystal." The party started at three and Crystal wanted her guests to be able to come right in and eat, drink, and relax. At two-thirty the D.J. arrived and began setting up his equipment. He had an excellent outdoor sound system and an extensive musical library. Any song or instrumental piece one wanted to hear—he had it.

The guests began arriving shortly after three—except for Dorothy and Eddie, they came over shortly before three. Crystal was certain that Dorothy wanted to be the first one on the premises—before any guests arrived. Crystal told Sherry she still felt Dorothy was a nosy neighbor. Sherry dismissed this idea, saying Dorothy just wanted to be considered a member of the family.

By four o'clock, the party was in full swing. Among the guests were Marie's mother, Joy; Joy's sister and Marie's sister and her husband, who Crystal was meeting for the first time; Crystal's friends Adelia and Ricardo; and several of Crystal's aunts, uncles, and cousins. A niece and two of her nephews drove in from Flint, Michigan. Crystal had offered them one of her bedrooms, but they declined saying they had already booked rooms at a nearby motel. Quite a few of Eric's CTA buddies had been invited and they all came. The yard was filled with over seventy guests as Sherry had predicted. Crystal was overjoyed as Eric smiled and greeted relatives and friends.

Everyone was having a ball eating, drinking, dancing, talking, networking, and as the elders would put it, plain old "fraternizing." The two young ladies that served as hostesses, both wore navy and powder blue outfits. Sherry noticed they were watching Jay as he moved about the crowd, displaying his super entertaining personality he had inherited from his mother. Sherry made a mental note to let Crystal know which one of the young ladies might be a good "prospect."

Sherry's daughter, Carolyne, had begged so hard it was agreed that she could be a junior hostess. She was having big fun. Sherry's two sons followed Jay around trying to emulate him and trying to act like grown-ups. Sherry was glad when Leonardo gave them a few tips on how to keep on acting like the teenagers they were. Eric sat in a cushioned chair, at a table that had been set up just for he and Crystal along with their immediate family.

Crystal milled about mingling with the guests, but she occasionally glanced over to make sure Eric was okay. He was responding quite well to the attention his friends and relatives were giving him. Many of them had not seen him since the retirement party and expressed their gratitude to Crystal for including them in the anniversary celebration. Some brought presents but most brought cards containing various monetary gifts. Leonardo followed Sherry around like he was a tomcat and she'd been dipped in catnip.

At four-thirty the D.J. announced he was about to play the "Electric Slide," which was also the name of a popular line dance. He urged everybody to "get on up and get on down." Half of the women and a few of the men raced to line up and "get down." Eric didn't get up, but Crystal could tell he was having fun just watching. It had been a while since she had seen him laugh and pop his fingers the way he was doing. At that moment, she knew throwing the anniversary party had been just the thing to bring Eric back to himself. She went over and stood beside him. Occasionally she leaned down and kissed the bald spot in the middle of his head. He looked up and smiled at her.

Lady Sax came in and within minutes she had her saxophone out and was blowing a tribute to Crystal and Eric—"The Anniversary Song." This brought back memories for Crystal, and she wished she and Eric could dance like they'd danced on the cruise. While Lady Sax was performing, Anna and Abraham took to the floor and performed a beautiful dance duet. When they were finished, Anna took the D.J.'s mike and turned to Eric and Crystal.

"Mom, that dance was dedicated to you and Dad. Since I'm not good with words, I hope the dance expressed how much I love you both and wish you many more years of good health, wealth, and marital bliss." She handed the mike to Abraham who said, "I second that emotion." The guests laughed and applauded. Crystal leaned down and kissed Eric on the top of his head as she fought to hold back the tears. As if on cue, Mark went and picked up the mike.

"Mom, Dad, I give thanks to God who saw fit to join you two together. The fact that you made a commitment and continue to keep that commitment is in itself a commendable feat. That commitment allowed us to grow up with a spiritual foundation in an atmosphere of love, appreciation, and respect. Neither of you ever put anything or anyone before your family. Mom, you taught me to be prayerful and always trust in God. Dad, you've taught me what it really means to be a man. Together you both taught me the importance of being responsible, respectable, and humble. Dad, I knew you loved Mom by the way you treated her. Through your actions, I've learned that honesty and family values should be at the apex of all we aspire to be. Mom, I knew you loved Dad by running our household but yet never making him feel he was less than the head of our house. I really don't know two people who love each other more. And I love you both. May love continue to sustain you." Crystal was now visibly fighting to hold back the tears as Shaun picked up the mike.

"Mom and Dad, you are the two people I love most in this world. No offense to you, honey," he said, pointing to Marie. "I don't think I could have chosen better parents if the choice had been mine," he continued. "That is excluding the Rockefellers." Shaun paused, knowing he'd drawn laughter, and then continued. "But really there isn't a price tag on what you have taught me. You equipped me with the tools to survive in a world where survival depends heavily upon the choices we make. As we pay homage and celebrate your thirty years of committing your lives to each other, we want you to know that we think you are the word "marriage" personified. Happy anniversary." Crystal smiled while a tear that managed to escape settled upon her cheek. Shaun passed the mike to Jay, who was standing nearby awaiting his turn.

"Well Mom and Dad, like Anna, I am not big on words either. That's why I patiently looked for just the right Hallmark card that said what I wanted to say. But since I accidently left the card in L. A., I'll have to use my own words. When I think about the sacrifices both of you have made and the examples you've set, I realize you were preparing us to become productive, self-sustaining individuals who loved, and respected you, ourselves, and the people we came in contact with. If we have not learned to apply these things to our daily lives, it is not your fault. Today we are proud that you stayed together—not because of us your children, but because of the love and commitment you made to each other. I love you. Happy anniversary,"

Jay looked around to hand the mike off to Tony. Finally he saw Tony approaching. "Man, get on up here. What are you waiting for?" When he saw Tony had a sheet of paper in his hand he continued, "He's probably written a book. Come on man and keep it brief. Remember, it's a party, not a Sunday morning church service."

Tony snatched the mike from Jay, pretending to be miffed. After pausing, he displayed a smile. "Crystal and Eric," he paused again and then spoke to the guests. "That's what I call them. Crystal is my godmother. I do have a real mother, who I love and respect too." He looked back down on the paper he was about to recite from. Then he looked up again. "I'm not good with elegant words, but I wrote this poem in honor of you." He began to read:

"THIRTY YEARS AND A LIFETIME TO GO"

Thirty years ago today, you made a vow that you would love each other and stay with each other somehow. Through thick and thin and through good and bad, you managed to survive on what you had. By the grace of God I have experienced a love that has an unbreakable foundation, a gift from above. It is a mixture of your life experiences and your commitment to each other. A life time of service you pledged to one another. Crystal, it is your big heart and your love and compassion; Eric, it is your firm hand and willing heart that helps bless you with your possessions. My soul has been filled with an unconditional love. A love that could only have been sent from above. Family does not always come with a blood line. It sometimes comes with a heart and soul line. My commitment to you is to be the best God-sent-son. So wherever you go and whatever you do, my prayer is that God's grace will see you through. I'm not your blood, we know 'tis true. But there's plenty of love between me and you. Oh, and theres one more thing I

want you to know, I'm wishing you thirty more years and
a lifetime to go.

As Tony handed the mike to Sherry, the guests all stood and applauded. Crystal finally allowed the tears to fall. Eric stood up and walked toward Sherry with his hand outstretched as he reached for the mike. The guests cheered and applauded and then fell silent as they anxiously waited for Eric to speak. Crystal smiled with wild anticipation as he took the mike. Feeling Eric was really back to his old self, she stood beaming proudly. She didn't even bother to wipe away the tears. She knew her husband had finally returned. This was the day she had been waiting for.

Eric spoke into the mike. "That was good, but I know a poem too." He began to recite. "I got a gal in Kansas City, she's got meatballs on her titty. She's got ham and eggs between her legs, and boy ain't she pretty." Eric laughed loudly and a few of the guests laughed with him, including Leonardo, while others either gasped or remained silent or tried to stifle their laughter. Eric turned to Sherry, who wanted to laugh too but the startled and embarrassed look on Crystal's face made her decide it would not be a good idea. "Thank you for bringing me to this party, honey," Eric told Sherry and grabbed her and kissed her right on her lips.

Crystal looked as if she wanted to cry—for real. The D.J. played a loud popular song with a fast beat and several couples began to dance. Shaun walked over and took Eric's arm and guided him back to his seat. He gave Crystal a "look" and she responded by hugging Eric as she sat down beside him. She couldn't hide her look of disappointment and defeat. No one left, and the party continued until the scheduled time it was to come to an end. Mark had snickered at Eric's poem, but Jay and Anna didn't think it was funny at all. Shaun had been discussing Eric's health with Tony, so he was neither shocked nor surprised. In fact, he had laughed with Mark and Shaun. The festive mood of the guests had not been affected by Eric's performance. In the end, friends and relatives all thanked Crystal for inviting them and assured her they'd had a ball. They sounded sincere, and Crystal accepted their compliments graciously.

By eight o'clock, the last guest had left and most of the clean-up had been done. The caterer and her crew had cleaned up after themselves. Leonardo, Sherry, and the other two hostesses had stayed and helped Crystal with what little she had to do. Afterwards they said goodnight and Leonardo winked at Crystal and said he would be spending the night on Sherry's sofa. Shaun's wife Marie had left with her family. Shaun had assured her that one of his brothers would bring him home later. Mark, Shaun, Jay, and Anna gathered in the dining room to discuss what all of them, with the exception of Shaun, had just found out about their father's health.

"Talk about a show stopper, that was some poem Dad ended the party with," Mark said.

"He didn't end the party. The guests continued to enjoy themselves," Shaun said defensively.

"I know Mom was embarrassed. By the way, shouldn't she be down here?" Anna chimed in.

"She's upstairs putting Dad's pajamas on," Shaun informed them.

"You mean laying them out for him," Jay corrected him.

"I mean putting them on him," Shaun said emphatically. "How come he can't put them on by his self?" Anna asked.

"Sometimes he forgets how to put them on," Shaun answered.

"Forgets? He can't remember how to put his pajamas on? He didn't have a problem remembering the words to that poem. Mark wasn't that the poem that caused you and Shaun to get a whipping for teaching it to Jay? Look how long ago that was, and Dad still remembered it," Anna reminded them.

"Shaun, you mean he's losing his memory? Is that how to explain his behavior at the party? Jay asked.

"Yes, Dad has dementia," Shaun said unemotionally.

"Dementia, what's that?" Anna asked.

"It's a form of Alzheimer's," Mark said.

"Mom told you that?" Jay asked.

"She didn't have to tell me. He did some crazy stuff the last time they spent Christmas in L.A. Mom tried to cover it up."

"He's had dementia that long? They haven't spent Christmas in L.A. in two years," Jay exclaimed.

"Mom has been in denial longer than that. She didn't want to face the fact that all the years they have spent together will soon be erased from his memory—like they never existed. He probably won't remember her or us," Shaun said somberly.

Jay's eyes began to swell with tears, "How can he forget us? He lives and breathes for us."

"Mom spends most of her waking hours caring for him and that's after working all day. She really needs some rest." Shaun said.

"You moved back here, why haven't you helped her get some?" Anna snapped.

"I've got a job and a wife, and I do help her," Shaun snapped back.

Jay took up for Shaun, "Why don't you move back here? You ain't doing anything in New York."

"You don't know what I do in New York," Anna said putting her face close to Jay's.

"I know you've been there going on six years, Miss-I-Wanna-Be-A-Dancer."

"Hey man, why don't you ease up off of her?" Mark said, feeling the need to come to Anna's defense.

"This is an A and B conversation, C your way out." Jay spat at Mark.

"You don't have to defend me, Mark. I can defend myself. And so what are you doing that's so great in L.A. "Mr.-Why-Should-I Marry-One-Woman-When-I-Can-Stay-Single-And-Screw-Them-All?" Anna spat at Jay.

"Come on now, all of you calm down," Shaun said, trying to quell the quiet discussion that had somehow turned into a loud, uncontrolled argument. "Mom never allowed us to fight when we were growing up, why start now? Can't you see she's got enough to deal with? I know you are trying to understand what's happening to Dad. We all came home to celebrate a happy occasion only to find out it is a not so happy occasion." Crystal was about to enter but hearing that part of the conversation, she stopped to listen to more.

"Let's get something straight right now," Anna said. "Believe me, I love Mom and Dad. They adopted me and made me a part of this family, showering me with as much love and affection as they gave the rest of you. Don't think I don't appreciate that. I do, but I don't feel it is the obligation of the children to take care of their aging parents. That's my opinion and I have a right to have one just like everybody else."

"I agree with Anna," Mark said, "No matter what her reasons are. But I do feel we should help our parents in any way we can without giving up our own lives."

"Why not, they gave up theirs for us," Jay said with unmistakable resentment.

"Not totally," Anna said with defiance. "It was their responsibility to take care of us. It may sound harsh, but we are not obligated to take care of them. There comes a time in everybody's life when a painful decision has to be made."

"Are you saying our dad should be put in a home?" Jay was livid. "Girl, you've lost your damn mind! Mom would never agree to do that. You act like you don't even know her." Crystal decided she'd heard enough. She entered the dining room as Eric headed unnoticed into the den. She began speaking as she entered.

"Maybe she doesn't know me, but I know me."

"Mom, we were just discussing how we could help you with Dad," Jay said, hoping she hadn't heard the entire conversation. But Crystal had heard as much as she needed to hear. She knew it was time to draw the bottom line.

"I have enough help. I'm grateful that Shaun came back to help me, I didn't ask him to. Well ... maybe in a way I did, but I haven't asked the rest of you to come home and help me and I won't. Mark, I heard you say this was not a happy occasion. I beg to differ with you. This is a very happy occasion. Your father and I celebrated thirty years of loving each other. I still love him and he still loves me, and that makes us both very happy. Believe me, whatever my husband—your father—is going through, he and I will go through it together. Through it all, I will handle it. End of discussion. Now I'm going in the kitchen to fix us some snacks. Shaun, come give me a hand." Suddenly they heard a loud crash coming from the den. They all rushed in to find the bookcase lying on its side and papers and books strewn all over. Jay entered first.

"What are you doing in here, man?"

"Nothing, I'm just trying to find my insurance papers," Eric said, his tone more frustrated than angry.

"What insurance papers?" Crystal asked.

"The insurance papers for my Buick," Eric answered.

"You don't own a Buick anymore, Eric. We own a Toyota."

"You own a Toyota, I own a Buick," Eric insisted.

"You don't own a car, Eric," Crystal said, trying hard to stay calm.

"Damnit, woman! I know what I own, and I don't intend to drive around and have an accident and let somebody sue the shit out of my ass!"

"Eric, the kids are here. They've never heard you swear at me like that," Crystal said, still trying to remain calm. Eric turned away from Crystal and opened the drawer to a table and began pulling papers out and throwing them on the floor. "Stop it, Eric! You don't drive anymore. I drive and I have insurance on the Toyota."

"That's some shit. I do drive. I drove this morning and I had insurance this morning." Suddenly Shaun stooped down and picked up some papers.

"Wait, what's this? Here they are, Dad. You were right. See, I found your insurance papers. They were right here all the time." He handed the papers to Eric.

"Whew! Thanks, son. I knew they were down here somewhere. See, I told you," Eric said, sticking his tongue out at Crystal. "I'll take them upstairs and put them in a safe place."

"Yeah Dad, you go do that," Shaun urged.

Eric headed back upstairs.

Mark could no longer hold his laughter.

"Man, those weren't insurance papers," Jay said.

"I know," Shaun said laughing.

"Okay Shaun, stop laughing and help me stand this bookcase back up," Mark said, as he tried to stop laughing himself.

"Alright, but tell Mom to stop laughing," Shaun playfully ordered.

"I'm not laughing," Crystal said, still trying to remain calm.

"Well you should be," Shaun said, his tone becoming serious as he stopped laughing.

"Why should she be laughing?" Anna asked.

"Because crying won't change a thing," Shaun replied.

"And I guess laughing will?" Anna was asking a question rather than stating a fact.

"No," Shaun replied, "But if she laughs through her tears sometimes, she might see some of the humor in this and she'll feel better. She can control her own inner emotions." Crystal displayed a weak smile. "That's better, Mom. I'll go check on Dad. Anna you help Mom fix the snacks," Shaun said as he headed upstairs to check on Eric. Jay, Anna, and Mark followed Crystal into the kitchen.

"As much food as there was at the party, tell me why are we about to have snacks," Anna said.

"Don't pretend like you don't want any as much as you like to eat," Mark said teasing her. Besides, I ate at five and it's almost ten. It's feeding time again, and Mom knows best." Anna later told Mark that she was glad Crystal had put an end to the previously heated debate that was about to get out of hand. If Crystal did hear her when she said the care of aging parents was not the responsibility of the children, she hoped Crystal knew it didn't alter the fact that she loved and appreciated both she and Eric's devotion toward her.

Crystal had meant what she'd said too. She really didn't want to have that discussion—not tonight, not ever again—with her children or anyone else. It is my burden and I intend to carry it come hell or high water. Case closed.

It was almost midnight when Crystal finally announced it had been a long day and she was going to turn in for the night. She suggested that Mark do the same. Anna had already joined Abraham, who had laid down earlier complaining of fatigue after doing most of the driving from New York. Jay had retired shortly after finishing his snack. He went to bed early as a child and he hadn't changed much as an adult. Crystal had waited up until Mark got back from driving Shaun to his mother-in-law's. Mark agreed he was tired too. As they climbed the stairs, Mark stopped and turned to her. For a moment, neither spoke.

"It's going to be alright, Mom."

"I know," she said.

Mark hugged her. "I love you and Dad."

"I know that too, and we love you more," she said smiling.

Crystal entered her bedroom. The night light helped her find her gown and led the way to the bathroom where she prepared for bed. She had been careful not to wake Eric. She turned the light out in the bathroom. She knew the nightlight would be enough to lead her to the bed. Crystal also knew she would be sleep as soon as her head hit the pillow. As she entered the bedroom again, she was startled to see Eric leaning against the wall, pushing it with both hands. Crystal looked at him for a moment, not quite sure of what he was trying to do.

"Honey, what are you doing?" she asked.

"I'm trying to keep this damn wall from falling."

"Turn it loose, it's not going to fall," Crystal said quietly, not wanting to wake the others.

"I'm not going to let this damn thing fall."

"You can't just stand there all night holding up the wall."

"If I turn it loose, it'll fall and kill us both."

"It isn't going to fall," she said, hoping he would take her word for it and come to bed.

Eric continued to push against the wall. Crystal tried to remove one of his hands but he raised his voice, ordering her to watch out or the wall would come down and crush them both. Exhausted and not knowing what else to do, Crystal turned and crawled into bed. Suddenly, she burst into laughter. Then she was quiet. Shaun had said laughing would make her feel better—it didn't.

"Okay honey, I'll just lie here and see how long you're going to stand there. You'll get tired and see that the wall is not going to fall." She continued to watch him for a while but soon dozed off. Maybe it was because even when she was asleep Eric was always on her mind that she awoke thirty minutes later to find him still holding on to the wall.

"Honey, please come to bed," she coaxed. When Eric didn't respond, Crystal decided she would try to sleep in intervals. The clock on the dresser displayed 1:30 a.m. She woke up several times to find Eric still standing against the wall. At four o'clock she awoke, glad to see that he had finally stopped holding up the wall. But he hadn't come to bed. Fearing the worse, Crystal jumped up and checked the bathroom. He wasn't there. She rushed down the stairs praying he hadn't decided to go outside. She had forgotten to put the extra locks on the doors. Entering the den, Crystal was relieved to find Eric sitting in the dark.

"Honey, are you okay?"

"I'm fine," he answered."

"Aren't you sleepy?" she asked, wondering, If not, then why not?

"I was waiting up for you," he said.

"It's almost morning. The kids will be getting up. They'll probably want to spend some time with you, and you'll be too sleepy," she warned.

"The kids are here?"

"Yes, yesterday was our thirtieth wedding anniversary. They all came home for the party."

"I'm sorry I didn't buy you a present," Eric said sadly. Crystal moved through the darkness and sat beside him on the sofa. Placing her arms around him she said, "You are my present, and everything you have ever done for me and our children has been my presents. I know you love me. No one on this earth loves me more than you."

"I love you because you love me," Eric said earnestly. At that moment Crystal felt he was as close to being his old self as he would ever be again. She remembered what Sherry had said and decided to take advantage of the moment.

"Yes, yes I do love you. You deserve to be loved. You've always worked to provide for us. You never disrespected me or called me out of my name. You never got drunk or stayed out all night gambling or chasing other women. You always helped me around the house, trying to make my burden lighter. You washed, ironed, cooked, and cleaned. We always worked side by side. You've never abused me or our children. I am so grateful, honey, and I love you very, very much. I am truly blessed to have you for my husband and ..."

Eric's snoring interrupted Crystal. She hoped he'd heard most if not all of what she'd said. Without waking him, she curled up beside him. She closed her eyes and smiled as sleep took control of her too.

Nine
Dementia—Stage Three Continues

SEVERAL MONTHS HAD PASSED SINCE THE ANNIVERSARY PARTY. Whenever Crystal and Sherry discussed the event, Crystal would tease Sherry by asking her if she had any more bright ideas since placing Eric in familiar surroundings bombed. Sherry reminded her that at least her family and friends had been made aware of Eric's condition.

Crystal was glad their children were honoring her wish by not discussing Eric's health or his future care. They called her every week, just to check on them. Every time one of them would get close to mentioning Eric's dementia, Crystal would change the subject. Though no longer in denial, Crystal still refused to admit that at some point she might not be able to continue caring for Eric. Whenever she felt like throwing in the towel, she would repeat her vows ... "In sickness and in health ..."

During their last visit to his office, Dr. Winter had tried to suggest different options Crystal should consider, but again she reiterated that a nursing home was not an option. Dorothy was still helping but she was showing signs of fatigue, and Shaun's job was requiring him to put in more overtime. Shaun's wife Marie offered to come over in his place but then she had to work on Saturday, the day Crystal really needed someone. So

Crystal continued to, as she called it, "roll with the punches."

Crystal didn't work summer school because she wanted to stay home with Eric. She had asked Dorothy to come over for only three or four hours a couple days a week. But now it was the fall semester and she felt guilty about being glad she was back at work. She defended her feelings by telling herself she had spent every evening and all day on Friday, Saturday and Sunday with Eric all summer long, except for the few Saturdays she did get to shop with Sherry. She also took Eric out for short walks around the neighborhood. Many of the neighbors made friendly gestures; a wave or a pleasant greeting as they passed.

Although September was just ending, Crystal found herself thinking about Thanksgiving. Maybe the kids could come home again. She wouldn't invite anyone else, just them—and Sherry of course. Crystal didn't know what she would do without Sherry.

She started to call her friend but decided not to bother her since this was the Saturday they didn't go shopping. She opted to relax in the den and watch the Saturday afternoon movie with Eric. Crystal thought she was going to watch the movie, but she dozed off ten minutes after the movie began. She hadn't been sleep no more than thirty or forty minutes, but when she awoke Eric was gone. She became upset when she found the front door open. He's at Dorothy's, she thought. Why didn't she just bring him back home? She knew I would come looking for him.

Crystal rang Dorothy's bell. She decided she would give her a piece of her mind. When Dorothy opened the door, she still had her hat and coat on. She told Crystal that she and Eddie had just returned home from shopping and they had no idea where Eric might have gone. Crystal really panicked.

Crystal searched up and down the street, to no avail. She jumped in the car and drove around for at least an hour. She even stopped by the neighborhood police station. They suggested she check the area hospitals. She returned home but still no Eric. She called several hospitals to no avail. Shaun was at work, so she couldn't call him. Finally in desperation, she called Sherry, who immediately rushed over.

"What's up," she asked as Crystal met her at the door. "On the phone you sounded ..." She stopped, alarmed by Crystal's appearance. "What the ...? You look terrible."

"You'd look like this too if you'd been kept up for two days and two nights with very little sleep, and now Eric is missing."

"What do you mean missing," she asked, hoping it wasn't what she was thinking.

"We were sitting here in the den watching a movie, and I must have dozed off. When I woke up, the front door was wide open and he was gone." Sherry didn't say it, but she knew this would happen. She had often heard that people who had dementia or Alzheimer's were prone to wandering off.

"Did you call the police?" she asked.

"No, I went to the station. They said I should check with the hospitals—which I did. No luck there either. I don't know what else to do."

"What about Dorothy? Did you check with her?" Sherry asked.

"Of course, that was the first place I checked after checking all over this house. I even looked in the backyard. Dorothy said she hadn't seen him."

"I thought you said she was nosy. Of all the times for her not to be looking. You said she sees everybody and everything that goes on over here."

"She does but she wasn't home. She and Eddie went shopping. I couldn't call Shaun, so I had to call you. Sherry, I'm scared. He's out there alone. He probably doesn't remember where he lives, or who he is for that matter. Something terrible could happen to him." Crystal started to cry. "It's all my fault. I failed him. I vowed to take care of him and I failed him!"

"Stop crying. It's not your fault. Girl, you're tired. You can't watch him twenty-four-seven. I thought Shaun came over on Saturdays."

"He had to work," Crystal said, still crying.

"I thought Dorothy watched him some Saturdays" Sherry said.

"No, I don't bother her on Saturdays. Besides, I probably won't be bothering her at all; I might have to quit my job. Dorothy said she didn't know if she could continue caring for Eric."

"Why?" Sherry asked.

"She said he cusses at her and tries to hit her."

"I thought Dorothy had gotten used to Eric and had him under control," Sherry said. Crystal nodded.

"At one time she did, but lately he's gotten worse."

"Well, maybe you ought to think about ..." Knowing what Sherry was about to suggest, Crystal cut her off.

"No, I'm not putting him in a nursing home!" Ignoring Crystal's growing anger, Sherry calmly said, "You might have to."

"I'm telling you I won't," Crystal said emphatically.

"And I'm telling you that you can't work and take care of him. Look at you. Shaun helps you, Dorothy helps you, and you still look like three rainy days, an earthquake, and several aftershocks."

"You're not funny, Sherry."

"Honey, I'm not trying to be."

"You don't understand, he needs me, he depends on me. I vowed, in sickness and in health, 'til ..."

"... til your death do you part? Crystal, you may as well face it. Mark has a family, Anna has her career, Shaun has a wife who is probably going to start her own family soon, and Jay's transfer may never come through. They have already lost one parent. And if something happens to you, they are not going to take care of Eric."

"They won't have to because nothing's going to happen to me. I will take care of my husband. He is not going into a nursing home!" The telephone interrupted what was headed for another heated debate. Crystal rushed to answer. "Hello? ... yes ... yes ... oh thank God ... I'll be right there. Come on, Sherry," Crystal said, slamming down the phone.

"Where to?" Sherry asked as she rushed to keep up with Crystal.

"The police station, they've found Eric." Sherry insisted she should do the driving. She told Crystal that an accident might slow them down. Sherry knew Crystal was not in the mood for humor, but she was just trying to keep her calm. Arriving at the police station Crystal jumped out of the car almost before it stopped. Sherry had to run to catch up with her. They entered the station and found Eric sitting on a bench. His eyes lit up when he saw Crystal.

"Honey, am I glad to see you. When I got off from work, I came outside and some son-of-a-bitch had stolen my car."

"Eric, you don't work and you don't have a ..." Sherry nudged Crystal.

"Eric, as soon as we saw that your car had been stolen, we reported it. You can ride home with us," she said, giving Crystal the "look."

"Thank you," Eric said, "I sure would appreciate that." A police officer standing nearby said, "Ma'am, it's a good thing you came in earlier and reported him missing. He didn't have any I.D. on him, but the picture you left helped us to identify him. He's a little confused but he seems to be okay." Crystal thanked the officer and took Eric by the hand, leading him toward the door. At the door, Eric snatched away.

"What about my wallet? One of them son-of-a-bitches stole my wallet with my money in it."

The police officer spoke up, "Ma'am, like I told you, he didn't have any identification, no wallet, and no money."

"You're a liar," Eric yelled, "I had money right here in my pocket." Sherry cleared her throat and Crystal took the hint. She opened her purse and said, "I have your wallet and your money right here in my purse, honey."

"Good," Eric said. "The nerve of you guys, trying to steal my shit!" he yelled at the policemen before Crystal pushed him out toward the street. "Will they call me when they find my car," he asked Crystal as she helped him into Sherry's back seat.

"Yes, they'll call you," she said. She wasn't angry; in fact, she was very happy that he was safe and unhurt.

When Sherry pulled up in Crystal's driveway, Dorothy came rushing out to express her joy that Eric had been found. For the first time, it became apparent to Crystal that Dorothy really cared about them. She's not just a nosy neighbor—maybe a bit too inquisitive at times—but she really cares, Crystal thought as she assured Dorothy that Eric was okay. Dorothy offered to go in with them, but Crystal said they would be fine. She just wanted to get Eric inside and fix him a bite to eat. Dorothy made Crystal promise to call her if she needed her. Seeing the admiration in Dorothy's eyes and hearing the genuine sincerity in her voice, Crystal smiled as she promised and thanked Dorothy for caring.

While Sherry helped Crystal prepare dinner, they found humor in the trip to the police station.

"Did you see the expression on that cop's face when Eric accused him of taking his wallet?" Sherry laughed.

"Yes, and did you see Eric ball up his fists like he was going to punch one of them in the face?"

"Yes, I was afraid they would forget about his age and condition and lock him up." Crystal laughed so hard she almost knocked over her coffee. Suddenly she stopped. "I can't believe I'm standing here with you laughing at my poor husband."

"That means you're getting there," Sherry said.

"You and Shaun are always telling me that. Getting where?" Crystal asked, but she knew exactly what Sherry was referring to.

"You're getting to the point where you can laugh sometimes. You're finally realizing that no matter what kind of hand life deals you, you have to play it to the best of your ability and smile through it all."

"But I still want to cry," Crystal said, sounding as if she was ready to do it that very moment.

"Go ahead, cry," Sherry urged.

"But I thought you wanted me to laugh," Crystal reminded her.

"So, do both."

"You know something," Crystal said, now sounding very serious. "I'm tired of you and Shaun telling me to laugh through my tears. I can't go around laughing and crying at the same time. What will people think?"

"They'll think you've found a way to cope. You just might be an inspiration to others who are facing the same situation." When dinner was ready Crystal started setting the table.

"Don't set a place for me," Sherry said, I've got to go home and prepare my own dinner." Crystal realized she had taken Sherry away from her own responsibilities.

"I'm sorry, just because you're here at the drop of a hat doesn't mean you don't have your own family obligations. Thank you for having my back."

"Will you stop thanking me? If we're supposed to be family, then you are one of my obligations. Besides, I'm also your friend. I just do what friends do."

Lying in bed that night, Crystal tried not to think about all of the harm that could have come to Eric. She silently thanked God for keeping him safe. She also reminded herself to keep all doors locked from now on.

Since the next day was Sunday, other than the fact that it had been a while since they had gone to church, something compelled Crystal to get up and get herself together and attend the eleven o'clock service. Although the church was only a block and a half away, she decided to drive the short distance. Eric was beginning to walk a bit slower and slightly unsteady. The fact that his vision was poor didn't help either. Lately, Crystal always held Eric's arm in case he stumbled. She often thought about the couple she had seen in the park. She remembered how the woman assured the older man he could depend on her.

Crystal was glad she had decided to attend church. Eric smiled and clapped his hands throughout the singing. The choir sang a song that he especially liked "Jesus Will." Ironically, the sermon that Sunday was taken from the book of Daniel. It was the biblical story of Shadrach, Meshach, and Abednego and their refusal to serve king Nebuchadnezzar's golden image. Crystal would later describe it as "unshakable faith," the kind of faith she knew she had to have in order to sustain her during the challenges she was now facing up to.

After church, Eric's mood seemed to be a bit more pleasant. That evening, Sherry called to check on them. She was glad to hear they had gone to church and the effect it had on Eric. She suggested they do it more often. Crystal promised they would.

The holidays were nearing and although it was Crystal's favorite time of the year, she no longer felt excited with anticipation. Lately, Eric seemed more agitated than ever, and she didn't know what to do to lift his spirits. His attitude was beginning to affect Crystal's mood too. Plus, she hoped Eric wouldn't say or do anything to cause Dorothy to give up. She had really begun to rely on her.

Crystal hoped and prayed the tiredness and stress she was experiencing would go away and not affect her work with her students. Most of them were good, conscientious students. There were some things that she usually overlooked, but now they were beginning to get on her nerves. She thought about calling Dr. Winter's office to make an appointment but changed her mind. Instead she decided a hot soak in the tub was probably what she needed. Crystal checked her messages, said goodnight to Rene, and headed for home. Since Rene hadn't given her any messages from Dorothy, she assumed everything was all right—at least she hoped so.

At home, Crystal heaved a sigh of relief when she found both Eric and Dorothy in good spirits. Dorothy said goodnight and after dinner, Crystal settled down in the den with Eric for an hour of TV. She paid very little attention to the program on TV as she sat thinking about how she would pamper herself in the bathtub as soon as she put Eric to bed. When the phone rang, she couldn't believe that Sherry wanted to come over this time of night to tell her about some bright idea she had. Sherry sounded excited, so Crystal told her to come on over but to make it quick. She decided to be standing in the doorway when Sherry arrived. She smiled as she thought, I'm going to let her know I'm in a hurry to get on with my plans so she'd better be quick. Standing in the door, she smiled again as she thought, Maybe I'll just stand here and not let her in. I should make her tell me her idea from here.

IT WAS A GOOD THING SHAUN HAD KEYS TO THE HOUSE. When Crystal did not answer the door, he entered and rushed up the stairs two at a time. Crystal was just regaining consciousness when Shaun entered the bathroom. Eric was sitting in the tub calling Crystal's name. Crystal was still on the floor beside the tub. Her upper torso was wet. Her forehead was bleeding from a large swollen knot containing a small cut. She told Shaun she was all right, but seeing the blood from the cut on her head and both of her arms hanging limp, he knew she was not all right.

He picked Crystal up and sat her in the chair beside the bed and called Sherry, asking her to come over right away. Then he picked Eric up out of the tub, dried him off, put on his pajamas, and put him in the bed. Crystal admitted she was now in pain. When Sherry arrived, Shaun asked her to stay with Eric while he took Crystal to the nearby emergency room.

Hours later, Shaun and Crystal returned from the hospital. Crystal's left arm was in a short cast and a sling. Her right arm was in a cast up to her elbow. A Band-Aid covered the cut on her swollen forehead. Shaun led her into the den where Sherry was watching television. Sherry's face showed both shock and dismay when she saw Crystal. While still staring at Crystal, she told them the bath must have been very soothing because Eric had gone right to sleep. Crystal plopped down on the sofa. For a moment no one spoke. Crystal just sat, looking at Shaun and then at Sherry. Finally she said, "How come no one's laughing? Or maybe I should cry first and then laugh. Right?"

"Mom, there are things we can and should laugh about, but what happened to you tonight isn't very funny. I'm really concerned."

"Your whole family is concerned," Sherry admitted. "Your cousin Betty called, and when I told her what had happened, she said if you don't put Eric in a nursing home, she's going to do it for you."

"She can't run my house," Crystal snapped.

"You can't either, with your wrist fractured and your other arm broken in two places," Shaun responded. Sherry covered her mouth stifling a gasp. "Mom, you know I love Dad, but like Anna said, there comes a time when painful decisions have to be made."

"He's right, Crystal," Sherry said. Crystal looked at them, shaking her head.

"I can't do that to him," she said, tears swelling in her eyes. "I can't put him away. I don't care what you say, I can't do it."

"You're not putting him away," Sherry said.

"Mom, Dad needs to be where he can get professional care."

"And I can give him that. I can give him professional care and loving care." Crystal said, her voice trembling as it was beginning to rise, mostly with passion rather than anger.

"Mom, he's become more than you can handle."

"I love him, Shaun," Crystal said, beginning to sob uncontrollably. "I can't do that to him! Why can't you understand that? He's my life and I'm his life."

"But Mom, he's slowly forgetting all of that."

"Stop it! Don't tell me that! He'll never forget me. He'll never forget all the things we've meant to each other. All the years ... all the struggles ... all the challenges, every obstacle we've had to overcome. We've got plans ... hopes ... dreams..."

"Come on, Mom." Shaun tried to calm Crystal to no avail.

"You're asking me to put the only man who truly loves me, the only man that I truly love ... in a nursing home where he'll be mistreated, abused, and forgotten about, and you want me to calmly agree to that?"

"Listen Mom, I'll call Marie and let her know I'm spending the night. I'll call in sick in the morning. You need to get some rest, some sleep."

"Yes," Sherry agreed, "you really need to rest. I can stay here too; I just need to call home and let the kids know."

"No, you both can go home. I can sit up and watch Eric," Crystal said, fighting hard now trying to convince her own self that she could handle the situation.

"Look Crystal," Sherry said, looking at her friend and hoping she could make her understand. "It's time to throw in the towel. If you have to stay awake all night and watch Eric, you need to face reality."

"That's what she's been doing, Sherry, staying awake half the night watching him. That's why she's in the shape she's in. And that's why she needs to make that decision," Shaun concluded.

"I won't do it, I won't," Crystal cried, almost screaming. "Please don't ask me to do that. I can't put him away, I can't!" Crystal was on her knees now, almost hysterical. "Lord, tell me what to do. Give me a sign, Lord! my

God, please give me a sign!" Crystal looked so pitiful, so helpless. Shaun looked as if he were about to cry too. Sherry went to Crystal and put her arms around her, tears swelling in her eyes.

"Honey, he's given you so many signs. You're just not paying attention to them." Crystal turned and looked at Sherry with tears flooding her eyes and streaming down both cheeks.

"Would you have put Herbert in a nursing home? Would you?"

"I don't know," Sherry said, letting her tears flow. "I honestly don't know. Every situation is different." Sherry wiped away Crystal's tears, holding her as they rocked back and forth. Suddenly they heard noises coming from upstairs. Then they heard a series of loud thuds. They remained quiet as they listened. Again they heard the noises only this time they were even louder. Shaun started up the stairs, but Crystal pushed past him and rushed up, almost stumbling, unable to use her arms to steady her balance. Shaun stayed right behind her hoping she wouldn't fall but knowing he was prepared to catch her. Sherry followed them. When they had reached the top, they saw Eric standing in the doorway of the bedroom. He was wearing a pair of Crystal's pantyhose and had one of her bras on backwards with a glove on each foot.

"Don't go in there," he said pointing toward the bedroom. "Put on your coats; we have to go to the police station right away. We've been robbed." Crystal pushed pass Eric and entered the bedroom. Shaun and Sherry followed. Every dresser drawer was pulled out and thrown on the floor. Clothes, papers, jewelry, shoes, hats, perfume bottles, and every other personal item that could be named were strewn about the room. Toilet paper had been pulled in from the bathroom until there was no more on the roll. Eric's ties and belts were hanging from the curtain rods and ceiling light fixtures. Buttons, spools of thread, paper clips, rubber bands, hair pins, safety pins, and various other paraphernalia cluttered the floor. Crystal just stood looking at the havoc Eric had wrecked upon the room. Shaun and Sherry also just stood looking. Sherry knew that while she thought he'd been sleeping, he had been very busy. She wondered why she hadn't heard anything until now. No one spoke—except Eric.

"See, I told you, we've been robbed. We gotta hurry down to the police station and make a report. Maybe they can catch those sons-of-bitches."

It was Thanksgiving now. Sherry still prepared Thanksgiving dinner but it wasn't the big dinner she had planned, and she didn't invite any outsiders. It was just her, her children, Leonardo, and of course Crystal. Before they ate dinner, Leonardo drove Crystal to the We Care Nursing Home, where they sat and visited with Eric. They watched him eat the plate of food Sherry had sent. He still possessed a healthy appetite. Eric was glad to see them and at times sounded like his old self but it was obvious he didn't realize where he was or that it was even Thanksgiving.

Crystal was just happy that he still knew who she was. When they first entered Eric's room, Leonardo saw that Crystal was on the verge of crying. He joked with Eric and before the tears could escape her lids, everybody was laughing. Shaun and Marie stopped by. Crystal was glad they did, but she was deeply moved when Dorothy came in bringing Eric a miniature peach cobbler. Eric was delighted and stopped eating the turkey and dressing to dig into the cobbler. He didn't remember who she was, but he smiled and thanked her.

That evening, Sherry convinced Crystal to stay all night at her house. She really didn't want her friend to spend the rest of the holiday in that big house alone.

During the days that followed, Marie and Dorothy took turns staying in the house with Crystal, helping her to do the things her casts prevented. Marie and Shaun didn't move in but they were there every other day. And of course Sherry was there every day. Shaun insisted that Crystal spend the Christmas holidays with he and Marie and her family but not before he agreed to take her to see Eric every single day. They tried hard to make her smile and enjoy the season, but she hadn't been ready to accept the sudden change in her life; it showed in everything she said and did.

Crystal's wrist and arm were in casts for several months, leaving her no choice but to give orders about the care she wanted and expected from the nursing home staff. She visited Eric every day, sometimes twice a day, making sure he was treated both kindly and efficiently. Crystal took a leave of absence from teaching until she could decide what to do with the rest of her life.

Winter arrived and the cold, snow, and icy weather did little to lift Crystal's spirits. Sherry knew that when Crystal wasn't at the nursing home, she spent a lot of time sitting at home crying; whenever she was alone. Sherry tried very hard to convince her that it was not a healthy thing for her to do.

After the casts were removed, Dorothy continued to come over for a few hours each day. Crystal had depended on Sherry and Dorothy to help her do almost everything. She couldn't stop herself from thinking, Maybe if I had listened earlier to what everyone was telling me to do, I wouldn't be depending on others to take care of me now. But in the final analysis, Crystal knew she would do it the same way if she had to do it all over again ... Well, maybe not exactly the same way, she thought to herself.

Crystal's children called often, and Shaun took over doing the household chores that needed a man's wit and brawn. Tony came by at least twice a month. He would run outside errands when necessary and sometimes just sit with Crystal talking about the good times they'd had and assuring her that everything was going to be all right. Crystal said if it hadn't been for Sherry, Dorothy, Shaun, and Tony, she didn't know what she would have done. She realized that God answers prayers in different ways. He answered hers by sending her the people she needed. Sherry came by every weekday to drive Crystal to visit Eric. Shaun took her on weekends. Crystal wouldn't think of missing one day. Sherry didn't talk much about Leonardo. When Crystal asked, Sherry would say everything was okay but Crystal could hear in her friend's voice that something was amiss. Since Sherry didn't seem to want to discuss it, Crystal didn't push it. She felt when Sherry was ready, she would confide in her, and she still prayed Leonardo wouldn't break Sherry's heart.

As another year passed, Crystal tried not to think about what used to be but it was hard because the future looked cold and bleak. A few months after Crystal's casts were removed, Shaun and Marie moved in with her. She didn't know what prompted the move, but she was ecstatic. It was as if she had been born again—figuratively speaking. Dr. Winter had even commented on the positive change that had occurred in her appearance and attitude.

Soon Crystal was driving again and interacting with Shaun and Marie as a family unit. She loved to cook, and Shaun and Marie certainly enjoyed and looked forward to the fruits of her labor. Crystal joined a theater organization, attended church regularly, and volunteered to mentor aspiring young actors. And of course, she continued to visit her husband. She wanted to join a support group but decided it would be too painful. In the future, she might decide to do that, but not now. She still maintained Eric's appearance by keeping his hair combed; shaving him; trimming his fingernails and toenails; putting oil and lotion on his hands, arms, legs, and feet; and keeping him and his surroundings smelling fragrant and fresh. During those days, Crystal prayed a lot. Her faith was as strong as ever, but she now knew that God had the master plan and she like everyone else had to bow to his will. She realized that God had kept her healthy and well in order for her to keep her commitment and continue to take care of Eric. She also realized that although Eric was not the same person she had married, he was still in that body and she still loved him even more than before—if that was possible.

ANOTHER SPRING HAD FINALLY ARRIVED, and Crystal was glad that Shaun and Marie had settled in and were treating her home as if it were theirs. She felt she might even return to work after the summer. She would still be able to visit Eric every day. In her heart she kept the hope alive and the belief that Eric would get well enough to come home. She also thought about retiring and bringing him back home to spend the rest of her days caring for him herself.

One afternoon, Sherry went in with Crystal to visit Eric. Crystal hadn't noticed any change in Eric before, but on that day he seemed to have deteriorated overnight. The CNAs who gave him care admitted that Eric had stopped talking and refused to get out of bed and go sit in the dining room with the rest of the residents. When Crystal looked at Sherry, she knew instantly what she was thinking. But she also knew Sherry was not going to put it into words. Sherry jumped right in, helping Crystal with the routine care she gave Eric every day. That was one of the many times Crystal was so grateful to have a friend like Sherry. After a few days of their combined TLC, Eric seemed to improve. It was as if through Sherry he was realizing the meaning of true friendship. Eric began looking much better and even agreed to sit and eat in the dining room. Crystal's own spirits were uplifted, and her looks of despair were soon replaced with smiles. She even shared her hopes of bringing Eric back home with Sherry. Not wanting to discourage her friend, Sherry agreed it just might be possible.

It was the middle of March. One afternoon Crystal returned home from visiting Eric and checked her answering machine. There was an urgent message from Jay asking her to call him right away. Praying that nothing serious had happened, Crystal returned his call. She always became anxious when she heard messages like that. Her children were so far away. She prayed every day that they be kept safe from harm. When Jay answered the phone, Crystal was glad to hear his voice had an upbeat tone.

"Hey Mom, guess what? I'm getting married." He hadn't waited for Crystal to guess. Crystal literally screamed with delight. She started bombarding him with questions.

"Who is she, where did you meet her, how long have you known her, when is the wedding, will it be here in Chicago?"

"Whoa, hold on there, Sapphire," he joked. "Please, one question at a time."

"Son, that is wonderful news. You don't know how much this has lifted my spirits, no—it has lifted my very soul. Thank you, Jesus." Jay could hear Crystal's voice fighting to maintain control. She didn't want to cry—not now. "Well, I'll try to cover all of your concerns. Her name is Delores. She was the blind date Al introduced me to. I met her when I came home for you and Dad's anniversary party, but I didn't get a chance to tell you. The wedding will be in August, and we are getting married in Chicago since that's where she used to live and that's where you want us to get married. Now go sit down and catch your breath, and stop crying and praying.

Tomorrow you can start making out your guest list. I'll be home next week. Love you. Oh, and don't tell Dad. I want to tell him myself. Gotta go now, bye."

Before Crystal could say anything else, Jay had hung up. To say Crystal was happy would truly be an understatement. One would think she was the one getting married. She dialed Sherry and almost screamed the news through the phone. Sherry shared Crystal's excitement. Right away they began to set a date when they would go shopping for their outfits. Of course they admitted they would have to wait until they knew the bride's color scheme. Sherry was so happy to hear the joy in her friend's voice again. Crystal had told her she was praying for a miracle. This must surely be it.

"Wait until we tell Eric," Sherry squealed.

"No no, we can't," Crystal cautioned, "Jay wants to be the one to tell him." Sherry said she understood and promised that Eric wouldn't hear it from her. Crystal could hardly wait for Shaun and Marie to get home. She even called Dorothy, whom she now considered part of the family. Dorothy shared her excitement, reminding Crystal to be sure to let her know if there's anything she wanted her to do. Crystal promised she would. When Shaun and Marie heard the news they were equally as happy. Shaun teased Crystal. "Our family will go down in history as the 'partyingest' bunch of party animals in the universe."

"Yes, if there is such a word as 'partyingest,'" Crystal said, laughing.

The next day, Crystal called and asked Sherry to come over and help her compile her guest list. Sherry reminded her they had plenty of time but also urged her not to forget to put Adelia and Ricardo on the list.

"Don't worry, I intend to invite everybody I know—well maybe not to the wedding but certainly to the reception," Crystal said, excitement oozing from every pore on her body. She told Sherry that she hoped Jay's bride-to-be would agree to get married in her living room. She reminded her that ever since she and Eric had bought the house she had hoped to one day have a wedding there. The bride could march down the winding stairs and enter the huge living room that was certain to be decorated in silk and floral splendor.

"You're preaching to the choir. You were really hoping I would get married in your living room, and I probably will if Leonardo ever sets the date."

"Speaking of Leonardo, you haven't been mentioning him lately. Shall I ask why?"

"That's because you and I have been busy making sure Eric's needs were addressed, and I really didn't want to burden you with our problems."

"Problems, what problems could Sleeping Beauty and Prince Charming possibly be having?"

"Well," Sherry said hesitating, "it seems those 'loose ends' Leonardo kept mentioning had to do with dissolving a marriage he had neglected to mention."

"You're kidding?" Crystal's voice revealed her shock. "He never told me or Eric. We never knew!"

"He kept it from me too, which is causing me to have misgivings about our relationship since he's proven to be a bit dishonest," Sherry admitted, sounding woeful.

"A bit dishonest? That is an understatement. It's ... it's like he lied. He misrepresented himself, and in my book that's lying," Crystal exclaimed.

"Since he's still married, that would certainly prevent our getting married."

"Duh uh! How long were you going to carry this around before you told me," Crystal asked, her voice full of compassion.

"I couldn't tell you. You have your own hill to climb. It wouldn't be fair." Sherry had set aside her own personal challenges in order to pitch in and help Crystal with Eric. Thinking about this made Crystal realize the true depth of their friendship. Vowing she would always be there for Sherry too, Crystal assured her that Leonardo probably had a good reason for not revealing his secret marriage, and she believed everything would be all right. She told Sherry that Leonardo had confessed his sincere love for her and her children and wanted more than anything to make her his wife. Finally she admitted that no matter how dishonest he seemed, she believed Leonardo really meant what he'd said. Sherry assured Crystal that she too believed Leonardo and intended to listen to his explanation with an open mind.

As promised, Crystal didn't tell Eric about the wedding, but Jay changed his mind about telling him too. When he went to visit Eric on several occasions prior to the wedding day, Eric was in bed and did not get up. Nor did he once ask Jay when he was going to get married. Jay figured there was no use telling his father that he was finally getting married. He was disappointed that Eric did not remember the one thing he wanted most for his youngest son. Jay asked Crystal to promise him that she would do whatever it takes to insure that his father be allowed to attend his wedding. Crystal said, "Son, that's a given. There's no way I would let him miss it. When you get married, and he's still on the planet earth, he'll be there."

Delores lived in a nearby suburb of Chicago. Crystal liked her the minute she laid eyes on her.

"Jay, she's beautiful," Crystal said as she opened the door for him and Delores.

"What did I tell you? Move over Halle Berry!" Jay said, grinning from ear-to-ear. Delores smiled, blushing at the compliment.

Crystal led them into the living room where she had a tray of refreshments she had prepared for what Jay insisted would be an informal introduction to his future wife. Oh what would I have given for Eric to have been able to hear those words, Crystal thought as she didn't even try to hide the joy and excitement she was experiencing. When Crystal learned Delores was from Belize, she thought to herself, These young men of mine don't mind integrating. One has a Mexican, one has a semi-Asian, and now a Belizean. What are their children going to be called? Whatever happened to 'I want a girl just like the girl that married dear old dad?'

Since the wedding was several months away, Delores agreed she would be happy to have Crystal's input in the planning. Crystal was ecstatic. Knowing his mother's passion for party planning, Jay was glad Delores had allowed his mother to help, but he silently prayed Crystal would not take over. This was Delores's first marriage too. Just as they had labeled all of the events they'd planned, Crystal said, "This will be the wedding of the century!"

Sherry was happy to see her friend so absorbed in the festive preparations. The house was being painted inside and out with new carpeting being replaced in every room. Since all the kids would be coming home and relatives living in distant cities would be coming in, Crystal wanted everything to be perfect.

Leonardo didn't tell Sherry until the week before Jay's wedding that his "loose ends" had been tied and he was now a fee man and he was all hers. Sherry was delirious with joy, but she decided not to tell Crystal until after Jay's wedding. She didn't want anything to take the focus off the one thing

Eric and Crystal had been praying for. Crystal hasn't been this happy and excited in months ... no years ... not since Eric's retirement party, Sherry thought as she too became caught up in the excitement. She smiled as she thought, I hope girlfriend will be just as excited when Leonardo and I get married.

On a beautiful Saturday in August, a white 1992 Cadillac stretch limousine pulled away from the We Care Nursing Home. The limo winded its way through early afternoon traffic in the southbound lane of the Bishop Ford Freeway. Finally reaching its familiar destination, the limo pulled into the driveway of Crystal and Eric's "mini-mansion." Several neighbors had gathered out front to take pictures. As the limo driver got out, Mark, Shaun, and Tony emerged from the house. Mark and Tony escorted Crystal inside, while Shaun manned Eric's wheelchair.

Inside, the foyer was beautifully decorated with fresh flowers which also adorned the banisters all the way up to the top of the stairs. The living room had been transformed into a wedding chapel with several rows of chairs on each side of a bridal isle containing dozens more beautiful flowers. The bride had chosen a soft rose and white décor.

As customary, the bride's family sat on one side of the aisle, while the groom's family was seated on the other. All sixty-five seats were filled. The overflow stood in the back of the room where they too could witness the ceremony.

Delores's mother, also from Belize, looked radiant in her beautiful two-piece, deep rose-and-cream colored dress she had allowed Crystal to select. Delores's father, originally from England, looked regal and handsome in his cream colored, double-breasted tuxedo with rose colored bowtie and cummerbund and cream patent leather shoes.

Shaun had placed Eric on the end of the first row of seats. Eric was handsomely dressed in a cream colored high-fashion tuxedo with a rose shirt, bowtie, and cummerbund; cream patent leather shoes completed his attire. Sherry and Leonardo were seated on the same row next to Eric and Crystal.

Crystal wasn't eavesdropping, but she clearly heard Leonardo when he leaned over and whispered to Sherry. "You know something, baby? We could have made this a double wedding."

"Right, now you tell me," Sherry replied, withholding a smile, pretending to be upset.

Crystal nudged Sherry as she whispered, "Girl, don't you realize that was a real proposal?" Sherry released the smile and let go with a big wide grin.

Dorothy and Eddie were seated on the second row directly behind them. Dorothy had attempted to coordinate her attire close to Crystal's, but the huge pink and red flowers in her dress didn't quite allow it.

Crystal wore a beautiful silk shantung deep rose and cream colored two piece dress, with matching rose-colored shoes. Sherry wore a soft pink form-fitting two-piece dress with matching shoes. Leonardo was eye-catching handsome in his double-breasted, off-white silk suit and off-white shoes.

The four bridesmaids—Anna, Leticia, Marie, and Marcy, Delores's sister—all wore soft light pink gowns. Monique, the maid of honor and Delores's oldest sister, wore a deep rose gown.

The groomsmen—Abraham, Mark, Shaun, and Miguel, Delores's brother—all wore cream-colored tuxedos with pink shirts, bowties, and cummerbunds, and cream-colored shoes. Al, Jay's best man, wore a cream-colored tuxedo with a deep rose shirt, bowtie, and cummerbund, with cream colored shoes. Jay wore white tails with a deep rose shirt, bowtie, and cummerbund, and white shoes.

The bride was breathtakingly gorgeous in a white lace and pearl flowing gown with a two-foot long train. As Jay had already proclaimed, Delores was as beautiful as a movie star.

Isaiah looked adorable in his cream-colored tux, serving as the ring bearer. Arielle, Delores's niece, looked angelic in a three-tiered, soft pink chiffon dress with matching accessories. As the flower girl, she would be sprinkling the pink and white rose petals down the aisle as she preceded the bride.

Lady Sax began to softly play "Always and Forever." Jay, Al, and Reverend Williams had already entered the room from the opposite direction and stood at the specially constructed altar.

The wedding party entered. The beautiful bridesmaids were escorted by the handsome groomsmen. The lovely maid of honor, carrying a uniquely arranged bouquet of pink, rose, and white flowers, marched down alone; followed by the adorable ring bearer and the angelic flower girl. Slowly the music changed to "The Wedding March", and the seated guests stood up. All eyes were on the radiant and beautiful bride as she entered. Jay stood looking at her with adoring eyes. Then he turned his eyes toward Eric and Crystal and smiled. Tears were swelling in Crystal's eyes. She thought Eric seemed to be aware of what was taking place, but she wasn't really sure.

Jay's smile said, "This one is for you, Mom and Dad." Crystal watched Eric's expression as the bride passed him, arriving at the altar. Eric looked directly at the bride.

"Who gives this woman's hand in marriage?" asked Rev. Williams. The bride's father stepped up and replied, "I do."

Suddenly, Eric leaned forward in his wheelchair. Loudly and very clearly, he said, "I do too." Everyone burst into laughter. Crystal laughed too—right through the tears that were now streaming down both cheeks.

LIFE TO LEGACY

Let us bring your story to life! With Life to Legacy, we offer the following publishing services: manuscript development, editing, transcription services, ghostwriting, cover design, copyright services, ISBN assignment, worldwide distribution, and eBooks.

Throughout the entire production process, you maintain control over your project because we are here to serve you. Even if you have no manuscript at all, we can ghostwrite your story for you from audio recordings or legible handwritten documents.

We also specialize in family history books, so you can leave a written legacy for your children, grandchildren, and others. You put your story in our hands, and we'll bring it to literary life!

Please visit our Web site:

www.Life2Legacy.com
or call us at:
877-267-7477
You can also e-mail us at:
Life2Legacybooks@att.net

10/13

CPSIA information can be obtained at www.ICGtesting.com
Printed in the USA
LVOW08s1811021013

355119LV00003BA/806/P